A Primer of
Human Behavioral
Pharmacology

APPLIED CLINICAL PSYCHOLOGY

Series Editors:
Alan S. Bellack, *Medical College of Pennsylvania at EPPI, Philadelphia, Pennsylvania,*
and Michel Hersen, *University of Pittsburgh, Pittsburgh, Pennsylvania*

A Continuation Order Plan is available for this series. A continuation order will bring delivery
of each new volume immediately upon publication. Volumes are billed only upon actual ship-
ment. For further information please contact the publisher.

A Primer of
Human Behavioral
Pharmacology

Alan Poling

Department of Psychology
Western Michigan University
Kalamazoo, Michigan

Plenum Press • New York and London

Library of Congress Cataloging in Publication Data

Poling, Alan D.
  A primer of human behavioral pharmacology.

  (Applied clinical psychology)
  Bibliography: p.
  Includes index.
  1. Psychopharmacology. 2. Psychotropic drugs. I. Title. II. Series. [DNLM: 1. Behavior—drug effects. 2. Psychopharmacology. QV 77 P768p]
  BF207.P64   1986   615'.78   86-16896
  ISBN 0-306-42186-0

© 1986 Plenum Press, New York
A Division of Plenum Publishing Corporation
233 Spring Street, New York, N.Y. 10013

Printed in the United States of America

Dedicated with love to my mother, Ruth Poling

Preface

Drugs and sex are two topics about which most people have strong opinions and weak understanding. Knowledge of each can be gained in many ways, all with associated rewards and risks. Like all textbooks, this one was written in the belief that reading can foster learning. The book is intended to introduce principles of behavioral pharmacology to readers with little or no knowledge of the discipline but with an interest in how drugs affect human behavior.

Gleaning anything of value from the text requires two things from the reader. The first is a willingness to accept an analysis of drug effects that shares little with folklore or common sense notions of drug action. The second is a willingness to accept the fact that the behavioral effects of drugs are complex and depend upon a sizable number of pharmacological and behavioral variables. Unless one is aware of these factors and how they determine a drug's actions, the behavioral effects of drugs can be neither predicted nor meaningfully explained. If it does nothing else, this volume will make it obvious that the behavioral effects of drugs are lawful and can be predicted and understood on the basis of well-established relations between empirical phenomena. Describing these relations and exploring how they allow behavioral pharmacologists to make sense of drug effects that are otherwise incomprehensible was a major goal in preparing the text.

The first of the eight chapters is a summary of the historical development of behavioral pharmacology. The second and third chapters introduce important concepts from the disciplines of pharmacology and behavioral psychology; these concepts, merged and blended, are the conceptual skeleton of behavioral pharmacology. Chapter 4 details the potential stimulus properties of drugs and shows how a drug's stimulus properties, many of which are learned, can determine its behavioral effects. Chapter 5 illustrates how nonpharmacological variables, such as response rate in the absence of drug, can modulate a drug's observed effects. That the research methods characteristically favored by behavioral pharmacologists can be profitably employed to evaluate behavior-change medications is the theme of Chapter 6. Chapter 7 provides an analysis of drug abuse from the perspective of behavioral pharmacology. The book ends with a brief speculation about the future of behavioral pharmacology. Taken together, the eight chapters present a broad overview of behavioral pharmacology, although no one topic is covered in exhaustive detail. For that I offer no apology; the text is a primer, not an encyclopedia. Nonetheless, sufficient references are cited to allow readers seeking further information to find it with relative ease.

Many people made significant contributions to the book, although I alone must bear responsibility for its weaknesses. I owe a special debt of thanks to Andy Lattal and Travis Thompson, who were my teachers in the finest sense of the word. I am also deeply indebted to several past and present students: Eb Blakely, Jim Cleary, Dawn Delaney, Deb Grossett, Earl Hall-Johnson, Mitch Picker, and Kathy Krafft stand foremost in having provided good data and better friendship. Finally, Eliot Werner, Timothy Shaw, and the entire staff at Plenum Press made production of the book not only possible but a pleasure as well. I appreciate their help.

National Institutes of Health Grant NS-20216 provided partial, and invaluable, support for the preparation of the book. I sincerely thank those individuals responsible for awarding the grant to me.

Contents

1

Historical Origins of Behavioral Pharmacology

"A drug is broadly defined as any chemical agent that affects living processes" (Mayer, Melmon, & Gilman, 1980, p. 1). Although the fossil record fails to reveal whether *homo erectus* used drugs, the writings of nearer ancestors reveal that *homo sapiens* has self-administered drugs throughout recorded history. No less authoritative sources than the Bible, the Koran, and the Talmud affirm that humans have long recognized drugs' ability to alter subjective internal states as well as overt behavior. In fact, our ancestors appear to have used drugs and to have speculated on their effects millennia before Christ and Mohammed trod the earth.

Among the more illustrious ancients who wrote about drugs was the Greek poet Homer, who told how the sorceress Circe used a hallucinogenic substance to create delusions in Odysseus' crew, making them think themselves swine. Homer also related that Pythia, princess of the Delphic oracle, inhaled a vapor (perhaps cannabis) to facilitate perception and that wealthy Scythians took vapor baths that were medicated with burnt hemp seeds and inhaled cannabis vapors which "fulfilled their deepest desires." Homer was even aware of drug interactions, for he wrote that the

Gods would occasionally intervene and supply an antidote, moly, which counteracted the effects of Circe's potions.[1]

Despite the longevity of human drug use, the scientific study of drugs spans little more than a century. The behavioral actions of drugs are better understood today than ever before thanks to the development of a general science of pharmacology and an offshoot of that science known as behavioral pharmacology. The purpose of the present chapter is to recount several events which contributed to the emergence of behavioral pharmacology. More detailed coverage of many of these happenings is provided by Caldwell (1970), Holmstedt (1967), Hordern (1968), and Pickens (1977).

What Is Behavioral Pharmacology?

The discipline known as behavioral pharmacology resulted from the seemingly unlikely wedding of traditional pharmacology and Skinnerian psychology and has existed for little more than three decades. Two fundamental principles integrate the field. The first is that the effects of drugs are lawful and thereby subject to scientific study. The second is that the behavioral effects of drugs merit attention in and of themselves. Behavioral pharmacologists assume that drugs are environmental events (stimuli) the effects of which, like those of other stimuli, can be understood (i.e., predicted and controlled) without recourse to reductionistic or mentalistic explanations. From this perspective, the study of drug effects should focus upon (1) determination of behavioral loci of drug action, (2) determination of behavioral mechanisms of drug action, and (3) determination of drug and nondrug variables that influence a compound's behavioral actions.

The term *behavioral loci of drug action* refers to the changes in overt behavior produced by a drug—what the drug actually

---

[1]Dr. James B. Appel called my attention to these examples, for which I am grateful.

does at the behavioral level. *Behavioral mechanisms of drug action* refers to the manner in which a drug affects responding and involves the stimulus properties of the drug itself as well as the manner in which the drug modulates the actions of nondrug stimuli. Behavioral loci and mechanisms of drug action will be fully analyzed in subsequent chapters. For now, the important point is that behavioral pharmacology is primarily concerned with relations between what might be considered as "input" variables, the administration of drugs, and "output" variables, changes in behavior, and the factors which modify these relations. Drug-induced physiological changes in the organism, "throughput" variables in our metaphor, are recognized to mediate the relation between input and output, but a lack of understanding of these changes does not prevent one from being able to predict, and in some cases control, a drug's behavioral effects.

It may at this point be judicious to point out that there is no clear and absolute distinction between psychopharmacology and behavioral pharmacology; the former term was in fact offered early on as a descriptor of a then yet to be developed science dealing with the behavioral effects of drugs (Macht & Mora, 1921). However, not all attempts to develop such a discipline adopted the research strategies and explanatory principles characteristic of Skinnerian psychology; those which did led to the emergence of the science herein called behavioral pharmacology. This term, popularized by Thompson and Schuster's (1968) textbook with the same name, makes it clear that overt responses, not inferred intrapsychic events, are of primary interest.

A crucial step in the development of behavioral pharmacology was the demonstration that behavior is lawfully related to measurable changes in the environment and can be explained without recourse to unobserved, hypothetical entities. Ivan Pavlov's justly famous studies of respondent conditioning were among the first showing the orderliness of overt behavior and its susceptibility to scientific analysis. One of Pavlov's students, Igor Zavadskii, conducted a study that is thought to be the first in the tradition of behavioral pharmacology. In this study, Zavadskii measured the effects of caffeine, cocaine, ethanol, and morphine on the re-spondently conditioned salivation of dogs (Laties, 1979). Zavad-skii's procedures share much with those used by behavioral phar-macologists today: A wide range of doses was studied, within-subject controls were employed, and effects were measured under a range of conditions. However, this line of research apparently held little appeal for the Soviets, and the emergence of behavioral pharmacology as an organized discipline awaited the birth of be-havioral psychology in America.

As an infant science, behavioral psychology attempted to dis-cover general principles of learning by studying seemingly simple organisms under controlled conditions. (Important historical de-velopments in behavioral psychology and the basic principles of the field are considered in Chapter 3.) As early as 1920, re-searchers at Johns Hopkins University examined how drugs in-fluenced maze learning by rats (Macht & Mora, 1921). However, systematic examinations of the behavioral actions of drugs oc-curred only sporadically from the turn of the century until its midpoint. In the 1950s, interest in the area skyrocketed; Pickens (1977) reported that between 1917 and 1954 only 28 studies ex-amining drug effects on learned behavior were published in English-language journals, whereas 274 such studies appeared from 1955 to 1963. The factors responsible for this remarkable increase are complex (see Pickens, 1977), but certain momentous happenings bear note.

By 1955, behavioral pharmacology had matured into an ac-cepted, if controversial, discipline. In two major books, Skinner (1938, 1953) had expounded the theme that behavior is orderly, therefore subject to scientific analysis, and had developed a tech-nology for this analysis. In 1956, the potential value of this tech-nology for studying drug effects was emphasized at a conference called Techniques for the Study of the Behavioral Effects of Drugs, sponsored by the prestigious New York Academy of Sci-ences and chaired by Skinner and Dews (*Annals*, 1956). Re-searchers studying drug–behavior interactions were quick to adopt Skinner's operant conditioning methodology, especially in the areas of drug self-administration and drug effects on the performance of learned behaviors. Funds for such endeavors indirectly resulted from the discovery of two remarkable compounds, chlorpromazine (Thorazine) and LSD.

Drugs and Psychiatry

Psychiatry is "the branch of medicine concerned with the study and treatment of mental disorders, including psychoses and neuroses" (*Webster's New Twentieth Century Dictionary*, 1979). "Mental disorders" are detected on the basis of unusual and troublesome behavior, thus behavior problems are ultimately the focus of the discipline.

Although a variety of drugs were prescribed for mentally ill individuals prior to the mid-1800s, their usual action was laxative, diaphoretic, or emetic. One of the first drugs with direct behavioral activity to be introduced into psychiatric practice was "dawamesc," a flavored paste of hashish which de Tours began using in 1845 to "induce and study mental symptoms and to treat mental disease." Two years later, chloroform and ether inhalations were evaluated as treatments for psychoses and neuroses. Some beneficial effects were reported to occur early in treatment, but they disappeared with protracted exposure to the drugs.

Little more than a decade after the introduction of chloroform and ether treatments, chloral hydrate was reported to be of value in managing agitated behavior. This action, like that of chloroform and ether, was largely confined to the first days of exposure, therefore the use of chloral hydrate eventually came to be restricted to depressant and soporific (sleep-inducing) applications.

Hyoscyamine was first employed to manage psychotic individuals in 1875; five years later, cocaine treatment of morphine and alcohol addiction and, subsequently, a range of behavioral problems, become popular. The use of sodium bromide to induce sleep in mentally ill patients was first evaluated as a treatment in 1897; the first phenothiazine derivative, methylene blue, was introduced into psychiatric practice two years thereafter. Although these drugs were indeed behaviorally active, a point to which the current recreational popularity of cocaine bears witness, their effectiveness in dealing with behavioral problems was at best limited.

The same holds true of most of the compounds utilized by psychiatrists early in the present century, one in which behavior-change medications were ever more widely adopted.

In 1929, Bleckwenn gave sodium amytol its first psychiatric trial. Sen and Bose used rauwolfia alkaloids in India to manage psychotic behaviors as early as 1931, and Sakel began using insulin coma therapy four years later, first with morphine addicts and later with schizophrenics. Experiments with camphor-induced convulsions as a treatment for schizophrenia began in 1936; these studies led to the development of a new seizure inducer, metrazol. The first report of the use of a stimulant, amphetamine, in the treatment of emotionally disturbed children was published in 1937 (Bradley, 1937). Histamine was used by Marshall and Tarwater as a treatment for psychotic patients in 1938, but five years later three French psychiatrists reported success in treating a variety of psychiatric disorders with pyrabenzamine, an antihistaminic. The development of these pharmacological interventions, most (but not all) of which were eventually shown to be worthless, is discussed by Caldwell (1970).

One of the major achievements in pharmacotherapeutics had its beginnings in 1949 when the French surgeon Laborit began investigating pharmacological procedures for reducing postoperative shock in surgical patients. Laborit experimented with a variety of antihistaminics, including members of the phenothiazine class of chemicals. He noted that certain phenothiazines reduced the need for general anesthesia, decreased postoperative anxiety, and induced a state of sedation without loss of consciousness. However, he was not satisfied with these results and was convinced that a more useful drug could be found.

Paul Charpentier, a chemist with the French pharmaceutical company Sepia, synthesized it. The year was 1950 and the drug was chlorpromazine, a phenothiazine derivative with weak antihistaminic properties. Laborit recognized the psychiatric applications of chlorpromazine, but his efforts to encourage psychiatrists to use the drug met with considerable initial resistance. Nonetheless, in early 1952 several of Laborit's colleagues working at the military hospital in Paris reported a series of resounding successes in treating psychoses with chlorpromazine. Within the next few years, the use of chlorpromazine spread throughout Europe, North America, Australia, and the Soviet Union. A number of adequately controlled studies found that chlorpromazine was generally useful for managing the behavioral manifestations of schizophrenia and other psychoses, although not all schizophrenics benefit from the drug, some improve without it, and all who receive it are at risk for developing motor dysfunctions (see Berger, 1978).

After the synthesis of chlorpromazine, certain other phenothiazines were found to have antispychotic (or neuroleptic) properties; the same is true of some thioxanthenes and the butyrophenone, haloperidol (Haldol). According to Baldessarini (1980):

> The use of antipsychotic agents is extremely widespread, as is evident from the fact that several hundreds of millions of patients have been treated with them. While the antipsychotic drugs have had a revolutionary, beneficial impact on medical and psychiatric practice, their liabilities, especially their almost relentless association with extrapyramidial neurological effects, must also be emphasized. (p. 395)

The neuroleptics firmly established drugs as a major weapon in the psychiatrists' armamentarium. However, neuroleptics were not the only compounds that the mid-1950s introduced to clinical practice. Various anxiolytics (antianxiety agents), antidepressants, and stimulants, as well as the antimania drug lithium carbonate, found a place in clinical psychopharmacology during this period. Chlordiazepoxide (Librium), a benzodiazepine anxiolytic, was synthesized in 1947 and first used clinically in 1958 (prior to that time, barbiturates were favored for dealing with "anxiety"). Azcyclonal, a diphenylmethane derivative with antianxiety properties, was introduced by the neurologist Fabing in 1955. A final group of putative anxiolytics, the aminoalkanols, has been employed only recently; their efficacy is questionable (Klein, Gittelmlan, Quitkin, & Rifkin, 1980).

The class of drugs knows as monoamine oxidase (MAO) inhibitors, though rarely used today because of the threat of hypertensive crisis when combined with certain other medications or food rich in tyramine (e.g., aged wines and cheeses), were the first recognized antidepressants. Iproniazid, a MAO inhibitor originally used to treat tuberculosis, was found over 25 years ago to improve the symptoms of depression (Crane, 1957). Shortly thereafter, Kuhn (1958) introduced the prototypical tricyclic antidepressant, imipramine, to American psychiatry. This drug, serendipitously discovered during a search for alternatives to chlorpromazine, was followed in rapid succession by a number of other tricyclics.

The most recent appearance among the antidepressant medications is a class of drugs known as tetracyclic compounds. Representative of this class are mianserin and maprotiline (Claghorn, 1976). Although the novelty of the tetracyclic compounds has generated considerable interest, there is no conclusive evidence of their superiority relative to the tricyclics (Klein *et al.*, 1980).

Several stimulant medications are prescribed to control the inattention, hyperactivity, and disruptive behavior characteristic of attention deficit disorder (in years past, this set of behaviors was called hyperactivity, minimal brain dysfunction, or hyperkinesis). Stimulants which have been used for this purpose include amphetamine, dextroamphetamine (the racemic isomer of amphetamine, also known as d-amphetamine), methylphenidate (Ritalin), and magnesium pemoline (Cylert). One other drug, deanol, has also seen limited use.

Methylphenidate was first synthesized in Switzerland in 1956 and soon after appeared in American psychiatry. The effectiveness of the drug in controlling hyperactivity was quickly documented (Knobel, 1959), and methylphenidate became the drug of choice for the treatment of hyperactive children, although there is legitimate controversy as to whether any form of pharmacotherapy is needed to deal with the condition (O'Leary, 1980).

Magnesium pemoline is the newest of the stimulant medications used to treat attention deficit disorder. Its effectiveness was first established in a series of studies published in the 1970s (e.g., Conners, Taylor, Meo, Jurtz, & Founnier, 1972).

Psychiatrists at present have a veritable smorgasbord of drugs at their disposal. For the most part, behavioral pharmacology played only a minor role in the development and evaluation of these compounds. Behavioral pharmacologists were, however, instrumental in the development of *animal models*, which are assays that allow the clinical utility of a compound to be predicted on the basis of how it affects nonhuman subjects. Animal models were important to drug houses because they provided a means of discerning new, and profitable, compounds which duplicated or improved upon the actions of legally protected medications.

Perhaps the best known animal model is that used to screen drugs for neuroleptic properties. In this assay, rats or monkeys are trained under avoidance and escape conditioning procedures,[2] then their performance is compared in the presence and absence of the substance of interest. Neuroleptics interfere with avoidance responding at doses which do not affect escape responding; other drug classes fail to do so. (This actually is an oversimplification but aptly captures the rationale of the procedure.)

The success of the escape–avoidance conditioning paradigm for screening neuroleptics initiated a search for assays selectively affected by other drug classes. This search was only partially successful, and interest in animal models eventually faded as it became clear that they were not especially useful in the initial discovery of therapeutically useful compounds nor in elucidating why some drugs are useful in dealing with problem behaviors. Behavioral procedures involving nonhumans have nevertheless retained a place in drug houses' screening and evaluation of newly synthesized compounds. For example, drug self-administration

---

[2]Escape and avoidance conditioning are explored in Chapter 3. In brief, escape responses are maintained by the termination of stimuli that are present at the time the response is emitted, whereas avoidance responses are maintained by the postponement (or cancellation) of forthcoming stimuli.

procedures involving nonhumans are typically employed in initial evaluations of the abuse potential of drugs being considered for clinical application (see Thompson & Unna, 1977).

Beyond helping to devise drug screening procedures, and in the process gaining much information about the effects of many drugs in a variety of experimental paradigms, behavioral pharmacologists contributed greatly to the development of objective, scientific methods for evaluating the behavioral effects of drugs. Historically, behavioral pharmacologists have favored within-subject experimental designs in the tradition of Sidman (1960) and have insisted that drug–behavior interactions can be adequately assessed only when independent and dependent variables are operationally defined public events, accurately and reliably manipulated and monitored. To date, the approach to drug evaluation advocated by behavioral pharmacologists has not greatly influenced clinical drug assessment, although this appears to be changing as a science of clinical behavioral pharmacology emerges. The applicability of the research methodology of behavioral pharmacology to clinical drug evaluation is addressed in Chapter 6.

Drug Abuse, LSD, and Behavioral Pharmacology

Drug abuse, which can be generally defined as a pattern of administration of a drug that produces deleterious behavioral or physiological effects without producing compensatory medical benefit, is an ancient and vexatious problem. In America, production and abuse of alcohol began well before the Union was formed. The use and abuse of narcotics gained popularity sometime later, after the Civil War, and was by 1880 widely recognized as rampant. Three factors appear to have contributed to increased use of morphine and opium in this country (Ray, 1983). The first was the development of the hypodermic syringe in 1856. The hypodermic syringe allowed Civil War soldiers to inject morphine with ease, and they frequently did so to allay the pain, dysentery, and other miseries of war. The result: Many soldiers returned home physically dependent upon, and highly inclined to use, morphine.

A second factor that contributed to the use of opioids in America was the importation of Chinese laborers, many of whom smoked opium, as they had done in their homeland.

The wide distribution of patent medicines—potions bearing enticing labels like "Dr. A. L Taylor's Oil of Life," "Swain's Panacea," and "Dr. B. Brandreth's Life-Addition Pills and Quintessence of Sarsaparilla"—was the third factor that increased the use and abuse of narcotics (and other drugs) in the United States, for these patent medicines often contained opium or another narcotic in addition to alcohol and, in some cases, cocaine. The techniques used to market these concoctions were both innovative and effective (see Young, 1974), so effective, in fact, that many upstanding citizens who would never intentionally take "drugs" regularly used and became physically dependent upon a favored patent medicine, the ingredients of which were almost never advertised.

In part because of the problems associated with patent medicines, Congress in 1906 enacted the Pure Food and Drug Act, which required that drugs must be pure and accurately labeled. This act did not, however, limit the import of opium or other drugs. The Opium Exclusion Act of 1909 rendered illegal the importation and manufacture of opium or its derivatives for nonmedical purposes. The Harrison Act, passed in 1914, affirmed the principles set forth in the acts of 1906 and 1909 and further specified that dispensers of narcotics (which included cocaine) must register with the Bureau of Internal Revenue. At the time this act was passed, one American in 400 was addicted to opium or its derivatives (Ray, 1983).

Two Supreme Court decisions, one handed down in 1919, the other in 1922, established that physicians could not prescribe opiates to "addicts" even in the context of treatment. This precedent, along with the stipulations of the Opium Exclusion Act, ensured that there was no way in which an addict could legally obtain a narcotic. One result was the establishment of an illegal and profitable drug market which is very much active today. A second result was making criminals of a sizable number of otherwise lawabiding citizens; one-third of all individuals imprisoned in 1928 were guilty of breaking drug control laws (Ray, 1983).

Recognition of the problems created by imprisoning drug abusers without treatment goaded Congress into establishing in 1929 two centers for the treatment of persons who had broken a federal law and also were "addicted" to habit-forming drugs, which included opium and its derivatives, marijuana, and peyote.

Nine years prior to the establishment of these "narcotic farms," Congress had attempted to deal with abuse of another kind of drug, ethanol (beverage alcohol), by passing the infamous Eighteenth (or Volstead, after its author) Amendment. This amendment made illegal within the United States the manufacture, sale, transportation, and import of intoxicating liquors. Although the Eighteenth Amendment reduced per capita ethanol consumption in the years immediately following its passage, by 1930 intake had returned to about the 1920 level (Ray, 1983). In addition, enforcement of the amendment was costly, difficult, and often politically and otherwise foolhearty. After a brief and tumultuous life, the Eighteenth Amendment was repealed by enactment of the Twenty-first Amendment to the Constitution. Prohibition had failed utterly in its aim of reducing alcohol abuse.

Legislation designed to control the abuse of other substances, including the acts described above, also failed to prevent significant trafficking in opioids, cocaine, and marijuana, while the federal treatment centers faired little better in dealing with acknowledged drug abusers. In fact, from 1900 to 1960, a number of new drugs came to be popular on the street, bringing with them new and significant abuse problems. Amphetamines, for example, were first synthesized in the 1930s; twenty years later, they were recognized as having considerable abuse potential. Barbiturates and anxiolytics, too, eventually came to the public's attention as drugs capable of harming the incautious user and society at large.

It was LSD (lysergic acid diethylamide), however, and the small but colorful band of devotees who advocated its use that galvanized national attention to the "drug scene" and played a significant role in the development of behavioral pharmacology.

The contribution of LSD to behavioral pharmacology is an indirect and perhaps infamous one. First synthesized by Hoffman in 1953, this potent hallucinogen immediately aroused scientific curiosity concerning its usefulness in clarifying the mechanisms of psychosis, dreaming, creativity, and perception (Sankar, 1975). Self-administration of the drug also became popular, especially outside the alleged mainstream of Western society. Historically, LSD was associated with a social movement fostered by Timothy Leary and the hippie subculture. Obvious and supposedly abusive intake of LSD (who can forget the slogan, "Tune in, turn on, drop out?"), cannabis, and other drugs played a highly popularized role in this movement, which culminated in the social unrest of the Vietnam War era. Because this unrest and the attendant drug use aroused much public concern, federal funds became available for studies of drug self-administration and the behavioral effects of drugs. Some of this money was awarded to behavioral psychologists—men and women who claimed that drug–behavior interactions, including those responsible for drug abuse, could be profitably studied and explained through the research methods popularized by Skinnerian psychologists. The truthfulness of this claim will be explored in Chapter 7.

Drug abuse in America surely did not end with the Vietnam War, nor did attempts to control drug abuse by fiat die with the Eighteenth Amendment. At present, regulation of drugs with recognized abuse potential follows dictates set forth in the Comprehensive Drug Abuse Prevention and Control Act of 1970, which became effective on May 1, 1971. This act assigns drugs to one of five schedules (classes) according to their potential for abuse and whether or not they have medical uses. The maximum penalties for illegal manufacturing and distribution, or possession, of a drug are determined by the category to which it is assigned. Heroin, for instance, is a Schedule 1 drug: It has high abuse potential and no medical use. The maximum first offense penalty for the manufacture or distribution of heroin is 15 years imprisonment, a fine of $25,000, and a probationary period of three years after release from prison. Phenobarbital, in contrast, is a Schedule 4 drug with recognized medical use and relatively low abuse potential. The maximum first offense penalty for the manufacture or distribution of phenobarbital is three years in prison, a $10,000 fine, and one year of probation. Behavioral pharmacologists were, and remain, active in determining the schedules to which particular drugs should be assigned and in attempting to understand and treat drug abuse.

Behavioral Toxicology

Much of the impetus for the development of a science of behavioral pharmacology resulted from the discovery of drugs effective in the treatment of behavioral problems and from the widespread public awareness of the ubiquity and seriousness of drug abuse problems. A third, though perhaps weaker, impetus came from a growing concern with the effects of chemical contamination of the environment.

Individual concern with environmental pollutants has a long history, but only recently and through media exposure of tragedies like the chemical contamination that rendered a portion of Love Canal, New York, and all of Times Beach, Missouri, unlivable has the enormity and seriousness of the problem become apparent to the general public. And an enormous problem it is: Each year, according to Environmental Protection Agency (EPA) estimates, United States industries produce some 88 billion pounds—that is 44,000,000 tons—of toxic wastes, 90% of which are improperly disposed. In addition to the new wastes we generate each year, our nest is fouled with the excrement of the past:

> Experts estimate that toxic chemical wastes fester in as many as 50,000 dumps across the country and that 180,000 open pits, ponds and lagoons at industrial parks also bubble with witch's brews. EPA officials say that at least 14,000 of these sites are potentially dangerous—posing fire hazards, threatening ground water or emitting noxious fumes . . . experts estimate that the cost of cleaning up America's chemical dumps could run as high as $260 billion dollars. (*Newsweek*, 1983)

But what has any of this to do with behavioral pharmacology? A great deal, for the behavioral (as well as physiological) effects of exposure to many environmental contaminants are unknown. Consider, for example, polybrominated biphenyl (PBB). PBB made national news due to a series of events which began in southern Michigan early in May 1973. Through human error, PBB was substituted for magnesium oxide in a large batch of livestock feed prepared at a Farm Bureau Services' plant. The PBB contamination was not recognized, and the feed reached farms, cattle, and, eventually, many of Michigan's 9,000,000 residents (see Chen, 1979). Unfortunately, although it is known that high doses of PBB do palpable damage, the behavioral (and other) effects of low levels of exposure to this drug and to most other environmental contaminants are unclear. This creates significant obstacles for those charged with determining "safe" levels of environmental contaminants and for those evaluating claims that individuals have been damaged by exposure to pollutants and hence deserve compensation from the responsible party.

As early as 1969, researchers contended that the methods of behavioral pharmacology were appropriate for detecting deleterious effects of relatively low doses of toxins (Weiss & Laties, 1969). This branch of behavioral pharmacology, termed behavioral toxicology, has experienced considerable growth (see Evans & Weiss, 1978; Weiss & Laties, 1975), spurred recently by enactment of the 1976 Toxic Substances Control Act, which demands toxicological assessment of chemicals prior to marketing. As Evans and Weiss (1978) emphasize:

> Behavioral toxicology exemplifies how society now is demanding answers to new kinds of questions, requiring new approaches in toxicology. Regulatory agencies are being asked to make decisions about environmental quality and health risks, guided only by overt morphological and morbidity data. Few rigorous animal models are available to substantiate the kind of human symptoms and functional changes that occur with low-level exposure. It is here that behavioral studies in toxicology hold the greatest promise. (p. 450)

It is, perhaps, a sad commentary on current society that the growth of behavioral pharmacology was partially fueled by an emerging recognition of the problems that environmental toxins and recreational drugs pose for humanity and of our collective inability to deal effectively with these problems.

Pharmacology and Behavioral Pharmacology

Although behavioral psychology contributed greatly to the research methods and conceptual principles adopted by behavioral pharmacologists, any attempt to understand drug effects demands knowledge of basic principles of pharmacology. These principles, summarized in Chapter 2, arose from the application of scientific methods to the study of drugs which began midway through the nineteenth century with the work of Bernard in France, Schmiedeberg in Germany, and Abel in the United States (for histories of pharmacology see Holmstedt & Leljestrand, 1963; Schuster, 1962). These researchers and their successors made it clear, for example, that all drugs have multiple and dose-dependent actions; these are now basic tenets of behavioral pharmacology. In addition, the concepts of tolerance and physical dependence, as well as the receptor model of drug action, come from traditional pharmacology. These concepts form an integral part of the thinking of behavioral pharmacologists (e.g., Thompson & Schuster, 1968). The point to be made, of course, is that developments in classical pharmacology were (and are) instrumental in shaping behavioral pharmacology.

Milestones in Behavioral Pharmacology

It is unlikely that any five behavioral pharmacologists could reach a consensus as to what events constituted milestones in the field, each would probably opt for her or his own work. Nevertheless, the philosophical underpinnings, methods, and explanatory models of behavioral psychology were initially made public in a small number of books and journal articles. Table 1 provides a chronological listing of several publications which appear to have made seminal contributions to the field. Certain

Table 1
Selected Milestones in the Development of Behavioral Pharmacology

Year	Event
1955	Dews publishes an article presenting data indicating that the effects of drugs can be rate-dependent, that is, determined by the rate of occurrence of the response in the absence of drug.
1956	The New York Academy of Sciences sponsors a conference called "Techniques for the Study of the Behavioral Effects of Drugs." Basic research methods and explanatory principles of behavioral pharmacology are described by participants, who include Dews, Herrnstein, Miller, Morse, Sidman, and Skinner.
1957	The Behavioral Pharmacology Society is founded, the first (and only) professional association devoted entirely to the field.
1959	Skinner publishes an important chapter arguing that studies using the methods of operant conditioning to study drug effects in nonhumans are of value in understanding the actions of drugs used to treat the mentally ill.
1964	Thompson and Schuster publish a paper showing that monkeys not previously exposed to morphine will self-administer the drug; the study is the first of many in this general area.
1968	Thompson and Schuster publish *Behavioral Pharmacology*, the first text devoted to the subject.
1971	The second behavioral pharmacology textbook appears, Harvey's *Behavioral Analysis of Drug Action*.
1971	The fact that drugs have stimulus properties like those of other environmental events is made clear in an edited text (Thompson & Pickens).
1975	Iverson and Iverson publish *Behavioral Pharmacology*, which overviews the discipline.
1975	An edited volume devoted entirely to behavioral toxicology is promulgated (Weiss & Laties).
1977	Another major text in the general area of behavioral pharmacology is marketed (Seiden & Dykstra).
1977	The *Advances in Behavioral Pharmacology* series (Thompson & Dews) is initiated. This series provides current reviews of specific research areas.
1978	*Contemporary Research in Behavioral Pharmacology* (Blackman & Sanger), an edited text offering general summaries of research in several significant areas, appears.

other events (e.g., professional meetings) of exceptional importance are also listed. Even though many significant developments
in behavioral pharmacology are omitted from the table, anyone
familiar with the material presented in the publications listed
therein could justifiably claim a sound fundamental understanding of the field.

Concluding Comment

History is created as it is retold: The cowboy's history of the
American West is decidedly not that of the Lakota Sioux. The
history of behavioral pharmacology provided in the present chapter is similar to that offered by others (e.g., Pickens, 1977) and
does highlight events that obviously contributed to the
emergence, growth, and definition of the field. Like all histories,
however, it is neither complete nor unbiased.

Regardless of how it came to be so, behavioral pharmacology
is at present a viable discipline. A proliferation of books and journal articles disseminates information concerning the behavioral
effects of drugs, and universities offer courses and curricula in
behavioral pharmacology. Although laboratory investigations
with nonhuman subjects remain an important source of information, behavioral pharmacologists have recently begun to address
how drugs affect human activities. The balance of this book describes the rudiments of this analysis.

CHAPTER

2

Basic Principles
of Pharmacology

The preceding chapter introduced the science of pharmacology and made the point that the behavioral actions of drugs cannot be understood without knowledge of basic pharmacological principles. The purpose of the present chapter is to provide an introduction to these principles.

Labeling and Classification of Drugs

All drugs are chemicals and have *chemical names.* The chemical name of a drug provides a complete description of the molecule and is derived from a set of rules outlined in *Chemical Abstracts.* Although the chemical name of a drug is precise, it is likely to be long and cumbersome. Consequently, the use of chemical names in pharmacology and related disciplines is largely restricted to newly synthesized compounds which have not received *generic names.*

The generic name of a drug is its official name as listed in the *United States Pharmacopoeia.* Generic names are assigned by the United States Adopted Name Council; they specify a particular chemical structure and are in the public domain. Generic names are shorter and more easily pronounced than chemical names and are usually employed in scientific writing. The convention of referring to drugs by generic names will be followed throughout this text, although *brand names* also will be noted when they are likely to be familiar to readers.

The brand (or trade) name of a drug specifies a particular formulation and manufacturer of a generic chemical. Brand names are protected by trademark laws and are controlled by the Food and Drug Administration. Brand names inevitably are simple and typically suggest a drug's therapeutic application. Elavil, for example, is the trade name of a tricyclic antidepressant (amitriptyline), a "mood elevator."

Abused drugs are frequently assigned *slang names* by those who self-administer them. Slang names are imprecise—any of several stimulants are "speed" in street argot—and are apt to vary with time and geography. Table 2 shows the chemical, generic, trade, and slang names of an abused drug which has recently garnered considerable attention.

Drugs may be classified on the basis of their chemical structure, their physiological actions, their behavioral effects, or their therapeutic usage. Each mode of classification is problematic. Classification according to chemical structure is unambiguous but is not consistently meaningful since drugs with similar chemical structures often produce vastly different physiological and behavioral effects. Classification according to behavioral effects would be useful to the clinician, but insufficient data have been collected concerning the behavioral effects of many drugs, and furthermore most drugs have multiple and complex behavioral

Table 2
Chemical, Generic, Trade, and Slang Names of a Commonly Abused Drug

Chemical name	Generic name	Trade name	Slang name
Phencyclidine 1(1-phencyclohexy) piperidine	Phencyclidine	Sernylan	Angel dust

Table 3
Generic and Trade Names of Several Drugs Commonly Prescribed
to Manage Behavior[a]

NEUROLEPTICS	ANTIDEPRESSANTS
Phenothiazines	MAO inhibitors
Chlorpromazine (Thorazine)	Isocarboxazid (Marplan)
Fluphenazine (Prolixin)	Phenelzine (Nardil)
Mesoridazine (Serentil)	Tranylcypromine (Parnate)
Thioridazine (Mellaril)	Tricyclics
Trifluoperazine (Stelazine)	Amitriptyline (Elavil)
Butyrophenones	Desipramine (Norpramin)
Haloperidol (Haldol)	Imipramine (Tofranil)
Thioxanthenes	Nortriptyline (Aventyl)
Chlorprothixene (Taractan)	Trimipramine (Surmontil)
Thiothixene (Navane)	Tetracyclics
ANXIOLYTICS	Mianserin
	Maprotoline (Ludiomil)
Glycerol derivatives	
Meprobamate (Equanil, Miltown)	ANTIMANIA DRUGS
Diphenylmethane derivatives	Lithium carbonate
Diphenhydramine (Benadryl)	STIMULANTS
Hyrodxyzine (Atarax, Vistaril)	Amphetamine (Benzedrine)
Benzodiazepines	Dextroamphetamine (Dexedrine)
Chlordiazepoxide (Librium)	Magnesium Pemoline (Cylert)
Diazepam (Valium)	Methylphenidate (Ritalin)
Flurazepam (Dalmane)	
Oxazepam (Serax)	

[a]Drugs are grouped according to therapeutic usage with the mentally ill.

actions that are dose-dependent. Classification according to physiological action encounters similar difficulties in that relevant data are frequently lacking, and most drugs act by means of multiple physiological mechanisms.

The most common classification of drugs is according to therapeutic usage. Table 3 lists a number of drugs according to their usual application in psychiatry. Although this system of classification is plagued by imprecise and overlapping categories and a lack of consensually accepted criteria for determining such categories, the system is widely employed and is of practical value in therapeutics. However, it must be recognized that some drugs

have no recognized therapeutic usage; such drugs are often classified according to their most prominent behavioral effect in humans (e.g., as hallucinogens).

In addition, the behavioral and physiological effects of all
members of a given therapeutic class are by no means identical.
Although some general statements can be made safely about the
actions of a given drug class, for example, tricyclic antidepressants, care must be taken to ensure that the idiosyncratic actions
of individual agents are not overlooked. This caution is of particular significance when one recognizes that pharmacologists frequently describe the actions of a class of drugs by referring to the
documented effects of a well-studied member of that class. Chlorpromazine (Thorazine), for instance, is commonly taken as the
prototypical neuroleptic (Baldessarini, 1980), and its actions are
assumed to closely resemble those of other members of the class.
They do, but there are differences which should not be ignored.
Chlorpromazine, for example, appears more likely than piper-
acetazine to produce extrapyramidal motor disturbances, although each is appropriately used to reduce the problem behaviors of individuals described as psychotic (Baldessarini, 1980).

Physical Properties of Drugs

The physical properties of a drug refer to its molecular weight
and structure, form (solid, liquid, or gas), solubility, purity, and
stability. These aspects are important in preparing and storing
drugs, although compounds used therapeutically usually come in
standardized preparations which may suggest that little knowledge of their chemical or physical properties is required for effective use. However, it is well established that pharmaceutical for-
mulations of a drug which are chemically equivalent (i.e., meet
the chemical and physical standards established by regulatory
agencies) are not necessarily biologically or therapeutically equivalent (Mayer *et al.*, 1980). Two preparations are *biologically
equivalent* if they produce similar concentrations of drug in
blood and at the site of action and *therapeutically equivalent* if
they produce equal benefit in clinical trials.

Seemingly trivial aspects of the drug preparation, such as the hardness of a tablet or the solubility of a capsule, as well as the inert agents with which active drug is combined, can determine how readily a drug enters the blood. The importance of such factors is shown in the results of a study conducted by Desta and Pernarowski (1973), who measured the time it took for 60% of the active ingredient in two brands of chlorpromazine hydrochloride tablets to be released. They found a sixfold difference between the two drugs; apparently, not all chlorpromazine is created equal.

The issue of therapeutic equivalence has become particularly important with the introduction of generic drugs. In the United States, patent laws ensure that a company that has developed a new chemical (or a new use for an old chemical) has for a period of 17 years protected control of that product. After that time, anyone is free to market the drug, although any brand name associated with it continues to be protected. If a patented drug has been profitable, it is likely that many companies will begin to produce it as soon as the period of protection afforded by patent laws expires. Although this may seem to be no more than good old American capitalism, there is no assurance that these new preparations are biologically or therapeutically equivalent to the original formulation. If they are not, the demonstrations of safety and effectiveness required by the Food and Drug Administration for the original preparation may not generalize to other brands. Perhaps cognizance of this issue contributes to physicians' preference for prescribing brand name drugs, which accounted for over 80% of all prescriptions written in 1982 (Ray, 1983).

The Fate of a Drug

The fate of a drug involves what happens to it after entering the body. After entry, a typical drug is absorbed, distributed, biotransformed, and excreted. In *absorption,* the drug enters the bloodstream. *Distribution* involves the movement of the drug through the bloodstream to its site of action, the place where it combines with protoplasm to produce an effect. *Biotransformation* refers to changes in the chemical structure of the drug characteristically produced by enzymatic action in the liver. Most drugs are biotransformed; the majority are inactivated in the process, but some are changed to an active form. *Excretion* refers to a drug's exit from the body, usually in urine.

Each step in the fate of a drug involves passage across cell membranes. The cell membrane is a thin (80 Angstrom) sheet of lipids and proteins organized in a mosaic structure. Drugs can cross cell membranes by passive diffusion or by active transport. In *passive diffusion*, drugs move through aqueous channels in the membrane, which is called *filtration*, or by dissolving in the membrane, from an area of greater concentration to an area of lesser concentration. In *active transport*, energy is used to move a substance across a membrane; this movement need not depend upon a favorable concentration gradient. (Facilitated diffusion, though very similar to active transport, does require a favorable concentration gradient. The uptake of glucose is an example of this process).

A number of factors influence the movement of drugs through passive diffusion. One is the concentration gradient: All else being equal, the greater the difference in concentration across a membrane, the more rapid the rate of movement. However, most drugs are too large to pass through channels in membranes and therefore must diffuse across the cell membrane. Drugs which are highly lipid-soluble do so readily; drugs which are highly water-soluble do not. Most drugs are weak acids or bases and are present in body fluids in both ionized (charged) and nonionized (electrically neutral) forms. In general, nonionized (or un-ionized) molecules are lipid-soluble and can diffuse across membranes, whereas ionized molecules cannot.

Because ionization impedes the passage of molecules across membranes, the movement of partly ionized drugs across membranes is a function of the pH of the internal environment and the pK_a of the drug. Put simply, the pK_a of a drug is the pH at which one-half of that drug's molecules occur in ionized form. The importance of pK_a and environmental pH is readily apparent if one considers that weak acids (pK_a of 3 or 4) are well absorbed from the stomach, an acidic medium, whereas weak bases (pK_a of 8 or

9) are poorly absorbed from the stomach but well absorbed from the less acidic intestines.

Though the factors which influence the passage of drugs across membranes are complex, it can be asserted in summary that (1) lipid-soluble molecules cross membranes more rapidly than water-soluble molecules, (2) un-ionized molecules cross membranes more readily than ionized molecules, (3) small molecules cross membranes more readily than large molecules, and (4) molecules which are actively transported cross membranes with ease. Detailed coverage of the variables that control the passage of drugs across membranes is provided in any good pharmacology text (e.g., Goth, 1984). Before leaving this topic, however, it should be noted that the passage of many drugs out of the bloodstream and into the central nervous system (CNS) is restricted by the unique physical structure and arrangement of endothelial cells of the brain capillaries and pericapillary glial cells. These features are responsible for the so-called *blood—brain barrier,* which largely prevents strongly ionized molecules from entering the CNS from the circulatory system. Highly lipid-soluble drugs cross this barrier with ease, however; cerebral blood flow is the only factor which limits their entry into the brain.

Absorption and Route of Administration

A drug must enter the body before it can be absorbed; the manner in which it does so is termed the *route of administration.* *Oral (enteral) administration* involves entry through the alimentary canal; the primary *parenteral* routes involve intraveneous, subcutaneous, and intramuscular injections. Certain drugs (e.g., nicotine) are commonly taken by inhalation, others (e.g., cocaine) are administered by being placed in contact with the membranes of the mouth, nose, or rectum. The intraperitoneal route, where drugs are injected into the peritoneal cavity, is commonly used with nonhumans but, being rather painful in bipeds and posing the risk of serious infection, has few human applications.

Rate and pattern of drug absorption are determined by route

of administration. Figure 1 shows the relations between four common routes of drug administration and plasma concentration of a typical drug. Plasma concentration directly determines the magnitude of drug effect; it is clear in Figure 1 that the rapidity, duration, and magnitude of a drug's effect are dependent upon route of administration.

In humans, convenience argues for the use of the oral route. However, many drugs are not absorbed when taken orally. Stomach enzymes digest some drugs, such as insulin, and others do not pass readily through cell membranes and consequently do not gain entry into the blood. Even when drugs are orally effective, this route may be troublesome (Julien, 1981). First, some drugs irritate the stomach lining, producing nausea and even ulceration. Second, although a known amount of drug may be taken

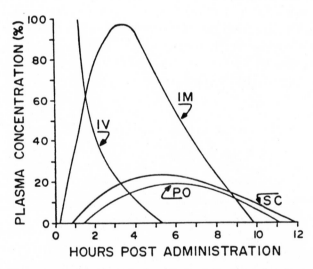

Figure 1. Plasma concentration of a hypothetical drug as a function of route of administration and time following drug administration. Routes of administration are abbreviated as follows: *IV* = intravenous (into a vein), *IM* = intramuscular (into a muscle), *SC* = subcutaneous (under the skin), *PO* = oral (through the alimentary canal). The general relations shown are typical of many drugs, although specific time courses of change in plasma concentration vary widely.

orally, the amount of drug actually entering the blood cannot always be estimated accurately. Individuals differ with respect to absorption of orally administered drugs, and absorption in a given person is affected by several factors, including stomach and intestinal pH and the presence of food in the stomach. Finally, as previously discussed, absorption is influenced by the physical characteristics of the preparation. Liquids usually are absorbed more readily than solids, although the two dosage forms sometimes are used interchangeably. Particulars of manufacture also influence absorption; different brands of the same drug may be absorbed at widely different rates. These factors limit the precision with which an orally given drug can be administered.

Parenteral drug administration is more precise, although rate of absorption following intramuscular or subcutaneous injection may vary widely as a function of (1) local blood flow, (2) the vehicle in which the drug is dissolved, and (3) injection volume. Intravenous drug administration allows for the immediate and accurate production of desired drug serum levels, since no absorption is involved. However, because of the immediacy of effects when this route is employed and the need for sterile techniques, intravenous injection is dangerous unless appropriately employed.

In addition to the routes described above, drugs are sometimes administered sublingually (i.e., through the oral mucosa), by direct injection into the brain, and topically by placing on the skin. These routes are described in detail elsewhere (Mayer *et al.*, 1980).

Distribution of Drugs

Once a drug is absorbed, it is distributed throughout the bloodstream. Parts of the body which are richly perfused, such as the heart, liver, brain, and kidneys, receive most of the drug shortly after absorption; the drug may reach muscle, skin, and fat considerably later. To reach their final sites of action, most drugs pass from small arteries to the capillaries, then through the capillary walls to the extracellular fluid, where they diffuse and eventually contact the cells they affect. With the vast majority of drugs (the exceptions are those few with nonselective actions, such as the denaturing of proteins), at a given point in time only a tiny fraction of the total amount of drug in the body is at the site of action and thereby producing an effect. The rest is located elsewhere in the body, and (as subsequently described) may leave the body without ever reaching the site of action.

The same factors which influence drug absorption determine the ease with which drugs will pass out of the circulatory system. In addition, some drugs selectively bind to plasma proteins; such protein-bound drugs are essentially trapped in the circulatory system. Other drugs selectively concentrate in fat, bone, or muscle, which impedes their distribution to other portions of the body. The barbiturate thiopental (Pentothal), for example, is highly lipid-soluble and thus is readily sequestered in fat cells. As the manufacturer points out, "Repeated intravenous doses lead to prolonged anesthesia because fatty tissues act as a reservoir; they accumulate Pentothal in concentration 6 to 12 times greater than the plasma concentration, and then release the drug slowly to cause prolonged anesthesia" (*Physicians' Desk Reference*, 1982, p. 559).

Biotransformation and Elimination

Many drugs are not readily eliminated from the body in their original form but after being *biotransformed* into more polar and less readily lipid-soluble metabolites are readily excreted. Biotransformation of most drugs occurs in the liver and may involve the nonsynthetic reactions of oxidation, reduction, or hydrolysis, or synthetic (conjugation) reactions, in which the drug or its metabolite couples with an endogenous substrate such as an amino acid. Describing these reactions is beyond the scope of the present text; they are clearly outlined by Goth (1984) and Mayer *et al.* (1980). For our purposes, it suffices to note that although biotransformation often results in the production of biologically in-active and readily excreted metabolites of the parent compound, as when morphine is altered through conjugation to morphine glucoronide, biotransformation also can result in metabolites which are as active or even more active than the parent com-pound. A good example of this is the biotransformation (through reduction) of chloral hydrate to trichloroethanol, which produces hypnotic effects identical to those of the parent compound.

The kidneys are the primary site of drug excretion, although the lungs, the skin, and the intestines are involved in the excre-tion of a few compounds. The kidneys are marvelously effective organs, charged with maintaining an appropriate internal en-vironment. In doing so, they must rid the body of the by-products of metabolic activity and of excessive quantities of sodium, po-tassium, and chloride but at the same time conserve necessary levels of these substances along with water, sugar, and other sub-stances essential for life. The manner in which this is accom-plished involves three processes: glomerular filtration, active tu-bular secretion, and passive tubular reabsorption. These pro-cesses are such that water-soluble, ionized molecules are excreted more readily than lipid-soluble, un-ionized molecules. That being the case, alteration of urinary pH can dramatically affect the rate of excretion of some drugs by altering the ionized fraction. For example, changing the urinary pH from 6.4 to 8.0 changes the fraction of nonionized salicylate, a strong acid and the active in-gredient in aspirin, from 1% to .04% and increases the rate of excretion by 400–600% (Mayer *et al.*, 1980). Because of this, administration of sodium bicarbonate to produce an alkaline urine and more rapid drug excretion is a part of the treatment for children suffering from the real and common medical emergency of salicylate poisoning.

A number of factors in addition to urinary pH can influence the rate of excretion of drugs. Among them are diseases of the liver or kidneys and the age of the individual. In general, hepatic and nephritic disease interferes with the biotransformation and excretion of drugs. These activities also are frequently impaired in the very young and very old, whose livers and kidneys do not function optimally. With some drugs, biotransformation and excretion differ significantly across species.

Drug Kinetics and Dose-Dependent Drug Effects

Pharmacokinetics is the branch of pharmacology concerned with the absorption, distribution, biotransformation, and excretion of drugs. "These factors, coupled with dosage, determine the concentration of drug at its sites of action and, hence, the intensity of its effects as a function of time" (Mayer *et al.*, 1980, p. 2).

The effects of all drugs are dose-dependent: the amount of drug that is administered determines both qualitative and quantitative aspects of its effects. At low enough doses, all drugs fail to produce observable effects; at high enough doses, all drugs produce toxic (harmful) effects. Actions observed between these end points typically are of greatest interest to pharmacologists, although toxic effects inevitably merit attention.

A common designation of drug dose is units of drug per unit of body weight, for example, 0.05 milligram *d*-amphetamine per kilogram body weight (0.05 mg/kg). Another designation of drug dose may produce more consistent results across patients; it is units of drug per unit surface area of the body. This designation is nonetheless uncommon. Drug blood (or plasma) level is a useful description of dosage with certain drugs (e.g., lithium chloride) and is favored for them.

The relation between drug dosage and the magnitude of effect is typically expressed in one of two ways. When the response of interest is discrete (i.e., the response either occurs or fails to occur), it is common to present the dose—response relation as a percentage of total exposed subjects who evidence the response. Figure 2 shows dose—effect curves for the hypnotic action of two hypothetical drugs, *A* and *B*. From this figure, the *median effective dose* (ED_{50}) of each can be extrapolated. This is the dose at which 50% of the subjects evidence the response of interest

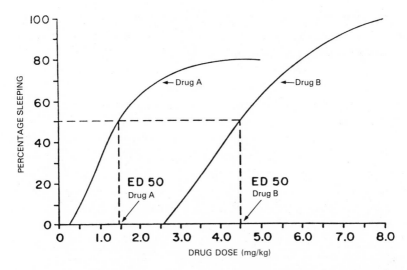

Figure 2. Percentage of subjects who were induced to sleep at each dose of two hypothetical drugs. The ED_{50} dose of each drug is illustrated by the dashed line and is the dose at which 50% of the subjects fell asleep within a specified period (e.g., 1 hour). The figure also shows that drug A is more potent, but drug B has greater peak efficacy.

(sleep) and this dose is indicated in Figure 2 by a dashed line. The maximum effectiveness, or *peak efficacy*, of each drug is also apparent. At its most effective dose, Drug B induced sleep in 90% of the subjects, whereas no dose of Drug A induced sleep in more than 75% of the subjects. Therefore, Drug B has the greater peak efficacy. Note that peak efficacy is not synonomous with *potency*. Potency refers to the amount of drug required to produce an effect of given intensity, frequently the ED_{50} dose. The ED_{50} dose of Drug A is lower than that of Drug B, therefore A is more potent. In clinical practice, however, peak efficacy is more significant than potency. Within limits, the actual amount of drug taken matters less than the magnitude of the effect produced by the most effective dose.

Another inference that can be drawn from an illustration like Figure 2 involves the mechanism of action of the drugs. If the shape of the functions and the maximum effects produced are similar, then it is likely that the drugs are acting by means of the same physiological mechanism (e.g., heroin and morphine affect the body through the same mechanisms, but the former is more potent than the latter). In the hypothetical example in Figure 2, the sedatives probably act through different mechanisms.

When response (effect) measures are continuous, dose–response relations usually are plotted with magnitude of effect on the y axis and dosage on the x axis. Such figures are interpreted just as when the ordinate depicts percentage of subjects evidencing an effect. (In figures showing dose–effect relations, dose is frequently but not necessarily scaled in logarithmic units; log transformations may convert sigmoidal dose–response curves to linear ones.) Figure 3 depicts an actual dose–response curve published by Sprague and Sleator (1977) showing the relation be-

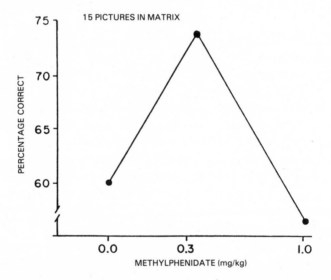

Figure 3. Effects of methylphenidate on picture recognition by hyperkinetic children. Children were briefly presented with a matrix of 15 pictures and a few seconds later were required to indicate whether a test picture had been presented in the matrix. Each data point represents mean percentage of pictures correctly recognized by 20 individuals across 240 tests. From Sprague & Sleator (1977). Redrawn and published by permission of the Association for the Advancement of Science and the authors.

tween dose of methylphenidate (Ritalin) given to hyperactive children and learning in a picture recognition task.

Dose–response relations are crucially important in evaluating all drugs. Any of a wide range of relations, linear or curvilinear, may be obtained between the amount of drug given and the magnitude and type of the resultant effect, and it is difficult to predict the nature of a dose–response relation *a priori* or following administration of fewer than three doses. For example, the dose–response relation shown in Figure 3 is the shape of an inverted U. If Sprague and Sleator had presented data only for the placebo (no drug) condition and the lower (0.3 mg/kg) drug dose, one might have assumed that higher drug doses would have further increased accuracy, a prediction not supported by the actual data.

The magnitude of any one response varies with drug dose; the range of responses produced also varies with the amount of drug taken. This is an important consideration in evaluating the safety of a compound. In general, the probability of adverse *side effects* (effects other than those for which a drug is taken) varies directly with drug dose. The relative safety of a drug increases as the distance between the dose required to produce the desired effect and the dose that produces damaging side effects grows. This relation is codified in the *therapeutic index* (TI), which usually takes the form therapeutic index = median lethal dose / median effective dose (abbreviated as $TI = LD_{50} / ED_{50}$), although more conservative measures are sometimes favored. Relative safety increases with this ratio, but the therapeutic index is misleading unless the dose–response curves for lethality (or other undesired effects) and the desired effect fail to overlap across all or nearly all of their lengths.

Time Course of Drug Action

Although drug dosage is a strong determinant of observed effects, the actions of a given dose will obviously vary over time. Each substance has a characteristic *time course of action*, which is determined by its physical properties, the dose administered, the route of administration, and organismic variables that alter the body's response to the drug. Since the magnitude of a drug's observed effects is directly related to drug blood levels, it is common practice to describe the time course of action of a substance by refering to alterations in drug blood levels across time. Table 4 shows how blood levels of a hypothetical drug might change over time following intravenous injection. Elimination of this drug, and many real ones, is analogous to the disappearance of a radioactive isotope by physical decay. Just as the rate of disappearance of a radioactive isotope is readily expressed as the time needed for one-half of it to decay (the half-life), the rate of disappearance of a drug may be described in terms of its *biological half-life*. The biological half-life, typically abbreviated as $T_{1/2}$, is readily calculated by measuring the time required for a given plasma level to decline by 50%.

Close examination of Table 4 will reveal two important points. The first is that the decline in drug level describes an exponential decay curve. That is, the change per unit time is a function of the concentration of the drug such that "the mean drug concentration in any hour divided by the concentration in the previous hour is a constant" (Goth, 1974, p. 23). When this occurs, *first-order kinetics* are said to obtain. For those drugs which follow

Table 4

Total Amount (Mg) of a Hypothetical Drug in Blood
at Various Times after Intravenous Injection[a]

	Time after injection (hours)						
	0	4	8	12	16	20	24
Total drug (mg)	400	200	100	50	25	13	7
	800	400	200	100	50	25	13

[a]This drug has a half-life of 4 hours and follows first-order kinetics. Although the drug would remain in the blood at a low concentration for an extended period, observable effects would disappear well before all of the drug was eliminated (e.g., when total mg drug fell below 25 mg).

first-order (exponential) kinetics, and most do, doubling the dose increases the duration of the drug's action by one half-life. This is the second significant point made evident in the table.

Although first-order kinetics are observed with many drugs, for some, maximum rate of elimination does not vary with dosage. In such cases, *zero-order kinetics* are said to hold, and elimination half-time varies directly with dosage. The anticonvulsant phenytoin (Dilantin) and ethanol (beverage alcohol) are two drugs which follow zero-order kinetics.

Tolerance and Physical Dependence

As noted earlier, a number of factors can influence the time course of action of a particular drug. Repeated administration of that substance, or of another compound, is one such factor of considerable importance. When a drug is given repeatedly, a *chronic* (as opposed to *acute*, or widely spaced) administration regimen is in effect. With chronic exposure, *tolerance* sometimes appears. Tolerance is evident when either (1) repeated administration of a given dose produces a progressively smaller effect or (2) a response of the magnitude initially produced by a given dose is produced only by administration of a higher dose (i.e., the dose—response curve is shifted to the right with chronic exposure). Figure 4 shows the development of tolerance to a hypothetical drug.

Pharmacologists conventionally differentiate *metabolic* (or kinetic) tolerance and *pharmacodynamic* (or cellular) tolerance. The former occurs when exposure to a drug increases the subsequent rate of its metabolism and excretion, a process which often involves enzyme induction. The latter is evident when adaptation to a drug occurs at a cellular level so that a given level of drug at the site of action produces weaker responses on subsequent exposures. Metabolic and pharmacodynamic tolerance are not mutually exclusive but appear together with certain drugs, such as nicotine.

A third type of tolerance, *behavioral tolerance*, occurs when

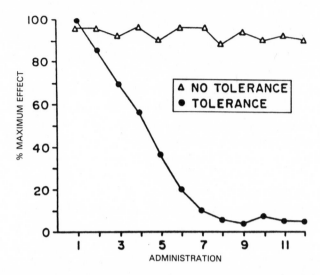

Figure 4. The effects of repeated administrations of a drug that produced tolerance and another drug to which tolerance did not develop. When tolerance occurs,
the effects of a drug lessen with repeated administrations, although the rapidity
and magnitude of this effect may vary.

responsiveness to a drug lessens only when a learned response
has been emitted in the drug state; drug exposure *per se* is not
sufficient for the development of behavioral tolerance.

In some cases, repeated exposure to one drug lessens the
effects of a second substance. When this occurs, *cross-tolerance*
is evident between the drugs. Cross-tolerance usually occurs
within groups of drugs with related mechanisms of action and
effects. Cross-tolerance occurs, for example, between the hallucinogens LSD, mescaline, and psilocybin and between the sedatives
pentobarbital, ethanol, and chlordiazepoxide (Librium) but does
not occur across these groups.

The rapidity with which tolerance develops and the extent to
which it occurs depend upon the drug in question, the response
being measured, and the conditions of exposure. Many drugs produce their greatest effect when initially given, with tolerance
rapidly developing. *Tachyphylaxis* is the technical term given to
tolerance which appears rapidly.

A phenomenon opposite to tolerance in behavioral outcome can result from repeated drug administrations. This is *accumulation*, wherein a drug is taken in more rapidly than it can be inactivated by the body, resulting in increasing blood levels and overt effects. Accumulation is a significant problem with substances not readily excreted by the body, for instance heavy metals and a variety of other environmental hazards.

Tolerance is often discussed together with *physical dependence*, since the two often but not inevitably appear coincidentally. Physical (or physiological) dependence describes the state of an organism in which abrupt termination of repeated drug administration is followed by a withdrawal syndrome. The withdrawal or abstinence syndrome is a confluence of signs (observable changes) and symptoms (changes reported by the individual) which emerge following abrupt termination of drug administration. An implication of the term *physical dependence* is that the chronic presence of the drug has altered the individual in such a way that normal functioning requires continued presence of the drug. Measurable disruption of normal activity induced by drug withdrawal includes physiological responses (e.g., diarrhea and vomiting when opioid administration is discontinued or tremors and convulsions when barbiturate administration is discontinued), overt behavioral responses (e.g., drug-seeking behavior), and subjective responses (e.g., self-reported dysphoria and craving for the drug).

The most prevalent explanation of the withdrawal syndrome is that the continuous presence of the drug causes cellular adaptation and therefore intense rebound responses are released when the drug is abruptly removed. Consistent with this notion is (1) the fact that withdrawal responses are usually in a direction opposite to the responses produced by a drug (e.g., the CNS depression produced by ethanol is replaced by convulsive activity, or the constipation produced by opioids is replaced by diarrhea) and (2) the feasibility of explaining tolerance, a frequent concomitant of physical dependence, as resulting from cellular adaptation. An important pharmacological characteristic of any drug is whether or not it produces physical dependence and, if so, the nature of the withdrawal syndrome associated with the drug. For example, a distinct withdrawal syndrome follows abstinence from chronic exposure to either the opioids or the barbiturates. Amphetamine withdrawal is characterized by a different and less dramatic syndrome in which eating and sleeping occur.

Whereas the occurrence of a withdrawal syndrome is generally taken as the hallmark of physiological dependence, tolerance is frequently taken to be an integral part of the state of physiological dependence. This assumption is often correct. However, tolerance, and behavioral tolerance in particular, may occur in an organism in which no measurable physical dependence is present (*National Institute on Drug Abuse*, 1978). Also, the development of tolerance may or may not covary in a parallel fashion with the development of physiological dependence. The one common feature of tolerance and physical dependence is that together they imply a change in the state of an organism which results from chronic drug administration. Furthermore, both tolerance and physical dependence are important considerations when drug self-administration occurs. We will return to this topic in Chapter 7.

Drugs, Receptors, and Neuronal Activity

Although the fact comes as a surprise to the layperson, pharmacologists generally acknowledge that drugs cannot qualitatively alter the function of cells. The response to a drug is within the framework of normal physiological function and is limited by the capacity of the cell to respond. In the case of most drugs, cellular function (and, as an eventual consequence, behavior) is altered through a chain of events that is initiated by the formation of a bond between the drug and some cellular constituent referred to as the *receptor*.

Cellular constituents which serve as drug receptors include proteins, nucleic acids, and the lipids of cell membranes. "The binding of drugs to receptors, in various cases, involves all known types of interactions—ionic, hydrogen, van der Walls, and covalent" (Gilman, Mayer, & Melmon, 1980, p. 29). Individual receptors show specificity in that only a limited number of drugs combine with them. *Agonist* drugs combine with receptors to produce a characteristic effect; such drugs have *affinity* (i.e., they combine with a receptor) and *efficacy* (i.e., they affect the function of that cell). Other drugs, termed *antagonists*, interact with the receptor or another cellular component to reduce the action of an agonist. If this action can be overcome by increasing the concentration of the agonist, the antagonism is termed *competitive*. Competitive antagonism usually involves the antagonist's combining reversibly with the receptor cell. Although the antagonist has no efficacy, it reduces the actions of the agonist by competing for receptor sites.

In contrast to competitive antagonists, *noncompetitive antagonists* prevent the agonist from having an effect at any concentration. This action may involve the antagonist's irreversibly combining with the receptor, or interacting with a cell so as to prevent the initiation of an effect following the formation of the agonist—receptor complex. The mechanisms whereby formation of a drug—receptor complex modulates cellular activity have been disclosed only within the past decade. These mechanisms involve cyclic nucleotides (cyclic AMP and cyclic GMP), are rather complex, and will not be considered here. The interested reader is directed to Nathanson and Greengard (1978) for a clear and informative coverage of this topic.

Although receptors will combine with exogenous drugs, they are usually occupied and activated by endogenous substances. These substances provide the means whereby cells interact and are responsible for the coordination and integration of bodily function. Understanding the physiological mechanisms through which drugs affect behavior demands knowledge of the processes through which this integration occurs. Unfortunately, our present knowledge of these processes is rudimentary and incomplete.

We do know, however, that the human brain contains approximately 10 billion cells called neurons. These neurons, along with those in the spinal cord, make up the central nervous system. Transmission of information in the CNS is electrochemically mediated. In its resting state, the inside of each neuron is negatively charged (about −70 millivolts) with respect to its outside. This *resting potential* is the result of the unequal distribution of ions within and outside the neuron. In the resting state, the neuronal membrane is relatively impermeable to sodium, which is positively charged, but easily crossed by potassium (positively charged) and chloride ions (negatively charged). In addition, the membrane is always impermeable to the large organic ions (negatively charged) which are sequested within the cell. Because of these properties and the action of the "sodium pump," which actively extrudes sodium from within to outside the neuron, in the resting state sodium is found at high concentrations outside, and organic anions at high concentrations inside, the neuron. As a passive consequence of this distribution, potassium ions are in excess within the cell and chloride ions in excess outside it. The net result of this distribution is the resting potential.

If the neuron is perturbed in particular ways, as when an endogenous substance combines with receptor material on its membrane, the permeability of the membrane to specific ions may be altered and its electrical potential may consequently change. This change may involve either *hyperpolarization* (i.e., an increase in potential) or *depolarization* (i.e., a decrease in potential). If the depolarization is of sufficient magnitude (such that the potential is reduced to about −40 millivolts), the membrane may become very permeable to positively charged sodium ions, which begin to enter the neuron.

As the sodium ions rush in, an *action potential*, or nerve spike, is generated. This wave of electrical activity, which is approximately 60 millivolts in magnitude and lasts less than one millisecond, passes rapidly and without decrement along the neuron until that cell ends. (After the action potential has ended, the permeability of the neuronal membrane to sodium decreases, the sodium that has entered is extruded, and the resting potential is eventually restored.) There, at the *synapse*, where this presynaptic nerve cell is in close proximity to a postsynaptic cell, a naturally occurring chemical *neurotransmitter*, synthesized in the body and stored in the presynaptic cell, is released.

This neurotransmitter dissipates across the synaptic cleft (a fluid-filled "gap" between neurons) and combines with receptor material on the membrane of the postsynaptic neuron. Neurotransmitters which depolarize the postsynaptic neuron and others which hyperpolarize it can be released from the same neuron. As Julien (1978) notes, "All cells in the nervous system receive impulses from both excitatory and inhibitory synapses. Indeed, the exquisite beauty of the nervous system is maintained by this delicate balance between excitation and inhibition" (p. 222). Depolarization of the postsynaptic neuron by the formation of a neurotransmitter–receptor complex is referred to as an *excitatory postsynaptic potential; inhibitory postsynaptic potential* is the name assigned to hyperpolarization produced in this manner.

A handful of chemicals are known to function as neurotransmitters, and many others are likely candidates for the role. Among the best studied neurotransmitters are norepinephrine, dopamine, acetylcholine, serotonin, and gamma aminobutyric acid (GABA). Acetylcholine and norepinephrine serve as neurotransmitters in the peripheral nervous system (PNS), as well as in the CNS, and much of what is known concerning their actions arose from studies of the PNS, which includes the somatic nervous system and both (i.e., the sympathetic and parasympathetic) branches of the the autonomic nervous system.

Among the major ways in which drugs can affect neurotransmission are the following:

1. By interfering with the synthesis of the neurotransmitter. The use of levodopa to treat Parkinson's disease involves such an action. Parkinson's disease produces tremor, bradykinesia, rigidity, and postural defect and is the result of a relative deficiency of dopamine in the striatal tracts of the brain (Bianchine, 1980). Levodopa is a metabolic precursor of dopamine; giving it to patients with Parkinson's disease increases dopaminergic activity in the striatal tracts and thereby alleviates symptoms.

2. By interfering with the storage of the neurotransmitter. Reserpine, which comes from an Indian climbing shrub (*Rauwolfia serpentina*), has such an action. This drug

interferes with the storage of serotonin and of the cate-
cholamine neurotransmitters norepinephrine and dopamine. Once used to manage schizophrenia, reserpine frequently produces severe and intractable depression and is
currently restricted in use to the management of hyperten-
sion not adequately controlled by other therapies (Weiner,
1980).

3. By interfering with the release of the neurotransmitter.
   One of the actions of cocaine is to facilitate the release of
   the neurotransmitter norepinephrine.

4. By interfering with the inactivation of the neurotransmitter. If a neurotransmitter were to bind eternally to receptor
   material, each receptor could modulate cellular function
   only once. However, enzymatic action provides a mechanism whereby the bond can be broken. Dopamine and
   norepinephrine, for example, are primarily inactivated at
   synaptic sites by the enzyme monoamine oxidase (MAO);
   the enzyme catechol-O-methyltransferase (COMT) also de-
   grades these neurotransmitters. MAO inhibitors such as
   pargyline (Eutonyl) were once commonly used as antidepressants and today are occasionally used as antihyper-
   tensives.

   Active reuptake into the presynaptic neuron also can
   inactivate a neurotransmitter. This process, as well as enzymatic action, is responsible for the inactivation of dopamine and norepinephrine. One of several posited actions
   of d-amphetamine is to interefere with the re-uptake of
   these transmitters; this action appears to be shared with
   cocaine.

5. By interfering with receptors. As noted previously, drugs
   can combine with receptors as either agonists, in which
   case they affect the cell, or as antagonists, which, having
   affinity but no efficacy, do not directly alter cellular function. Such antagonists do, however, block the access of
   neurotransmitters to receptor sites. Neuroleptics such as
   chlorpromazine (Thorazine) and thioridazine (Mellaril)
   produce their antipsychotic effects by blocking dopami-

nergic receptors, an action shown in stylized form in Figure 5.

Unfortunately, blockage of dopamine receptors produces undesirable as well as desirable effects; the former include a range of serious motor dysfunctions. The production of a wide range of effects is not unique to neuroleptics: It is a fundamental tenet of pharmacology that *all drugs produce multiple effects.* In part, this simply reflects the fact that one neurotransmitter controls a range of physiological functions. Moreover, a given drug may alter the function of several different neurotransmitters, each of which can activate a number of receptors with different effects.

It has become apparent in recent years that all of the receptors with which a particular neurotransmitter will combine are not alike. Receptor subtypes can differ with respect to location in the body, relative affinity for particular drugs, and the physiological activities which they control. For example, two types of dopamine receptors, D_1 and D_2, have been isolated. The relative anti-

Figure 5. Stylized drawing of a neuroleptic drug's (N) blockade of receptors (R) activated by the neurotransmitter dopamine (D). Due to its configuration, the neuroleptic is able to combine with the receptor, but formation of this complex does not directly modulate cellular activity. Dopamine better "fits" the receptor, and formation of this complex directly affects subsequent cellular activity. Receptors are located on the membrane of the postsynaptic neuron, dopamine and neuroleptic molecules not attached to a receptor are afloat in the extracellular fluid.

psychotic efficacy of antipsychotic drugs appears to correlate highly with their affinity for D_1, but not D_2, receptors. Receptor subtypes have also been described for acetylcholine, serotonin, GABA, and norepinephrine, as well as for opioid drugs. These latter receptors are known to bind with endogeneous morphine-like substances termed endorphins (a term coined from *endogenous morphine*).

Further discussion of receptors is beyond the scope of the present chapter, as is coverage of the effects of drugs on cells other than neurons (e.g., effectors and sensory cells). An excellent and contemporary review of drug and neurotransmitter receptors has been provided by Solomon (1984), who pioneered work in the area. Extensive coverage of the physiological and biochemical actions of a wide range of drugs is provided by Gilman, Goodman, and Gilman (1980) and by Goth (1984).

Drug Interactions

The preceding section introduced agonist and antagonist drugs. When an agonist and an antagonist are given in combination, their effect is always less than that produced by the agonist alone. The ability of naloxone to prevent or reverse the respiratory depression produced by heroin is an example of such an interaction and one of practical value in treating victims of heroin overdoses.

When an agonist and an antagonist drug are given together, their effects are *infraadditive,* that is, less than predicted on the basis of an arithmetic summation of their individual effects. Drugs produce *additive* effects when the magnitude of the effect produced when the drugs are given together approximates an arithmetic summation of the effects of the two agents given alone. *Supraadditive,* or synergistic, effects occur when the combined effects of two drugs are greater than the sum of the effects of the two agents given alone. For example, both carbon tetrachloride and ethanol damage the liver, but the extent of the damage produced by the two together is much greater than predicted on the basis of the actions of the individual agents.

Drugs can interact through a variety of mechanisms in addition to those previously described. In functional antagonism, two chemicals produce opposite effects on the same physiological functions, whereas in dispositional antagonism one substance alters the fate of another so that less of it reaches the site of action. Finally, direct chemical interactions between substances also can occur, as when chelating agents combine with heavy metals and thereby prevent or reverse the binding of these metals to body ligands. Melmon and Gilman (1980) carefully review these and other drug interactions.

Individual Differences

A wide range of nonbehavioral variables affects the actions of a given drug. Since these variables are not necessarily consistent across individuals, considerable variability may be evident in the behavioral and physiological responses of different people exposed to the same drug regimen. Several factors which may affect an individual's response to a particular compound have been presented in this chapter. These include age, the presence of disease, and history with respect to the drug and other substances. In addition to these variables, genotype can influence the action of certain drugs, as can gender.

Although the effects of drugs are lawful and can in principle be predicted accurately, drugs are not "magic bullets" which selectively and inevitably alter particular behaviors. All drugs are to some extent nonselective in their actions, and the actions of all drugs can be modulated by nonpharmacological variables. Because of this, care must be taken to individualize pharmacotherapeutic treatments, and it must be recognized that general statements concerning the behavioral effects of drugs are likely to be limited in generality. Controlled investigations have, for instance, shown that neuroleptics are generally of value in dealing with the altered motor behavior, perceptual alterations (hallucinations), altered mood (flat affect), disturbed thinking, and unusual interpersonal behavior characteristic of those persons diagnosed as schizophrenic (Berger, 1978; Lickey & Gordon, 1983). According to Berger, two conclusions can be drawn concerning the pharmacological management of schizophrenia:

> First, maintenance antipsychotics can prevent relapse in many but
> not all patients with schizophrenia. Second, since some patients do
> not relapse on placebo, these patients do not require maintenance
> treatment. Unfortunately . . . it is not possible to predict with certainty which patients will relapse. (p. 977)

Nor is it possible to predict which individuals will exhibit one or more of the deleterious side effects commonly associated with these drugs.

Concluding Comments

Isolating the factors which determine how an individual will respond to neuroleptics, and to other behavior-change drugs, is a worthy goal that can be pursued at many levels of analysis. Considerable gains have been made in understanding the biochemical bases of mental illness and the effects of drugs on neurotransmission (see Baldessarini, 1977; Berger, 1978; Gordon & Lickey, 1983), and it may one day be possible to use biochemical assays to predict how an individual will respond to a particular drug. It may, however, also be possible to predict and explain drug effects without recourse to biochemistry. This possibility is explored in the balance of the present text.

CHAPTER

3

Overview of Behavioral Psychology

Behavioral psychology as it exists today is a young discipline.[1] Although its philosophical underpinnings have their origins in antiquity, most writers who review the historical development of the field begin their story about the turn of the present century.

Four men, Edward Thorndike, John Watson, B. F. Skinner, and Ivan Pavlov, played especially important roles in establishing present day behavioral psychology.

Watson is best remembered for questioning or, perhaps more accurately, attacking, the procedures and paradigms of the mainstream psychology of his day. In the book *Behaviorism*, Watson (1924) made a number of assertions that must have bordered on

[1]Throughout this and other chapters, the terms *behavioral psychology* and *behaviorism* are used to refer to the branch of psychology currently associated with B. F. Skinner and his colleagues. This is conventional and certainly more parsimonious than using the cumbersome if descriptive phrases "the experimental analysis of behavior" and "applied behavior analysis" to refer respectively to basic and applied Skinnerian psychology. It must be recognized, however, that the terms *behavioral psychology* and *behaviorism* can be more broadly construed and are sometimes used to refer to any and all of several different analyses of the factors which account for the actions of humans and other species. I hope that the present exposition will not reflect such catholicity.

the heretical in the eyes of most of his contemporaries. He wrote, for instance, "It is the business of behavioristic psychology to be able to predict and control human activity. To do this it must gather scientific data by experimental methods" (Watson, 1924, p. 11). These methods demand directly observable data, and Watson argued for a purely empirical psychology concerned only with how overt behavior (responding) changes as a function of other observable changes in the environment (stimuli). For him, dualistic explanations of behavior, wherein an unobservable mind (or soul, or other hypothetical entity) is given causal status, were simply and absolutely unacceptable. They remain so for many behaviorists today.

Yet Watson, despite the crucial importance of his work for the development of behavioral psychology, did not contribute greatly to an understanding of the learning process now called *operant conditioning*.[2] Watson apparently was much influenced by Pavlov's (e.g., 1910) work in respondent conditioning and primarily emphasized the relation of temporally antecedent stimuli to behavior. However, the fundamental assumption of operant conditioning is that the consequences of behavior in one situation are a powerful determinant of whether or not that behavior will subsequently recur in similar circumstances.

Teachers and trainers have always made use of this principle to produce desired behaviors in their charges, but it is Thorndike who usually receives credit for formally expressing the relation of responses to their consequences. He did so in the *Law of Effect* (Thorndike, 1911), today recognized (if only in paraphrase) by

---

[2]Behavioral psychologists assume that many important responses are controlled by operant conditioning, which will be discussed in detail later in the chapter. In general, operant conditioning occurs when behavior is controlled by its consequences, that is, by relations between responses and events (stimuli) which follow these responses in time. Respondent conditioning, wherein behavior is controlled by stimulus–stimulus (as opposed to response–stimulus) relations, also is responsible for the development and maintenance of significant responses. It too will be described in this chapter.

most undergraduate psychology students. This is an early version of the "law":

> Of several responses made to the same situation, those which are accompanied or closely followed by satisfaction to the animal will, other things being equal, be more firmly connected to the situation, so that, when it recurs, they will be more likely to recur; those which are accompanied or closely followed by discomfort to the animal will, other things being equal, have their connections with that situation weakened, so that, when it recurs, they will be less likely to occur. (Thorndike, 1911, p. 245)

Thorndike's Law of Effect did not much impress Watson, who criticized it in a discussion of how habits (learned responses) are acquired. He opined:

> Most of the psychologists, it is to be regretted, have even failed to see that there is a problem. They believe habit formation is implanted by kind fairies. For example, Thorndike speaks of pleasure stamping in the successful movement and displeasure stamping out the unsuccessful movement. (1924, p. 206)

One perhaps can understand Watson's displeasure with the mentalistic cant of Thorndike's law and the unfortunate "stamping" metaphor. Yet the fundamental message of the Law of Effect—that the consequences of behavior can powerfully affect learning and performance—stands as the cornerstone of the scientific psychology he so staunchly defended.

This psychology owes a recognized debt to Skinner, whose research revealed much concerning how behavior is affected by antecedent and consequent stimuli and whose writings broadly popularized these findings and their significance. In his first book, *The Behavior of Organisms* (1938), Skinner described most of the basic principles of operant conditioning. The importance of these principles for understanding human behavior was made clear in a sequel, *Science and Human Behavior* (1953).

> In *Science and Human Behavior*, using only the basic concepts of behavior analysis that appeared in *The Behavior of Organisms*, some results of his subsequent work with pigeons, and the material that subsequently went into *Verbal Behavior*, he managed to deal with a wide variety of human situations from a completely behavioral point of view, and very convincingly at that. It was this extension to all

aspects of human activity that, I think, provided behaviorists with
the encouragement necessary for them to begin contributing to the
areas of mental illness, mental retardation, and other applied fields.
(Michael, 1980, p. 4)

Science and Human Behavior may well have encouraged behaviorists to apply the findings of their science to the solution of
human behavior problems. However, they did so only sporadically
in the decade following its publication: Prior to the mid-1960s,
most research in behavioral psychology utilized nonhuman subjects and was intended primarily to increase understanding of the
factors that control behavior. Much of this research was reported
in the *Journal of the Experimental Analysis of Behavior* (*JEAB*),
founded in 1958.

By 1965, however, behaviorists were steadfastly attempting
to explain and treat problem behaviors in a variety of populations.
These early clinical endeavors were reported in a number of
sources, including texts edited by Ullmann and Krasner (1965)
and by Ulrich, Stachnik, and Mabry (1966). A new journal devoted
entirely to the publication of articles describing behaviorists' attempts to deal with significant problem behaviors, entitled the
Journal of Applied Behavior Analysis (*JABA*), appeared in 1968.

Basic research continued during the 1960s; much of it was
described in *JEAB* articles. Several books devoted to fundamental
principles of behavioral psychology and to basic research findings
also were published during this decade, and still more appeared
during the 1970s. Table 5 lists a number of happenings from
1935–1970 which contributed to the growth of behavioral psychology. More recent events are not included since they are numerous, and many of the more important ones will be addressed
in subsequent chapters.

The history of behavioral psychology is interesting in its own
right, and has been carefully considered elsewhere (e.g., Michael,
1980). However, for our purposes, knowing the history of the
discipline is less important that knowing its fundamental principles. The balance of this chapter provides a brief overview of these
principles. This section is intended for the reader with little or no
training in behavioral psychology; those conversant with the top-

Table 5
Important Happenings in Behavioral Psychology, 1935–1970

Year	Event
1938	Skinner publishes *The Behavior of Organisms*, which sets forth the basic principles of behavioral psychology.
1947	The first Conference on the Experimental Analysis of Behavior (behavioral psychology) is held at Indiana University. This conference led to the founding of the Society for the Experimental Analysis of Behavior, which publishes *JEAB* and *JABA*.
1948	Skinner publishes the controversial *Walden Two*, a novel describing a utopian society based on the principles of behavioral psychology.
1950	Keller and Schoenfeld publish *Principles of Psychology*, an influential introduction to behavioral psychology.
1953	*Science and Human Behavior* appears. In this text, Skinner extends to human behavior the analysis outlined in *The Behavior of Organisms*.
1957	*Schedules of Reinforcement*, by Ferster and Skinner, and Skinner's *Verbal Behavior* appear. The former makes clear the role of reinforcement schedules in controlling behavior, the latter provides an operant analysis of human verbal behavior.
1958	*JEAB*, the first journal devoted entirely to behavioral psychology, is founded.
1960	The research philosophy and methodology characteristic of behavioral psychology is described in Sidman's *Tactics of Scientific Research*.
1961	Bijou and Baer publish Volume I of *Child Development*, which offers a behavioral approach to a field traditionally dominated by cognitive theories. A programmed text describing basic principles of behavioral psychology also appears (Holland & Skinner, 1961).
1965	*Case Studies in Behavior Modification* (Ullmann & Krasner, 1965) is published. This edited text described the application of behavioral principles to the solution of socially significant problems.
1966	Two edited texts appear, one providing reviews of basic research in many areas of behavioral psychology (Honig, 1966), the other (Ulrich, Stachnik, & Mabry, 1966) describing clinical applications of behavioral principles.
1968	*JABA*, the first journal dedicated to publishing reports of the clinical application of behavior principles, is inaugurated.
1969	Skinner publishes *Contingencies of Reinforcement*, in which a number of important conceptual issues were addressed (e.g., the differences between rule-governed and contingency-shaped behavior).

ic can skip this material without significant loss. More detailed but nonetheless elementary introductions to behavioral psychology have been provided by a number of authors (e.g., Lutzker & Martin, 1981; Powers & Osborne, 1976; Rachlin, 1976).

Science and Behavioral Psychology

From the time of Watson's and Skinner's earliest writings, many behaviorists have proclaimed their approach to psychology unique, scientific, and invaluable. Barber (1976) says, "Hearst (1967), Krantz (1971), and others (e.g., Harlow, 1969) have noted that present-day behaviorists who adhere to the Skinnerian or operant conditioning approach appear to share a common paradigm" (p. 7). In this context, *paradigm* refers to "a conceptual framework and a body of assumptions, belief, and related methods and techniques that are shared by a large group of scientists at a particular time" (Barber, 1976, p. 4). The paradigm accepted by a scientist determines what is studied, how it is studied, and the manner in which obtained results are interpreted. For example:

> As Katahn and Koplin (1968) pointed out, the behavioristic paradigm emphasizes objective descriptions of environmental events, operational definitions, and controlled experiments while the cognitive paradigm seeks to construct a model of internal processes and structures that can lead to the observed output. These contrasting paradigms lead to different questions and to different ways of designing and conducting investigations. Furthermore, even if psychologists who adhere to these divergent paradigms obtain similar data—which is highly unlikely since they will conduct quite different studies— their paradigms will lead to divergent interpretations of the data (Katahn & Koplin, 1968). (Barber, 1976, p. 8)

The purpose of the present section is to introduce the behavioristic paradigm. Skinner (e.g., 1974) has provided further explanation and defense of the conceptual perspective summarized herein and should be consulted by the reader interested in the logical structuring of behavioral psychology or in behaviorism as a philosophy.

One of the fundamental assumptions of behavioral psychology is that the observable responses of living creatures are worthy of study in their own right. Behavior, whether it be the self-administration of heroin or a written response to a question on a personality inventory, is important *per se*, not because it reveals anything about phenomena at another level of analysis, whether physiological or mental. Because of this focus, great care is taken to ensure that any behavior of interest is clearly defined and precisely measured. To avoid vexing ambiguities concerning what is meant when a particular behavior is referred to, behavioral psychologists employ *operational definitions*. Simply put, the operational definition of a behavior is an exact specification of the way in which it is measured. The history of psychology has been marred by much fruitless debate concerning the meanings of such terms as *intelligence, learning,* and *aggression.* In large part, these debates have stemmed from linguistic imprecision; people shared a set of terms but used them differently. Such Babel can be avoided only by consistent operationalism coupled with an insistence that scientific psychology limit its study to measurable actions that can be scaled along physical dimensions. Behaviors commonly are quantified along the dimensions of *magnitude, latency, duration, accuracy, frequency,* and *rate* of occurrence.

Magnitude refers to the physical strength of a behavior, for example, the force exerted in a manual task. Latency refers to the time elapsed between some environmental event and the onset of a response. The time between the onset and offset of a response defines response duration; accuracy reflects the extent to which a response is controlled by prior stimuli. Performance on a pen-and-pencil intelligence test is a measure of response accuracy in that the appropriateness of a given response is determined by the stimulus (question) that preceded it. Frequency refers to the absolute number of times that a response occurs, whereas rate denotes the number of occurrences per unit time.

A second assumption of behavioral psychology is that to explain any behavior one must demonstrate that some aspect of that behavior—its magnitude, latency, duration, accuracy, frequency, or rate of occurrence—covaries with the magnitude of some other measurable variable. That is, the behavior of interest, termed the *dependent variable*, must be shown to differ obviously as a particular aspect of the environment, the *independent variable*, is altered along some physical dimension. This may be clarified by example. Consider a situation in which we want to determine the effects of the phenothiazine neuroleptic chlorpromazine on the tested intelligence of moderately mentally retarded children.

Our first task would be to devise some standard measure of the dependent variable "intelligence," for which the Wechsler Intelligence Scale for Children—Revised (WISC-R) might suffice. Our second task would be to determine how performance on this test varies as a function of the presence or absence of our independent variable, chlorpromazine. Thus, in view of our knowledge of chlorpromazine, we would choose a drug regimen (i.e., how and when the drug is to be administered), then measure intelligence in the presence and absence of the drug. Since drug effects are known to vary across doses, we probably would compare the effects of several clinically relevant drug doses, say, 0, 50, 100, and 200 mg.

Intelligence would be tested at each of these doses and the relation between drug dose and tested intelligence ascertained. However, we would probably want to determine the dose–response relation on more than one occasion before reaching any firm conclusions concerning chlorpromazine's effects on intelligence. It is always possible that variables unknown to the experimenter are affecting behavior in one or more of the conditions of interest, such that behavior differs in those conditions but does so because of some unknown *extraneous* variable, not the independent variable of interest. Ponder what might happen if chlorpromazine actually had no effect on tested intelligence, but our subject was deprived of sleep when tested at the 0 mg dose and consequently performed badly, but was well rested and hence performed better when tested at the other drug doses. Given this outcome, we might erroneously conclude that chlorpromazine increased tested intelligence at all doses. Such a conclusion would not be supported in further tests by other researchers and would have been avoided had we tested each dose on two or more occasions, barring the unlikely possibility that the child was again deprived of sleep when the 0 mg dose was tested and at no other time. Repeatability of observations is synonymous with believability in science, therefore we probably would want to give each dose at least twice. We might also arrange to do the same set of tests with more than one participant; if a similar dose—response relation was obtained across individuals, our faith in the generality of the relation would be enhanced considerably.

Let us assume, then, that we have decided to give 0, 50, 100, and 200 mg of chlorpromazine to two mentally retarded children and to measure intelligence as assayed by the WISC-R when each dose is given. Each dose is administered to each subject on two occasions, in a random or irregular sequence. Figure 6 shows three possible outcomes of this experiment. A clear *functional relation* is exhibited in the upper frames of this figure, where tested intelligence varies inversely with chlorpromazine dose for both subjects, during both determinations of the dose—response curve. The middle frames show data that fail to depict a functional relation; tested intelligence did not differ as drug dose changed. The lower frames depict an essentially uninterpretable dose—effect relation. Here, a given drug dose failed to produce consistent effects across the two subjects and across repeated administrations to the same subject. Further testing would be required to determine why these data were so variable. As discussed in Chapter 6, behavioral psychologists have long contended that the intensive study of individual subjects provides the best means of isolating sources of variability (i.e., extraneous variables), as well as determining the actions of independent variables. Acceptance of this approach to research is an important feature of behavioral psychology (see Sidman, 1960).

Once it is clear that an independent variable is functionally related to a dependent variable, prediction, control, and explanation of the dependent variable—the three goals of science—become possible. Prediction is possible because the value of the independent variable determines, in probabilistic fashion, the value of the dependent variable. Thus, all other things being equal, the probable value of the dependent variable can be predicted given knowledge of the value of the independent variable to which a person is exposed.

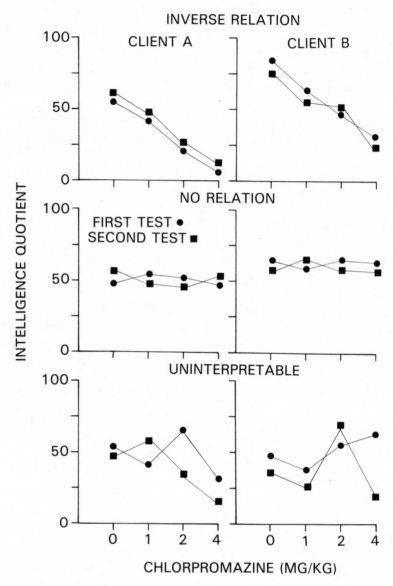

Figure 6. Three possible effects of chlorpromazine on the tested intelligence quotient of two mentally retarded children. A clear functional relation is evident in the upper frames; the data presented in the middle frames indicate that the two variables were not related; and the lower frames depict data that are essentially uninterpretable.

Remember, please, the functional relation between dose of methylphenidate given to hyperactive children and performance in a picture recognition task described by Sprague and Sleator (1977) and discussed in Chapter 2. Knowing their findings, we could predict that hyperactive children probably would be more accurate in picture recognition, or in performing a similar task, when given 0.3 mg/kg of the drug than when given either 0 or 1.0 mg/kg. If sufficient knowledge about the precise relation between the independent and dependent variable were available, we might also be able to quantify our prediction with fair accuracy.

In those cases in which the value of the independent variable is subject to manipulation, the value of the dependent variable can be controlled by selecting the value of the independent variable. The applied significance of scientific research stems from the disclosure of independent variables that are subject to manipulation by clinicians.

The notion that the description of functional relations provides an adequate explanation of behavior, or any other phenomenon, may not be intuitively obvious. However, in behavioral psychology as in science in general, it is held that something is "explained" when we can specify the events that "cause" it. As Eacker points out, "(A causal relation) . . . is the relationship between an independent and a dependent variable when the independent one may be prior to or contemporaneous with the dependent variable. In short . . . a causal relation is a functional one" (1972, p. 562). It must be emphasized, however, that any behavioral dependent variable is functionally related to a number of independent variables—no behavior has a single cause. Functional relations are most useful as explanations of behavior if (1) the relation between the independent and dependent variables is a potent one that occurs in many circumstances, and (2) the relation between the independent variable and the dependent variable is a general one that does not depend on idiosyncratic definitions or parameters of the variables in question. To be of any practical use, functional relations also must describe cause-and-effect sequences in which the independent variable is subject to manipulation.

A primary assumption of behavioral psychology is that behavior, including that of humans, is lawfully related to other physical events and is in that sense *determined.* Whether this assertion is true in all circumstances cannot be empirically determined, but it is abundantly clear that behavior can be *predicted* and hence understood only if it is functionally related to other events. Put simply, science, including the science of human behavior, must presuppose a deterministic universe.

A deterministic world coupled with the experimental method allows scientists to discover functional relations. To be useful in generally understanding behavior, however, specific functional relations must be organized and classified according to the general principles which they portray. Well-established functional relations constitute the laws of science. Such laws are tentative and data-based and vary along a continuum from molar to molecular. Molar laws express in a general way observed relations between classes of variables, whereas molecular laws specify in detail the functional relations between tightly delineated independent and dependent variables. Molecular laws are apt to be precise but limited with respect to generality and the range of phenomena for which they can account. In contrast, molar laws account for much data but tend to be imprecise unless they are very carefully conceived.

In general, as any science progresses it becomes increasingly parsimonious in that progressively fewer explanatory principles (laws) are required to account for a constantly expanding data base. At present, behavioral psychology has advanced to a point at which a considerable range of behavioral outcomes can be understood in light of a handful of explanatory principles. These principles are explored in the following section.

Respondent Conditioning

In *respondent conditioning* (also termed Pavlovian or classical conditioning), behavior is controlled through stimulus–stimulus pairings. (A stimulus is simply a physical event.) In this procedure, the presentation of one stimulus, termed the *unconditional stimulus* (US), characteristically elicits a measurable behavior termed the *unconditional response* (UR). The US–UR relation is "reflexive"; that is, in the absence of any specific training, the US elicits the UR in all (or nearly all) intact members of a species. In many cases, the unconditional response is of obvious survival value to the organism. For example, intense unconditional stimuli such as strong heat applied to the extremities elicit rapid limb withdrawal, which minimizes tissue damage.

Respondent conditioning, schematically represented in Figure 7, involves pairing a *conditional stimulus* (CS) with the unconditional stimulus. The CS can be any environmental change detectable by the organism being conditioned; this stimulus, however, must be neutral in the sense of not serving as a US prior to conditioning.

Under the respondent conditioning paradigm, the CS, through being paired with the US, comes to evoke a *conditional response* (CR), which often (but by no means always) is topographically similar to the UR. If, for example, a CS is respondently paired with a US (such as a blast of air into the eye) that elicits an eye

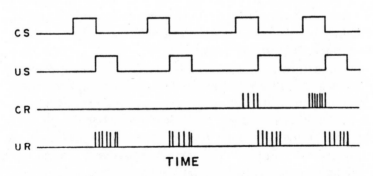

Figure 7. Schematic representation of a typical respondent conditioning paradigm. Note that from the onset each time the unconditional stimulus (US) was presented it elicited the unconditional response (UR), but the conditional stimulus (CS) only evoked the conditional response (CR) after having been paired with the *US* on a number of occasions.

blink, the CS eventually comes to evoke the eye blink as a CR. However, for this to occur, the relation between the temporal relation between the CS and US must be of a special sort. Specifically, the CS must be a "predictor" of the US (Hearst & Jenkins, 1974). This means in essence that the CS must closely precede the US in time, and the probability of the US occurring must be higher immediately after CS presentation than at any other time, although not all CS presentations need be followed by the US, nor need all US presentations follow the CS. Respondent conditioning does not typically occur if the CS follows the US (a procedure known as backward conditioning), or if the two are separated by more than a very brief period (when they are, the procedure is called *trace conditioning*).

When respondent conditioning does occur, the CS continues to evoke the CR only so long as the CS–US pairing is maintained; if CS–US contiguity is broken, conditioned responding eventually ceases. This phenomenon is known as *respondent extinction.*

If the CS is effective in evoking responding, stimulus generalization can be demonstrated. In stimulus generalization, stimuli similar to the CS along some physical dimension elicit conditional responses, even though these stimuli have never been paired with the US. In general, as the physical difference between the training CS and the stimulus being tested for generalization grows, the strength of the CR decreases (in respondent conditioning, strength typically refers to the magnitude, the duration, or, occasionally, the rate of the response).

Much is known about the factors affecting responding conditioning, and it is generally accepted that respondent conditioning is important in controlling certain human behaviors. Think, for example, about the set of physiological and behavioral changes collectively known as anxiety that most of us manifest upon entering our dentist's office. These responses resemble in many ways the unconditional responses elicited by the painful stimulation that the dentist typically, if unintentionally, provides—sweating, jaw clenching, and increased heart rate and blood pressure are likely to occur when we enter the waiting room and when the dentist's needle enters our jaw. In the former case, these responses are conditional responses elicited by the physical features of the waiting room, which have uniquely preceded dental work.

Operant Conditioning

Operant conditioning can be readily represented by a simple three-part model, as in Figure 8. Here, in the presence of some specific stimulus (termed the *discriminative stimulus*, or S+), a response produces a change in the environment. As a result of this environmental change, the future probability of occurrence of the response under similar conditions is altered.

The future probability of a response in a given circumstance typically is inferred from its measured rate of occurrence in similar past circumstances. If, after a particular form of response consequation, the rate of occurrence of a response increases, the operation of consequating the response is termed *reinforcement* and the specific consequence is termed a *reinforcer* (or a reinforcing stimulus). Consequences of a response may involve either the removal or delivery of a stimulus. When delivery of a stimulus increases the rate of occurrence of a behavior (or some other di-

Figure 8. Schematic representation of a typical operant conditioning paradigm. In the presence of some discriminative stimulus (S+) a response (R) occurs and produces (or at least is followed by) some change in the environment. Therefore, the future probability of occurrence of the response is either increased, in which case reinforcement is said to have occurred, or decreased, in which case punishment is said to have occurred.

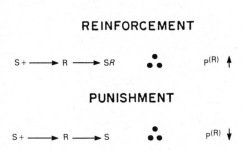

mension indicative of response strength), the stimulus is termed a *positive reinforcer* and the response-strengthening operation is considered *positive reinforcement*. *Negative reinforcement* also strengthens behavior but does so through the postponement or termination of delivery of a stimulus, the *negative reinforcer*.

A variety of environmental changes (i.e., stimuli) can serve as reinforcers. *Primary*, or unconditioned, reinforcers strengthen behavior in organisms without any particular history, which is to say in most "normal" members of a particular species. Many primary reinforcers are of direct biological significance. Air, food, and water are examples of positive reinforcers that fit into this category. Primary negative reinforcers, which organisms will *escape* (respond to terminate) or *avoid* (respond to postpone), include high-intensity stimulation in most modalities.

In contrast to primary reinforcers, *conditioned* (or secondary) reinforcers gain their ability to strengthen behavior through learning. Specifically, conditioned reinforcers are stimuli which are respondently paired with (i.e., immediately precede the delivery of) primary reinforcers or other established conditioned reinforcers. Money is a good example of a conditioned reinforcer.

For any two behaviors that occur with different probabilities (here, *probability* is defined as the amount of time spent engaging in the behavior), the opportunity to engage in the higher probability behavior will reinforce the lower probability behavior. Conversely, forcing an organism to engage in the lower probability behavior contingent on the occurrence of the higher probability behavior will punish the higher probability behavior. These two relations constitute the Premack principle (Premack, 1959) and are used to good advantage in applied settings.

Environmental events may reinforce (or punish) responses that precede them even if the response does not actually produce the reinforcer. A crap shooter who, for unknown reasons, says "Be there, baby" as he rolls the dice is apt to repeat the phrase under similar conditions in the future if the roll is a seven, even though there is no plausible mechanism whereby the verbal response could control the dice. Reinforcement of this type has been termed *superstitious*, adventitious, or fortuitous and probably controls many behaviors that appear counterintuitive. It must be noted, however, that explaining a behavior as being superstitiously reinforced is begging the question of how the behavior is actually controlled, unless the nature of the superstitious reinforcement is apparent (Lattal & Poling, 1981).

Reinforcers need not follow every occurrence of a behavior to determine the rate and pattern of its occurrence; intermittently occurring reinforcers can strengthen behavior. Specific relations among responses, environmental events, and the passage of time constitute *schedules of reinforcement*. Many reinforcement schedules occur naturally and can be artificially arranged. Only a few common schedules will be discussed here.

Fixed-ratio (*FR*) and variable-ratio (*VR*) schedules are response-based. In the former, a reinforcer follows every *nth* response, for example, every fifth response under an FR 5 schedule. So-called continuous reinforcement is an *FR* 1 schedule; all other schedules (except extinction) arrange intermittent consequation. Under a *VR* schedule, on average every *nth* response is followed by the reinforcer, although the number of responses required for reinforcement varies irregularly. Both of these schedules typically engender high rates of responding with protracted exposure. Postreinforcement (or preratio) pausing, the cessation of behavior following a reinforcer, is characteristic of performance under FR, but not VR, schedules.

In contrast to FR and VR schedules, fixed-interval (FI) and variable-interval (VI) schedules are time-based, although they do require emission of a specified response for reinforcement. The FI schedule specifies that the first response emitted after a given period has elapsed (e.g., 10 minutes under an FI 10-min schedule) will be reinforced. This interval usually is timed from the delivery of the previous reinforcer or the onset of some other stimulus. Relatively low overall response rates are typical under FI schedules; most responses are emitted toward the end of the interval, a pattern known as "scalloping." Variable-interval schedules specify that the first response emitted after some average period of time has elapsed will be reinforced; this interval varies irregularly around the mean value. These schedules generally evoke moderately high and very steady rates of responding.

"In differentiation schedules reinforcers are presented when a response or group of responses displays a specified property" (Zeiler, 1977, p. 203). The most commonly studied differentiation schedules are those which: (1) deliver the reinforcer only if the time between two successive responses (i.e., the *interresponse time*, or IRT) exceeds a specified value; (2) deliver the reinforcer only if the IRT is less than a specified value; or (3) deliver the reinforcer only if a certain response fails to occur during a specified period. Ferster and Skinner (1957) called the first two of these schedules the "differential reinforcement of low rates" (DRL) and the "differential reinforcement of high rates" (DRH), respectively, and Reynolds called the third "differential reinforcement of other behavior" (DRO). However, the designations DRL, DRH, and DRO are based on prediction of the patterns of behavior likely, but not certain, to occur under each condition; these designations inevitably confuse theoretical accounts of the schedules with the conditions for reinforcer delivery (see Lattal & Poling, 1981). Because of this, it seems preferable to substitute the description $IRT>t$ (interresponse time greater than t) for DRL, $IRT<t$ for DRH, and $d\bar{R}>t$ (duration of not responding greater than t) for DRO.

The patterns of responding that occur under differentiation schedules depend crucially on temporal parameters. In general, under $IRT>t$ schedules most responses occur with an interresponse time approximately equal to t, although response "bursting" soon after a reinforcer is delivered is common. High and consistent rates of responding frequently appear under $IRT<t$ schedules, whereas $d\bar{R}>t$ schedules of reinforcement typically result in a rate of responding lower than that which occurred in their absence. This last result may appear paradoxical; how can a schedule of reinforcement result in a lowered rate of responding? The answer is that, under the $d\bar{R}>t$ schedule, the response that is reinforced is a period in which a particular bit of behavior fails to occur. This response actually increases in frequency under the d$\bar{\text{R}}$>t schedule, which frequently results in a reduction in the rate of occurrence of the behavior whose absence defines the reinforced response (see Poling & Ryan, 1982).

Simple schedules can be combined to form complex schedules. Concurrent and multiple schedules are examples of complex schedules. *Concurrent schedules* arrange reinforcement simultaneously for two or more response classes. For example, under a concurrent VI 1-min FR 5-min schedule, left-key responses by a pigeon would be reinforced under the VI component, whereas right-key responses would be reinforced under the FR component. Concurrent schedules are especially useful for assaying choice (see de Villiers, 1977).

Unlike concurrent schedules, *multiple schedules* successively arrange two or more component schedules, each associated with a specific *discriminative stimulus*. Discriminative stimuli are environmental events that are uniquely correlated with particular schedules of reinforcement. They are antecedent stimuli and exercise control over responses which they precede in time. By convention, a stimulus correlated with the availability of reinforcement is termed the S+, whereas S− is the stimulus correlated with the unavailability of reinforcement. A condition in which responses never produce a reinforcer is termed *extinction*. Established responses eventually cease to be emitted under extinction conditions. The rate and temporal pattern of responding during extinction depend on the schedule that was in effect prior to extinction. For example, much more responding occurs following exposure to a VI 10-min schedule than following equal exposure to a FR 1 schedule. This illustrates the critical importance of historical factors in determining current performance.

Michael (1982) has devised a tripartite definition that fully describes the discriminative stimulus, which he defines as follows:

> It is a stimulus change which, (1) given the momentary effectiveness of some particular type of reinforcement (2) increases the frequency of a particular type of response (3) because that stimulus change has been correlated with an increase in the frequency with which that type of response has been followed by that type of reinforcement. (p. 149)

As an example of behavior control by a discriminative stimulus, consider a child who has not eaten since breakfast. The noon hour is approaching; the girl is hungry and food would serve as a positive reinforcer. She has previously acquired the response of asking adults for cookies, and both her father and grandmother are in the house. However, the father avoids between meal treats and in the past has not reinforced requests for cookies prior to lunch. The grandmother, in contrast, loves kids and cookies and has consistently given cookies when asked. Hence, with respect to the child's verbal response of "May I please have a cookie?" the father is an S− and the grandmother an S+ insofar as the request historically has been more successful in the presence of the latter. Because of this, the response is more likely to occur when the grandmother is about. This must, of course, be the case if she is actually serving as an S+.

As with respondent conditioning, stimulus generalization occurs in operant conditioning. Thus, stimuli similar to S+ may evoke the response previously reinforced in the presence of S+; in general, however, the probability of a stimulus evoking such behavior decreases as its physical similarity to S+ lessens.

To this point, no mention has been made of how operant responses are acquired. The fundamental process of operant response acquisition is called the *reinforcement of successive approximations,* or *shaping.* Shaping is a procedure whereby a terminal (target or desired) operant response is achieved by the systematic reinforcement of successively closer approximations thereto. Initially, the existing behavioral repertoire is reinforced on only a few occasions, after which a new criterion for reinforcement is adopted. This new criterion demands a response more similar in topography (form) to the target (desired) response than the previously reinforced behavior. Hence, if one is teaching a young child to say "dad," she or he might first reinforce any vocalization. Then, when babbling was occurring at a high rate, the teacher would selectively reinforce only "da" sounds, or the nearest observed approximation of that sound. Although it is possible that no response meeting the criterion for reinforcement will occur, this is unlikely. By failing to reinforce diffuse babbling, extinction has been arranged. In extinction, the variability of behavior increases, making it more likely that some *da*-like sound will be emitted. If, however, this does not occur, prompting (telling the child, "Say dad") and modelling the correct response ("dad, dad, dad") probably would serve to evoke the response. Once "da" had been voiced and reinforced on several occasions, a final criterion for reinforcement, emitting the "dad" sound, would be adopted and the child treated as described above.

Shaping is a potent device for evincing new responses, although other procedures, such as *response chaining*, are involved in the development of complex patterns of behavior. In chaining, a sequence of behaviors must be emitted before the primary reinforcer is delivered. In response chaining, only the terminal response is followed by a primary reinforcer; prior responses in the sequence simply provide an opportunity for subsequent responses to occur. Purchasing soda from a vending machine is a good example of response chaining. A sequence of several different responses is required to produce the drink, but only the final movement of the can to our lips is followed by the reinforcer that maintains behavior—a drink of artificially colored, flavored, and sweetened ambrosia.

In *backward chaining*, the terminal response is taught first, whereas *foreward chaining* involves teaching responses in the temporal order characteristic of the desired chain. Once the first response is learned, the next action in the sequence is taught. This initially involves delivering a primary reinforcer when the response occurs and shaping if necessary. After two sequential responses are acquired separately, they are combined into a chain. In the chain, completion of the temporally prior response is not followed by a primary reinforcer. Completion of this response simply establishes a stimulus condition that serves as an S+ for emission of the second response. This S+ serves as a conditioned reinforcer which maintains the first response. By continuing the process of having the occurrence of one response establish an S+ for a subsequent response, long and elaborate behavioral sequences can be established.

The foregoing has outlined in brief the fundamentals of operant conditioning. However, primary emphasis was placed on re-sponse-strengthening, or reinforcement, operations. At this point, punishment should be introduced. *Punishment,* like rein-forcement, is defined by its outcome (a decrease in the strength of a response) and may involve either the delivery or the removal of a stimulus. *Timeout,* which involves response-dependent institu-tion of a period of time in which one or more positive reinforcers are unavailable, is a form of punishment commonly used in clinical settings. *Overcorrection,* another clinically useful re-sponse-deceleration procedure, makes use of the Premack princi-ple to punish responding. Under overcorrection procedures, an organism is forced to engage in a low-probability behavior each time a response of higher probability is emitted. A final punish-ment operation, *response cost,* involves removing a positive rein-forcer that a person has earned whenever misbehavior occurs. An example of this is paying a child 10 cents for making his or her bed, but imposing a fine of 25 cents each time the bed goes unmade.

Punishment operations have been widely criticized when used to control human behavior. Surely such procedures can evoke aggression and avoidance and can be inhumane if poorly conceived. Response-suppressing operations nonetheless are a ubiquitous part of life and therapy and must be considered in attempts to explain behavior.

Several factors not previously discussed affect behavior under a given reinforcement (or punishment) schedule. The degree of deprivation relevant to the reinforcer maintaining behavior and the history of the person in question are obvious and strong de-terminants of behavior. Food is a more effective reinforcer if we have not eaten for a day than if we have just finished a five-course meal, and money is a reinforcer only for persons who have learned of its exchange value. Deprivation and history can be considered as antecedent, or setting, variables, in that they precede the re-sponse that they affect.

Michael (1982) has proposed that *establishing operation* (EO) be used as a general term for operations such as deprivation which (1) increase the effectiveness of a particular reinforcer and

(2) increase the likelihood of occurrence of behavior that has in the past been followed by that reinforcer. Although *drive* and *motivation* traditionally have been used to describe changes in an organism which produce these two effects, both terms implicate an inner state, rather than antecedent environmental change, as the primary determinant of responding. For this reason, *establishing operation* appears the best of the three alternatives.

Parameters of the reinforcement schedule under which an operant response is maintained, including the magnitude of the reinforcer, schedule value (e.g., number of responses required for reinforcement under an FR schedule), and concurrent response options, all exercise strong control over responding, as does an organism's history of exposure to that and other schedules. An organism's physiological state is another variable that influences performance in a given circumstance. For instance, illness can dramatically alter what is and is not reinforcing.

Knowing the variables that affect operant behavior enables scientists to examine how drugs interact with these variables to produce their characteristic effects. Over 25 years ago, Sidman (1956) wrote:

> A small amount of restraint in the form of systematic behavioral investigation prior to drug investigation cannot fail to bring some order into the accumulated facts of drug–behavior interaction. . . . A more precise delineation and classification of behavioral variables and the discovery of relations between behavior and other biological phenomena will lead inevitably to the elimination of a great deal of psychopharmacological investigation that now seems exciting but is actually little more than aimless wandering when compared to future potentialities in the field. (quoted in Thompson, 1982, p. ix)

At the present time, behavioral psychologists have a good, albeit imperfect, understanding of the variables that control behavior, and this understanding has been of real value in examining and explaining drug effects. However, much of the research conducted by behavioral psychologists (and by behavioral pharmacologists) has involved nonhuman subjects. In view of this, a brief discussion of how research with nonhumans can contribute to an understanding of human behavior, including drug effects thereon, appears in order.

Nonhuman Research, Human Research, and Meaningful Inference

The earliest research in behavioral psychology involved rats as subjects; pigeons later came to be used in the majority of investigations, although some researchers favored nonhuman primates and occasional studies were conducted with an unlikely melange of creatures. These include alligators, bees, blackbirds, cats, chickens, chinchillas, cows, crows, dogs, dolphins, ducks, Siamese fighting fish, goldfish, gerbils, goats, guinea pigs, hamsters, horses, mice, mynah birds, octopi, porpoises, quail, sea lions, turtles, and vultures (Grossett, Roy, Sharenow, & Poling, 1982).

Skinner (1953) notes that several disciplines ultimately concerned with humans, including medicine and physiology, make heavy use of nonhuman research findings. He also provides a good rationale for the use of nonhuman subjects in behavioral research:

> We study the behavior of (nonhuman) animals because it is simpler. Basic processes are revealed more easily and can be recorded over longer periods of time. Our observations are not complicated by the social relations between subject and experimenter. Conditions may be better controlled. We may arrange genetic histories to control certain variables and special life histories to control others—for example, if we are interested in how an organism learns to see, we can raise an animal in darkness until the experiment is begun. We are also able to control current circumstances to an extent not easily realized in human behavior—for example, we can vary states of deprivation over wide ranges. These are advantages which should not be dismissed on the a priori contention that human behavior is inevitably set apart as a separate field. (1953, p. 39)

Skinner acknowledged that the processes and laws which account for nonhuman behavior might be inadequate to account fully for human behavior. However, he rightly contended that whether this was so could be determined only by experimentation; whether or not processes demonstrated in nonhumans are applicable to humans might be determined by empirical test, but not by dogmatic assertion.

Within the past 25 years, many studies have demonstrated

that the basic processes of operant and respondent conditioning are operative in humans. That this is so is abundantly clear if one considers the range of problem behaviors that have been satisfactorily managed through the application of operant and respondent conditioning procedures (e.g., Leitenberg, 1978). Nonetheless, certain variables may affect the behavior of humans and nonhumans differently. Humans, for example, often respond at high and relatively high rates under FI schedules (e.g., Lowe, Harzem, & Bagshaw, 1978; Matthews, Shimoff, Catania, & Sagvolden, 1977). This pattern is rarely observed in nonhumans responding under FI schedules unless they are given unique histories, for example, a protracted period of FR exposure (Urbain, Poling, Millam, & Thompson, 1978).

As Poppen (1982) explains, several factors influence human performance under FI schedules. Unlike that of other organisms, human behavior is frequently *rule-governed*. Rule-governed behavior, fully described by Skinner (1969), requires a special reinforcement history and involves behavior controlled by the description of prevailing contingencies (relations among responses and other events), rather than actual exposure to these contingencies. (Behavior controlled by actual exposure to contingencies is called *contingency-shaped*.) It appears that humans exposed to FI schedules frequently self-generate rules and that these verbal mediators may contribute to the rate and temporal pattern of responding (see Poppen, 1982). Since they are covert, the role of such rules in controlling overt behavior is difficult to determine. However, it is clear that overt, experimenter-given rules can powerfully affect human operant performance (e.g., Baron, Kaufman, & Stauber, 1969; Lippman & Meyer, 1967).

The assumption that human operant behavior often is rule-governed, whereas that of nonhumans is not, may seem to imply that exploring operant behavior in nonhumans will tell us little about humans. Nothing could be further from the truth. Rule-governed behavior is itself operant behavior and can be explained in terms of basic operant processes—the same processes that control and can be readily demonstrated in the key pecks of pigeons and the lever presses of rats.

Rule-governed behavior can be explained in terms of behavioral principles most clearly examined in nonhumans, but the existence of the phenomenon underscores the need for studying humans as well as other species. Although behavioral researchers have published many studies examining the use of behavioral principles to deal with socially significant problem behaviors, they have published far fewer studies dealing with basic behavioral processes in humans. For example, Buskist and Miller (1982) present data showing that, from 1972 to 1981, less than 10% of the articles published in *JEAB, Animal Learning and Behavior,* and *Learning and Motivation* were concerned with the analysis of human operant behavior.

Concluding Comments

To date, most basic research in behavioral pharmacology, as in behavioral psychology, has involved laboratory animals as subjects, although basic research with humans is becoming increasingly common. Insofar as can be determined, drug effects in humans and nonhumans appear similar under comparable conditions. This does not, of course, imply that the effects of a low dose of *d*-amphetamine will necessarily produce quantitatively or qualitatively similar effects on the lever-pressing of rats and humans under, say, FI 2-min schedules of food delivery. If humans respond at relatively high and consistent rates under this schedule, which they are likely to do, whereas the rats produce textbook scallops, which also is probable, the drug is likely to produce rate decreases in the former subjects and rate increases in the latter. This is not, however, a species difference, but merely a manifestation of the rate-dependent effects of amphetamine, as described in the next chapter.

The point to be made is that one would expect parallel drug effects only when behavior was controlled by similar events and maintained at equivalent rates, regardless of the species in question. When human and nonhuman performances differ, similar drug effects are unlikely to be observed. At present, it appears that there is nothing about human behavior which makes it uniquely sensitive or impervious to drugs. Studies of nonhumans can therefore yield information useful in accounting for drug effects in humans and hence will be frequently referred to in subsequent chapters.

This does not mean, however, that all research in human behavioral pharmacology should be, or is, guided by the findings of basic research with nonhumans. Certainly some significant human behaviors cannot be reproduced or meaningfully simulated in other animals. For example, drug effects on self-reported "mood" or on the complex of behaviors taken to be indicative of a clinical state of schizophrenia can be examined only in humans, and there can be no meaningful human behavior pharmacology without the study of our own species. A major objective of the balance of this text is to summarize how such studies can be conducted within the framework of behavioral pharmacology.

Finally, a word on terminology. When relating experiments conducted with other species to the analysis of human behavior, many writers contrast *animal* or *infrahuman* research with *human* research, and compare *humans* with *animals* or *infrahumans*. This practice has utterly nothing to recommend it (see Poling, 1984). Humans are in fact animals, and it is not clear how other species are "less than" (i.e., *infra-*) human. When humans are compared to other species, the latter should be collectively designated as "other animals" (not simply as "animals") or as nonhumans, a term seemingly free of the misleading connotations associated with "infrahumans." Unless the lure of precedent becomes overwhelming, this convention will be followed throughout the present text.

CHAPTER

4

Stimulus Properties
of Drugs

A *physical stimulus* is any change in the environment that can be quantified through empirical means, whereas a *functional stimulus* is a physical stimulus that demonstrably affects behavior. Chapter 3 provided an overview of operant and respondent conditioning and emphasized that the functional properties of a physical stimulus are not immutable but depend critically upon prior and current circumstances. Electric shock, for example, may affect behavior by acting as a positive reinforcer, a negative reinforcer, an unconditional stimulus, or a discriminative stimulus. Given this, the behavioral effects of electrical stimulation are (a) complex, (b) situation-specific, and (c) amenable to analysis in terms of operant and respondent conditioning.

The same holds true for all other functional stimuli, including drugs. The notion that drugs have stimulus properties was first popularized in a 1971 text, *Stimulus Properties of Drugs*, edited by Thompson and Pickens. Contributors to this text demonstrated that drug effects often, though not always, depend upon a complicated interplay of environmental and pharmacological variables. The purpose of the present chapter is to summarize the potential stimulus properties of drugs and to consider how these properties can influence a person's response to a particular compound.

Drugs as Unconditional and Conditional Stimuli

An *unconditional stimulus* (*US*) is a change in the environment that reliably elicits an unconditional response (*UR*) in the absence of any special conditioning history, and hence in all or nearly all members of the species in question. Ipecac, for instance, when taken orally reliably induces vomiting in humans and therefore is used therapeutically as an emetic in the treatment of oral drug overdoses and in certain cases of poisoning.

Even when a drug affects behavior by acting as a US, environmental factors may modulate observed effects. Such an outcome is shown in Figure 9, which depicts the lethality of combinations of pentazocine (Talwin), a synthetic narcotic with mixed agonist and antagonist properties, and tripelennamine (Pyribenzamine), an antihistaminic, in mice housed after injection either individually or in groups of 16. Results are unambiguous: The combination, which is used on the street as a substitute for heroin (Poklis & Whyatt, 1980; Showalter, 1980), kills more mice when they are housed together than when they are housed alone. This finding suggests that individuals suffering from an overdose of what users term "T's and blues" should not be exposed to highly stimulating environments. Moreover, it makes clear that most if not all of the effects of drugs, including their ability to cause death at certain doses, can be influenced by nonpharmacological variables.

If a drug has *US* properties, a *conditional stimulus* (*CS*) that reliably precedes it may come through respondent conditioning to evoke a conditional response (*CR*). In many cases, the CR closely resembles in topography (form) the UR elicited by the drug. A cancer patient receiving chemotherapy in a physician's office may, for instance, eventually come to feel nauseous and vomit upon entering the office. Here, physical features unique to the office serve as a CS that reliably precedes exposure to a *US*, the

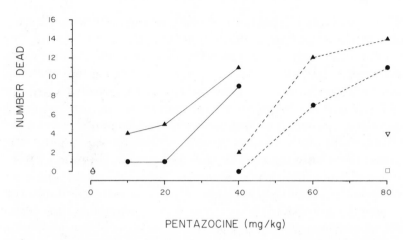

PENTAZOCINE (mg/kg)

Figure 9. Number of mice dead per group of 16, two hours after receiving an intraperitoneal injection of the listed drug or drug combination. Data are presented separately for mice housed individually or in groups of 16 after injection: (○) 40 mg/kg tripelennamine alone, individually; (△) 40 mg/kg tripelennamine alone, grouop; (□) 80 mg/kg pentazocine alone, individually; (▽) 80 mg/kg pentazocine alone, group; (●—●) 40 mg/kg tripelennamine and pentazocine individually; (▲—▲) 40 mg/kg tripelennamine and pentazocine group; (●—●) 20mg/kg tripelennamine and pentazocine individually; (△—△) 20 mg/kg tripelennamine and pentazocine group. Taken from Poling, Kesselring, Sewell, and Cleary (1983) and reproduced by permission of ANKHO International.

chemotherapeutic agent, which elicits the UR of vomiting. After a number of CS–US pairings, the CS begins to evoke a CR, regurgitation, much like the UR produced by the drug. That this is so is of obvious concern for patients receiving, and physicians administering, chemotherapy.

Although CRs and URs often are similar in topography, they need not be so. That this is the case becomes evident if one considers Siegel's (e.g., 1979a, b) work in the area of morphine tolerance. Among his findings are the following: (a) tolerance to morphine's analgesic effects can be attentuated by administering a series of saline injections prior to the drug regimen, or by giving saline as well as morphine injections during the chronic regimen; (b) saline injections following chronic exposure to morphine interfere with the retention of tolerance; and (c) animals that evi-

dence tolerance to morphine in one environment do not necessarily do so in another environment.

These findings cannot be explained in terms of morphine's
pharmacological properties alone. However, Siegel has offered a
model that accounts for them nicely. He proposes that stimuli
reliably correlated with drug administration are established as
CSs that come to evoke CRs which are opposite in direction to the
URs elicited by the drug US. These CRs compensate for the URs
elicited by the drug and, as they increase in magnitude with repeated CS–US pairings, reduce the magnitude of the observed
response to the drug, for example analgesia. Diminution of the
observed response with repeated administrations of a given drug
dose is by definition tolerance.

If one accepts Siegel's conditioning model of tolerance, the
seemingly counterintuitive effects of environmental stimuli on
the development and retention of tolerance are readily understood. The effects described in a (above) involve latent inhibition
(preconditioning exposure to the CS) and partial reinforcement
(following only a fraction of CS presentations with the US), those
in b respondent extinction, and those in c exposure to the US
alone.

It is known that tolerance can appear without respondent
conditioning—chronic drug administration surely can lead to increased drug inactivation (metabolic tolerance), usually through
enzyme induction, or a lessened response at the cellular level
(pharmacodynamic tolerance). Further, as discussed previously,
respondent conditioning can in some instances produce CRs similar to, not opposite in direction from, URs elicited by a drug (see
Solomon, 1980). For instance, there are several clinical reports of
humans who regularly self-administer drugs by intravenous injection exhibiting morphine-like subjective and physiological effects when saline was injected (e.g., O'Brien, 1975). Siegel's findings nonetheless underscore the importance of conditioning
factors in determining drug effects. These factors may even control the outcome of a drug overdose, As Siegel explains:

> A considerable amount of research has demonstrated environ-
> mental specificity in the display of tolerance: maximal tolerance is

observed when the drug is administered in the context of the usual predrug cues, but not in the context of cues not previously associated with the drug. An addict would be at risk for "overdose," according to this analysis, when the drug is administered in an environment which had not been previously paired with the drug.

Recently, the conditioning model of "overdose" was assessed both by interviews with addicts who are "overdose" survivors, and by a rat experiment (Siegel, Hinson, & Krank, 1978). The results indicated that drug-anticipatory CSs do indeed modulate tolerance to the pernicious effect of morphine. This conditioning model of tolerance, then, may be applicable to 'overdose' death. (1979a, p. 132)

If administration of a drug with discriminable sensory consequences predictably precedes exposure to a US, the drug may come to serve as a CS which, by virtue of respondent conditioning, reliably evokes a CR. That drugs can acquire CS properties in this manner is easily demonstrated in laboratory studies. For example, Turner and Altshuler (1976) trained rats under a variable-interval schedule of food delivery and then exposed them to a procedure in which d-amphetamine injections were explicitly or randomly paired with unavoidance electric shocks. For animals in the explicit pairing group, shocks were delivered only during sessions that were preceded by drug delivery. Animals in the random pairing group received the same number of injections and sessions in which shock occurred; however, drug injections did not reliably predict shock sessions. After shock sessions were terminated, d-amphetamine decreased the responding of animals in the explicit pairing group and increased the responding of animals in the random pairing group; the response rates of all rats were increased by the drug prior to sessions in which shock occurred. Turner and Altshuler interpreted these findings in terms of conditioned suppression. That is, in the explicitly paired group, the drug functioned as a CS that was respondently paired with a US, shock. Since the CRs elicited by the drug were incompatible with the required operant response (bar pressing), responding was suppressed relative to baseline conditions.

Although important human behaviors conceivably could be altered by drugs acting as CSs, situations in which this occurs are rare in the lives of most individuals, and this mechanism of drug action is rarely of practical or clinical significance.

Drugs as Discriminative Stimuli

A discriminative stimulus affects the probability of occurrence of a response by virtue of having been correlated with historical conditions where that response was to some extent successful in producing a stimulus change and affects behavior only if that stimulus change is currently effective (i.e., reinforcing or punishing). A drug is established as a discriminative stimulus ($S+$ or S^D) by reinforcing one response following drug administration and failing to reinforce that response when drug is not given, and one demonstrates that the drug is serving as a discriminative stimulus by showing that the response previously reinforced in the drug state occurs reliably when the drug is administered, but not when it is withheld. If a stimulus is reliably correlated with the absence of reinforcement for a particular response, that stimulus is termed an $S-$, or S^{delta} (S^Δ). Any drug that serves as an $S+$ or $S-$ must produce detectable subjective effects, or *sensory consequences.*

The discriminative stimulus properties of drugs have been studied in the laboratory for roughly 25 years, and research in this area has yielded a wealth of information concerning the sensory consequences of drugs and the biochemical mechanisms that mediate these consequences (see Ho, Richards, & Chute, 1978; Lal, 1977; Schuster & Balster, 1977). In these investigations, one response (e.g., depressing the leftmost of two levers) is reinforced when drug is given and another response (e.g., depressing the other lever) is reinforced following vehicle control administration. Under such two-response drug discrimination procedures, stimulus-appropriate responses usually are reinforced under an intermittent schedule, for example an FR 20. In this case, only responses that occurred prior to the emission of 20 responses on one or the other lever would be used in assessing whether the drug was serving as an $S+$. Subsequent responses would be excluded from this determination to prevent confusing control of behavior by an antecedent stimulus (the drug) with control of behavior by its consequences. If, for instance, right-lever responses were reinforced and left-lever responses extinguished during a test session, it would hardly be surprising if a subject emitted the vast majority of its total responses on the former lever. Such differential responding is *schedule-controlled*, not *stimulus-controlled*, and can occur in the presence as well as the absence of a putative discriminative stimulus.

There is almost infinite latitude in the range of behaviors that a drug can control by serving as an S+, and this helps to explain how a given drug can produce very different behavioral effects across individuals. Consider the behavior of different people who have drunk roughly equivalent quantities of ethanol (beverage alcohol). There are maudlin drunks, surly drunks, gross drunks, and lascivious drunks. Why? The reasons undoubtably involve the actions of multiple and interactive variables, historical as well as current. One factor likely to be of considerable importance is an individual's reinforcement history while drinking. Consider two 18-year-old college freshmen.

One plays shortstop on a local softball team and eventually begins to stop after games to sink a few beers with fellow players. For reasons that need not concern us, those individuals favor a bawdy good time and positively reinforce crude language, risque jokes, and the not-too-subtle double entendre. The initiate is shaped into emitting such behavior, which is heavily reinforced when it occurs. After a few drinking bouts, the foulness of the shortstop's mouth might well do Eddie Murphy proud.

Our second freshman is first exposed to ethanol in the company of self-proclaimed intellectuals who sniff brandy while pondering the arcane. These academics reinforce fine language and reference to the classics; "deposition of fecal boli" is their term for what dogs do on the lawn. The student whose drinking history is with this company is likely to behave rather differently when imbibing than the softball player considered earlier. That this is so has nothing to do with the direct effects of ethanol, which should be very similar in both students, but rather reflects unlike conditioning histories during drug exposure.

Note, however, that in the examples given above the drinking of ethanol and the sensory consequences affected thereby are but part of a complex of stimuli that are uniquely correlated with particular reinforcement contingencies. The likelihood that the softball player will play the rowdy during future drinking bouts depends upon the extent to which these bouts occur in situations that resemble in their totality the after-games milieu. In addition, if reinforcement contingencies change, discriminative stimuli eventually fail to control behavior. Should the shortstop's friends undergo a religious conversion and hence come to punish prurience, the player's behavior while drinking in their company— assuming that they did not turn away from beer in turning to god—eventually would change. If fact, should the group arrange sufficiently powerful contingencies of reinforcement and punishment, soon enough the shortstop would while drinking disparage filthy language and praise the lord with equal zeal. Unlikely though it is, this scenario emphasizes that the discriminative stimulus properties of a drug, and consequently its behavioral effects, can vary over time in the same individual, as well as across different people.

A study by Poling and Appel (1978), using rats as subjects, provides clear evidence that both qualitative and quantitative aspects of a drug's behavioral effects can be modified by changing its discriminative stimulus properties. In the first phase of this investigation, six rats were exposed to an FI 60-sec schedule of food delivery. d-Amphetamine, street "speed," at the relatively low dose of 0.5 mg/kg increased response rates of all subjects under this schedule (Figure 10).

In the second phase of the study, all animals were exposed to conditions in which an FR 20 schedule was in effect during some sessions and an FI 60-sec schedule was in effect during others. These conditions were arranged over a total of 63 sessions. For three subjects, the FR 20 schedule was in effect during 21 sessions, each preceded by an injection of 0.5 mg/kg d-amphetamine and the FI 60-sec schedule was in effect for 42 sessions, each preceded by saline injection; drug (FR 20) and saline (FI 60-sec) sessions occurred in an irregular temporal sequence. The remaining subjects also were exposed to the FR 20 schedule for 21 sessions and received d-amphetamine (0.5 mg/kg) prior to 21 of 63 sessions. For these animals, however, drug injections did not re-

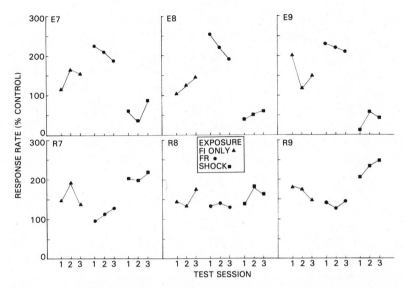

Figure 10. Response rates of individual rats under an *FI* 60-sec schedule of food delivery when given 0.5 mg/kg *d*-amphetamine. Each data point represents response rate during a single test session expressed as percentage of the mean control rate during baseline (nondrug) sessions. Conditions are labeled according to whether an *FR* 20 schedule or punishment was arranged during the training sessions preceeding drug testing. For rats E7, E8, and E9 the *FR* 20 schedule and punishment were perfectly correlated with *d*-amphetamine injections; for rats R7, R8, and R9 drug injections occurred randomly with respect to the *FR* schedule or punishment. Redrawn from Poling and Appel (1978).

liably precede either *FR* 20 or *FI* 60-sec sessions. That is, the FR 20 schedule followed 7 of the 21 injections of *d*-amphetamine (33%) and 14 of the 42 saline sessions (33%). At the end of this phase, 0.5 mg/kg *d*-amphetamine increased the response rates of all animals under the *FI* 60-sec schedule. However, the magnitude of the rate increase was much larger for those animals in which drug injection had been perfectly correlated with the *FR* 20 schedule than for those for whom the relation was random (Figure 10).

In the third 63-day phase, all animals were exposed to sessions during which responding under the *FI* 60-sec schedule sometimes was punished by electric shocks delivered under a *VI* 5-min schedule. For three subjects, each of the 21 punishment sessions was preceded by a 0.5 mg/kg injection of d-amphetamine; for the others, punishment sessions followed 7 drug injections and no punishment followed 14 drug injections. Thus, as in phase two, d-amphetamine was uniquely correlated with a change in environmental contingencies for three rats only. At the end of this phase, 0.5 mg/kg d-amphetamine substantially increased rates of responding under the FI 60-sec schedule when given to subjects for which drug injections and shock sessions were random with respect to one another. However, the drug actually reduced rates of FI 60-sec responding when administered to rats for which d-amphetamine and shock sessions had been perfectly correlated (Figure 10).

That d-amphetamine could increase or decrease the response rate of an individual animal under the same fixed-interval schedule, depending on the environmental contingencies with which the drug had been correlated and hence its discriminative stimulus properties, was the most interesting finding of the study just described. This result emphasizes that the behavioral effects of drugs, like those of other stimuli, may depend on the behavioral history of the organism as well as the current environment and the physical (i.e., pharmacological) properties of the stimulus.

Distinguishing Discriminative Stimulus Functions of Drugs

Remember that the definition of an $S+$ is tripartite. In some cases, changes in behavior produced by a drug may appear to involve its actions as an $S+$, but in actuality one or more of the defining features is missing. Consider a group of experienced middle-class American marijuana smokers. While smoking, they are quite likely to engage in verbal (and other) behavior indicative of hunger— "the munchies" in user argot (Ray, 1983). It is possible that this may reflect the actions of the drug as an $S+$, in which case users would have to have a history in which food-related responses were more successful (either in gaining food or some other reinforcer, such as verbal support from peers) in the presence of drug than in its absence. If such a history is lacking, the drug must be producing its effects in some other manner.

One way in which this might come about is if the drug acted as a deprivation-alterating variable. Michael (1982) has generally termed such variables *establishing operations (EOs)*. He defines an *EO* as "any change in the environment which alters the effectiveness of some object or event as reinforcement and simultaneously alters the momentary frequency of the behavior that has been followed by that reinforcement" (p. 151). (Establishing operations can also decrease the reinforcing effectiveness of a stimulus change, in which case the probability of occurrence of responses that had been followed by that reinforcement would decrease.) If in the foregoing example marijuana acted as an *EO* with respect to food-seeking responses, it would increase the likelihood of such responses by increasing the reinforcing value of food, not by having been correlated in the past with increased reinforcement for such responses.

That drugs can act as *EOs* is clear if one considers how amphetamines reduce food-seeking responses, or the manner in which polyethylene glycol (which reduces extracellular fluid volume) increases fluid-maintained operant responses. Although the control of behavior exercised by an *EO* can resemble that associated with an $S+$ or $S-$, it is important to distinguish the two functions. As Michael (1982) points out, "In everyday language we can and often do distinguish changing people's behavior by changing what they want and changing their behavior by changing their chances of getting something that they already want" (p. 154). Drugs can do both, but in the former case they are serving as an *EO*, and in the latter as an $S+$ or $S-$.[1]

Whether a drug is acting as an establishing operation or as a discriminative stimulus cannot be determined without knowledge

[1]The foregoing is a bare and simpleminded summary of establishing operations and of how drugs might affect behavior by acting as EOs. Readers sophisticated in behavior analysis will recognize that EOs can be established through conditioning and that a drug which acts as an EO can influence the reinforcing efficacy of conditioned, as well as primary, reinforcers. Moreover, EOs can alter the reinforcing value of negative as well as positive reinforcers. The important point in the present context, however, is simply that drugs can affect behavior by altering what traditionally has been termed "motivation" or "drive." Readers desiring further information concerning EOs and their behavioral effects should consult Michael (1982).

of the operant history of the person in question. One also must know a person's history to determine whether behavior in the presence of a drug involves discriminative stimulus control or entails what Skinner (e.g., 1969) has termed "rule-governed behavior." Rule-governed behavior occurs when an individual's behavior is consistent with verbal instructions describing reinforcement (or punishment) contingencies which that person has not directly contacted. For example, a motorcyclist's friend may say, "Don't ride in the rain; the road gets slick and its damned easy to wipe out." This rule describes relations among an antecedent stimulus, the presence of rain, the response of riding a cycle, and the probable outcome of that response, an accident. If the biker follows the rule and refrains from riding in the rain—and whether this occurs depends largely on prior experience with respect to the rule giver and the accuracy of similar rules provided in the past— the behavior is rule-governed. Rules can be provided by others or formulated by the individual whose behavior they are to control. Rule-governed behavior is of crucial importance to humans, for it enables us to behave effectively without requiring direct exposure to contingencies that might prove harmful or ineffectual. However, rule-governed and contingency-shaped behaviors are not necessarily identical; a person whose behavior is controlled by exposure to a verbal description of a contingency of reinforcement (or punishment) may not respond in the same manner as a person who actually has been exposed to that contingency. Moreover, rules can be faulty, fostering behaviors inappropriate for the situation at hand. Skinner (1969) provides detailed discussion of distinctions between rule-governed and contingency-shaped behaviors and of the importance of each in human endeavors.

What has any of this to do with drug effects? More than a little. Scientists have long known that a person's "expectations" can powerfully influence a drug's subjective effects (Wilkins, 1973). What, behaviorally, are expectations if not verbal rules? A novice American marijuana smoker is likely to be told by those introducing the drug that it will enhance the perception of color, taste, and sound. If the initiate has a history of following rules and is asked about the subjective effects of marijuana, the likely—

and rule-governed—response, quite apart from the pharmacological actions of the drug, is something like "It increases enjoyment of eating, having sex, and listening to music." A person not provided with a verbal description of the drug's alleged actions would not respond in this fashion. In this regard, it is interesting to note that the subjective effects of marijuana commonly reported by middle-class American users are rarely reported by Jamacian field workers (Dornbush, Freedman, & Fink, 1976), who in all likelihood are given different instructions concerning the drug's expected effects.

An individual's verbal reports concerning a drug's subjective effects may initially be rule-governed but if such reports are differentially reinforced in the presence and absence of drug, then the behavior is at least partially contingency-shaped, in which case the drug is serving as an $S+$. Consider for a moment the *placebo response*. Placebo, which in Latin means "I shall please," can be defined as "a substance or procedure that is without specific activity for the condition being treated" (Shapiro & Morris, 1978, p. 371), and placebo response as "the behavioral change of subjects receiving placebo" (Fisher, 1970, p. 37). A number of extensive reviews and analyses of the placebo response have appeared (e.g., Brody, 1980; Gadow, White, & Ferguson, 1986a, b; Jospe, 1978). For our purposes, it suffices to note that a substantial proportion of patients who receive a biologically inert placebo or a medication with biochemical effects unrelated to the condition being treated behave differently as a function of such treatment. Placebo-induced changes in behavior can be in a therapeutic or countertherapeutic direction and "vary significantly in different individuals and in any one patient at different times" (Melmon, Gilman, & Mayer, 1980, p. 47). The likelihood of a beneficial placebo response occurring appears to vary inversely with the severity of the condition being treated; the probability of any placebo response occurring is affected by a number of factors including the physical characteristics of the placebo and the intelligence and level of anxiety of the subject (see Rickels, 1968).

Conventional explanations of the placebo response are mentalistic: "Placebo effects result from the physician–patient relationship, the significance of the therapeutic effect to the patient, and the mental 'set' imparted by the therapeutic setting and by the physician" (Melmon *et al.,* 1980, p. 47). To a behaviorist, however, a patient's response to a placebo (or active drug) can be better understood in terms of (1) stimulus properties of the substance and its administration, (2) verbal rules concerning the substance's expected effects which the patient or other individuals (e.g., a physician) have provided, and (3) contingencies of reinforcement and punishment in effect at the time the placebo response is assessed. An individual's response to a placebo (or drug) can be mediated by the substance acting as a discriminative or conditional stimulus, or it can be an example of pure rule-governed or mixed rule-governed and contingency-shaped behavior. Since each of these behavioral mechanisms of action depends upon a particular conditioning history, the behavioral actions of a given placebo can vary dramatically across time within an individual, or across individuals.

Learning mediates the placebo response, but it surely is a real change in behavior, one manifested through physiological mechanisms. The physiological mechanisms responsible for most placebo responses are unknown, but it appears that *endorphins* (*endo*geneous *morphine*-like substances) mediate placebo-induced analgesia, for such analgesia can be abolished by narcotic antagonists (e.g., naloxone) which block endorphine receptors in the brain (Evans, 1981; Fields & Levine, 1981). Note, however, that this finding tells us nothing about the behavioral mechanisms responsible for the placebo response. A complete and revealing behavioral analysis of a subject's response to drug or placebo requires no recourse to biochemical events. That this is so in no way diminishes the value of physiological analyses of placebo (or drug) responses. Nor does it render meaningless research in *neuropsychopharmacology,* a discipline that attempts to explicate relations among environmental events (including drug or placebo administration), biochemical phenomena, and observed changes in behavior. Rather, it simply emphasizes that placebo effects, like those of drugs, can be examined at several different, and not necessarily overlapping or compatible, levels of analysis.

Drugs as Positively Reinforcing Stimuli

All reinforcing stimuli are stimulus changes that strengthen behaviors which closely precede them in time. *Positive reinforcers* involve adding something to the environment; *negative reinforcers* involve taking something away. What functions as a reinforcer for a particular person at a given time and place depends upon the individual's prior experiences and current circumstances.

Consider cigarette smoking. Early exposures to cigarettes typically are not in themselves positively reinforcing but may be repeated due to nonpharmacological reinforcers (e.g., peer praise) associated with the experience. With continued exposure, however, tolerance develops to certain unpleasant effects of smoking (e.g., nausea), and cigarette use may become positively reinforcing, due in no small part to the nicotine administered thereby. In this example, the reinforcing properties of smoking emerge gradually, through a process that involves interaction between the behavior of an individual (i.e., repeated administration) and the direct effects of a drug (nicotine). Behavioral actions of drugs which develop in this manner are frequently termed *functional* (as opposed to direct).

All drugs that humans self-administer without added inducement, including abused substances, are serving as positive reinforcers. Chapter 7 is devoted entirely to drug abuse and provides a detailed discussion of drugs as positive reinforcers.

Drugs as Negatively Reinforcing Stimuli

A drug is serving as a negatively reinforcing stimulus if an organism will respond to escape or avoid it. Monkeys, for example, regularly emit responses that prevent exposure to LSD (Hoffmeister, 1975), hence for them the drug is negatively reinforcing. Humans, too, regularly avoid contact with certain drugs, including prescribed medications. A diabetic child, for instance, may avoid painful premeal insulin injections by staying outdoors, safely away from the parent waiting to give the injection, or a schizophrenic may avoid exposure to a neuroleptic by vomiting soon after the medication is administered. In both cases, the result is failure to comply with an intended medication regimen.

Patient Noncompliance

Patient noncompliance is certainly a major problem of medicine (Haynes, Taylor, & Sackett, 1979; Marston, 1970). According to Sackett and Snow (1979), on average 38% of patients fail to comply with short-term medication regimens, and 46% fail to comply with long-term treatments. Yet the fact that patients frequently fail to take medications as intended by their physicians does not, in itself, indicate that these medications are serving as negative reinforcers. Remember that negative reinforcers strengthen behaviors that prevent or terminate exposure to them. A patient's failure to self-administer a medication may indicate simply that the drug is not positively reinforcing. Such a drug may have no stimulus properties whatever and surely need not function as a negative reinforcer.

Regardless of whether patient noncompliance results from a drug's negatively reinforcing properties or the absence of positively reinforcing properties, principles of behavioral psychology can be used to increase the likelihood of compliance. Research in this area is carefully reviewed by Masek (1982) and Epstein and Cluss (1982). A number of specific procedures have proven useful in increasing patient compliance. One involves careful monitoring of drug intake, a difficult but not impossible task, coupled with systematic reinforcement of appropriate drug taking and punishment of inappropriate self-administration. For example, a hypertensive patient and spouse might draw up a behavioral contract such that the patient gives the spouse $70 at the beginning of each week. Each day that the spouse actually sees the patient ingest scheduled medication, $10 is returned; any time medication is not taken in the approved fashion, $10 is sent to an organization despised by the patient. Here, short-term consequences are being arranged so as to support a behavior, adherence to a medication regiment, the assumed long-term consequences of which, good health, are too delayed to control behavior.

Providing appropriate rules for administering medications may also help to increase the odds of compliance. As discussed earlier, human behavior can be rule-governed as well as contingency-shaped, and it appears that much health-related behavior, including complying with doctors' orders, is of the former sort. A significant goal for researchers in behavioral medicine is to discern the conditions under which the likelihood of patients' rule following is maximized.

Determinants of Negative Reinforcement

Whether a given drug and dosage serve as a negative reinforcer depends upon prior and current conditions. The narcotic antagonist naloxone, for instance, at low doses typically does not serve as a negative reinforcer in subjects that are not physically dependent on opioids but will maintain avoidance behavior if physical dependence is present (e.g., Downs & Woods, 1975; Goldberg, Hoffmeister, Schlichting, & Wuttke, 1971; Goldberg, Hoffmeister, & Schlichting, 1972; Tang & Morse, 1975). In addition to the presence or absence of physical dependence, the schedule under which an opioid antagonist is administered can determine its stimulus function (see Goldberg, Spealman, & Shannon, 1982). For example, Downs and Woods (1975) initially exposed monkeys to conditions in which every 30th response terminated a stimulus associated with injections of naloxone. Responding was well maintained under this schedule. Responding also was well maintained for as many as 15 days in a subsequent condition in which responding produced naloxone injections (under a second-order schedule). Although responding eventually declined, these results indicate that, depending on current and prior circumstances, naloxone can serve as a positive or a negative reinforcer in the same subject.

A common misconception among individuals only minimally conversant with behavioral principles is the notion that a drug is serving as a negative reinforcer if it is self-administered by a person undergoing withdrawal symptoms, which are alleviated by the drug. The logic behind this analysis, albeit faulty, is as follows: Drug administration is an escape response which serves to terminate the aversive state of withdrawal, ergo the drug must be a negative reinforcer. Although it may be intuitively appealing, this analysis violates the convention of classifying reinforcers as positive or negative according to their *physical* characteristics, not their effects on some real or posited internal state of the subject. Moreover, if one applies the same illogic described above to the analysis of food-maintained responding, one is forced to acknowledge that food is a negative reinforcer since its administration terminates an aversive state, hunger. There is nothing to recommend such a mentalistic conception whether it is applied to the effects of food or of drugs, although this is not to deny the fact that withdrawal can play a role in drug self-administration. As discussed in Chapter 7, it surely can, but the mechanism involves an increase in the positively reinforcing value of the drug, not negative reinforcement.

If a drug serves as a negative reinforcer, stimuli that reliably precede exposure to it may come to serve as conditioned negative reinforcers. Conversely, a drug can acquire through conditioning negatively reinforcing properties if its administration predictably precedes exposure to an established negative reinforcer. Finally, drugs that serve as negative reinforcers also frequently serve as positive punishers, that is, as stimuli that reduce the future probability of occurrence of behaviors that lead to their administration. All of these actions can influence the observed drug effects within or across individuals.

Concluding Comments

Realization that drugs may possess stimulus effects acquired through conditioning, as well as the ability to affect behavior in the absence of conditioning (i.e., act as unconditional stimuli) has two important implications for understanding drug effects in humans. The first is that the behavioral actions of a given drug may differ dramatically across individuals, depending upon their conditioning histories with respect to it. One person may dance while intoxicated at a party because that response was richly reinforced in similar circumstances in the past, another may sing for the same reason. In both cases, ethanol would be affecting behavior as a discriminative, as well as an unconditional, stimulus.

The second implication is that a drug's behavioral actions within an individual may vary over time. Ethanol, for instance, possesses aversive taste properties and typically does not serve as a positive reinforcer upon initial exposure. With repeated exposure to the drug's pharmacological properties, however, it frequently comes to serve as a powerful positive reinforcer. As noted earlier, behavioral actions that develop through such an interaction of behavioral and pharmacological variables are termed functional, as opposed to direct, effects. Any attempt to account for the behavioral actions of drugs across individuals, or within an individual over time, is unlikely to succeed unless it considers functional as well as direct actions. Behaviorally active drugs are not magic bullets that selectively and inevitably change behavior in specifiable ways. They are, rather, stimuli and as such produce effects that may differ as a function of the conditions under which they are, and have been, administered.

CHAPTER

5

Drug–Behavior
Interactions

As discussed in the previous chapter, drugs can affect behavior by serving as functional stimuli. They also can modulate the effects of nonpharmacological variables. How they do so and the factors that influence these processes are the topics of the present chapter.

Drug Effects on Learning

From a behavioral perspective, learning refers to changes in an organism's behavior as a result of operant or respondent conditioning.[1] Learning can involve the emission of a topographically novel response, as when a new behavior is acquired through shaping, or the emission of a previously extant response under the control of a once ineffectual stimulus, as when a child who previously voiced "apple" when presented with the fruit is taught

---

[1]There obviously are many definitions of learning, and a good case can be made that learning need not involve operant or respondent conditioning. However, these processes, the latter in particular, appear to be involved in the majority of human learning.

to say "apple" upon seeing the printed word. The ability to learn allows animals to adapt rapidly to diverse environments; it is this ability that has enabled our species to colonize—and dramatically alter—the globe.

There are innumerable ways to study learning and drug effects thereon. Procedures that allow for a within-subject analysis of drug effects on learning are few, however, since with many assays of learning the response in question can be learned on a single occasion only. One procedure that does allow for repeated assessment of learning, and how it is affected by drugs, is the repeated acquisition of behavioral chains, or *repeated acquisition*, procedure.

Boren first described the repeated acquisition procedure in 1963; he also conducted the first study of drug (methylphenidate) effects on learning as assayed by the procedure (Boren, 1967). Since that time, the procedure has been used often and profitably by behavioral pharmacologists (see Thompson & Moerschbaecher, 1979).

The repeated acquisition procedure requires the subject to learn a sequence of responses (usually spatially defined) that changes during each test session. A study by Picker and Poling (1984), who were concerned with the effects of anticonvulsant drugs on learning in pigeons, illustrates how the repeated acquisition procedure can be used to assess drug effects. In this investigation, pigeons were tested in an operant conditioning chamber that contained three translucent response keys and a food dispenser. Food was earned dependent upon the completion of a four-response sequence. Each component in the chain (response sequence) was associated with a different key color, three response options were available during each component (i.e., left-key response, center-key response, right-key response), and the correct response for each component was defined by spatial locus. The sequence of responses designated as correct changed on a daily basis and could be determined only by trial and error. On Monday, for instance, the correct sequence might be peck left, peck right, peck left, and peck center, whereas the sequence center, left, center, right would be designated as correct on Tuesday.

With protracted exposure, the number of errors made by a subject in mastering a new sequence became relatively stable and provided a sensitive baseline against which drug effects could be assessed.

Figure 11 shows the effects of acute administrations of five anticonvulsant drugs on the performance of a single pigeon tested under the repeated acquisition procedure. Clonazepam, valproic acid, ethosuximide, and phenytoin produced generally dose-dependent decreases in responding whereas phenobarbital had little consistent effect on response rates. Phenobarbital and clonazepam produced dose-dependent increases in error rates. Although valproic acid and phenytoin generally increased errors relative to control values, this effect was not directly dose-dependent or consistent across subjects.

A within-sessions analysis of the distribution of drug-induced increases in errors revealed that the main effect of phenobarbital, clonazepam, valproic acid, and phenytoin was to increase errors during early acquisition (i.e., before the procurement of 15 or fewer reinforcers). Later in the session, a similar, and low, number of errors per reinforcer was made during drug and control sessions. This finding suggests that the drugs actually were interfering with learning.

With repeated exposure to the four-response sequence, the number of errors per reinforcer (food delivery) declined rapidly when drugs were not administered. Given this, if a drug were to slow responding so that few reinforcers were obtained, it might appear that learning was impaired relative to control sessions in which far fewer reinforcers were obtained. This confound can be avoided by recording in each session the number of errors made before the delivery of each reinforcer, which allows drug data to be compared with appropriate control data (i.e., data representing an equivalent number of reinforcers), as was done in Figure 11.

In contrast to the other anticonvulsants studied, ethosuximide had little effect on error rates. These results suggest that there are qualitative as well as quantitative differences in the effects of antiepilepsy drugs under the repeated acquisition procedure. They also are consistent with preclinical and clinical data

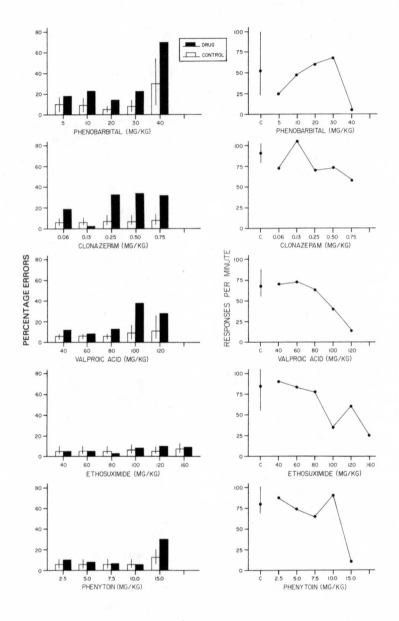

indicating that the majority of anticonvulsants can adversely affect learning, although this effect reportedly is not a major problem with ethosuximide at therapeutic doses (see Poling & Picker, 1986).

Global summaries of drug effects inevitably are dangerous, but a wealth of data suggest that many different compounds disrupt learning at doses that do not affect the performance of previously learned tasks (e.g., Sprague & Berger, 1980; Thompson & Moerschbaecher, 1979).

Most studies of drug effects on repeated acquisition have employed nonhuman subjects; however, the repeated acquisition procedure can be employed to analyze directly how drugs influence learning in humans. Thompson and associates, for example, have shown that benzodiazepines similarly disrupt learning in humans and pigeons tested under repeated acquisition procedures (Desjardins, Moerschbaecher, & Thompson, 1982; Thompson, 1975).

A problem sometimes encountered in using the repeated acquisition procedure with humans is very rapid mastery of new sequences; a human typically makes few errors in learning a simple sequence of three or four responses. This renders unlikely the possibility that drug-induced improvements in learning could be observed and may also reduce the likelihood that drug-induced learning impairment will be observed, since easy learning tasks appear to be less easily disrupted by drugs than are more difficult

---

Figure 11. Effects of phenobarbital, clonazepam, valproic acid, ethosuximide, and phenytoin on response rate and percentage of errors for one pigeon exposed to a repeated acquisition procedure. White bars in the left frame represent mean error percentage ({incorrect responses/incorrect responses + correct responses} × 100) during control sessions; the vertical line represents the range across these sessions. Error percentage for control sessions reflects performance during predrug sessions until a number of reinforcers equal to that obtained during the following drug session was earned. Dark bars in the left frame represent mean percentage of errors during initial exposure to the listed drug and dose. Data presented at C (right frames) indicate the mean rate of responding during control sessions; vertical lines represent the range across these sessions. Data are from Picker and Poling (1984).

ones. The difficulty of a repeated acquisition task can be increased by either (a) increasing the number of responses in the sequence or (b) increasing the logical complexity of the task (e.g., by defining correct responses in terms of multiple dimensions, such as color, brightness, and relative number of elements present, instead of spatial locus alone). Whether increasing task difficulty through these two operations would result in differential sensitivity to drugs is an interesting, and as yet unanswered, question.

Drugs Effects on Stimulus-Controlled Behavior

Learning involves the development of *stimulus control*, which "is observed when a change in a particular property of a stimulus produces a change in some response characteristic, as in the rate or probability with which a response occurs" (Rilling, 1977, p. 432). For example, the written stimulus "dog" is said to control the spoken word "dog" if the word is more often voiced in the presence of the written stimulus than in its absence.

Stimulus control occurs across a continuum. To illustrate this, suppose that a monkey's vocalizations are reinforced with food in the presence of a red light (S+) and extinguished in the presence of a green light (S−). The animal is then tested in the presence of lights of various colors and its rate of responding in the presence of various colors plotted as a *generalization gradient*. So long as the rate of responding to the S+ was higher than the rate of responding to the S−, stimulus control would be evident. In this case, it could be said that the animal *discriminated* between red and green or, synonymously, that it failed to *generalize* completely between the two colors. Only if vocal responding occurred when the red light was presented and at no other time would stimulus control be perfect. In all other cases, stimulus control would be imperfect and some degree of generalization evident.

Many factors influence the development and maintenance of stimulus-controlled responding. These include the training procedures employed, the physical characteristics of the stimuli used to control behavior, and the conditions under which stimulus control is assessed (see Rilling, 1977). It is recognized widely that drugs are capable of altering stimulus control, and studies of drug effects on stimulus-controlled responding—or, to use an older phrase, on discrimination and perception—are common in behavioral pharmacology (see Appel & Dykstra, 1977; Thompson, 1978).

Several procedures have been used to examine drug effects on stimulus-controlled responding. Among them are multiple schedules, stimulus-titration (or adjustment) procedures, matching-to-sample and delayed-matching-to-sample procedures, stimulus generalization procedures, discrete trial stimulus detection procedures, chained and related schedules, fixed-consecutive-number schedules, and repeated acquisition procedures. These techniques, which vary greatly in complexity and the kind of data they can provide, are described fully elsewhere (e.g., Appel & Dykstra, 1977; Thompson, 1978). Only the delayed-matching-to-sample assay and the fixed-consecutive-number schedule will be considered here.

Under the *delayed-matching-to-sample procedure* (Berryman, Cumming & Nevin, 1963), on each discrete trial a subject is presented with a number (e.g., two) of sample stimuli that differ in some physical aspect (e.g., color). Some time after presentation of the sample stimulus ends, two or more comparison stimuli are presented. A response to the comparison stimulus that matches (i.e., is physically equivalent to) the sample stimulus is reinforced; errors end the trial without reinforcement (and, in many studies, initiate a timeout). The delayed-matching-to-sample procedure allows for an evaluation of drug effects on the performance of a complex conditional discrimination. Moreover, since from a mentalistic viewpoint the subject can consistently respond correctly to the comparison stimuli only if the previously presented sample is "remembered," the procedure can be used to evaluate how drugs influence short-term memory.

A study by Picker, White, and Poling (1985) illustrates the use of a delayed-matching-to-sample procedure to analyze the effects of drugs, in this case the five anticonvulsants the effects of which under a repeated acquisition procedure were discussed in the previous section. In this investigation, pigeons were required to match stimuli (key colors) separated by 0.5, 1, 2, 4, or 8 sec, with each delay interval presented equally often during daily sessions. To provide a measure of response rate, five responses were required to extinguish the sample stimulus and (eventually) present the comparison stimuli. When administered acutely, clonazepam, valproic acid, ethosuximide, and phenytoin reduced rate of responding to the sample stimulus, whereas phenobarbital generally increased response rate (Figure 12). Phenobarbital, clonazepam, and valproic acid (Figure 12) produced dose-dependent decreases in overall accuracy (i.e., accuracy summed across all delay values). With these drugs, the relative magnitude of the accuracy decrement did not vary systematically with delay interval. Ethosuximide and phenytoin did not generally reduce overall accuracy, although the latter drug did so in some instances. The finding that clonazepam and phenobarbital impaired performance is consistent with earlier reports concerning the effects of benzodiazepines and barbiturates under the delayed-matching-to-sample procedure (Nicholson & Wright, 1974; Nicholson, Wright, & Ferres, 1973). Moreover, these results suggest that there are substantial differences in the effects of anticonvulsant drugs on stimulus-controlled responding as as-

---

Figure 12. Effects of phenobarbital, clonazepam, valproic acid, ethosuximide, and phenytoin on percentage of correct responses and rate of responding to the sample stimulus (i.e., on the center key) for individual pigeons. For the panels on the left, control data (indicated by C) are expressed as the mean percentage of correct responses ({correct responses/correct responses + incorrect responses} × 100) averaged across all five delays for the 10 sessions that preceded drug administration; vertical lines represent the standard error of the mean. Drug data are expressed as the percentage of correct responses for the two determinations at each dose and are averaged across all five delays. The panels on the right show the mean rate of responding to the sample stimulus during the 10 sessions that preceded drug administration (vertical lines represent the standard error of the mean) and during the two administrations of each dose. From Picker, White, and Poling (1985). Reproduced by permission of Springer-Verlag.

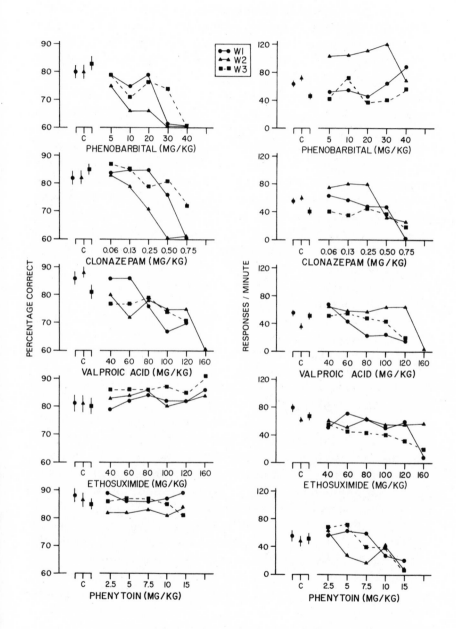

sessed by the delayed-matching-to-sample procedure, as well as under the repeated acquisition procedure summarized earlier.

The data collected by Picker and associates (Picker & Poling, 1984; Picker *et al.*, 1985) suggest that, unlike most other anti-epilepsy medications, ethosuximide has little effect on stimulus-controlled responding, even at doses that substantially reduce response rates. To explore this possibility further, Picker, Leibold, Endsley, and Poling (1986) compared the effects of ethosuximide and clonazepam, both anticonvulsants useful in the management of absence seizures, on the performance of pigeons exposed to two versions of a fixed-consecutive-number schedule. Although the preclinical behavioral pharmacology of ethosuximide is known to differ from that of clonazepam (Poling & Picker, in press), it is not clear to what extent the behavioral effects of these drugs can be modulated by strong stimulus control. The fixed-consecutive-number (*FNC*) schedule is one procedure that has been effectively employed to evaluate stimulus control as a determinant of drug action.

Under the *FCN* schedule, subjects are reinforced if they respond a fixed number of times (8–13 in the Picker *et al.* study) on one response key (work operandum), then emit a single response on a second key (reinforcement operandum). Premature switching or responding on the reinforcement operandum before the response requirement on the work operandum is completed resets the response requirement. In one variant of the *FCN* schedule, a discriminative stimulus (e.g., change in the color of key illumination) is correlated with the completion of the response requirement on the work operandum, whereas under the other no such stimulus change is arranged. The addition of the external discriminative stimulus substantially improves accuracy (percent of reinforced runs) without affecting overall rate of responding. Thus, any differences in drug-induced changes in accuracy under the two procedures cannot be attributed to differences in control rates of responding (i.e., rate-dependent effects) but rather reflects the stimulus control exercised by the external discriminative stimulus.

Several studies (e.g., Laties, 1972: Laties, Wood, & Cooper,

1981; Mechner & Latranyi, 1963; Szostak & Tombaugh, 1981; Wagman & Maxey, 1969) have shown that the addition of a discriminative stimulus reduces the disruptive effects of various drugs (e.g., d-amphetamine, methylphenidate, scopolamine, pimozide). Data presented in Figure 13 show that this also is the

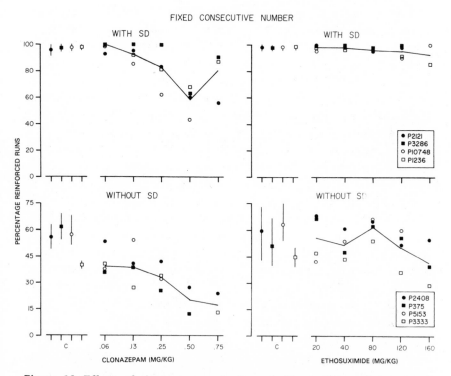

Figure 13. Effects of clonazepam and ethosuximide on the performance of pigeons under a fixed-consecutive-number schedule with and without an added discriminative stimulus. A reinforced run was one in which (a) pecking was begun on the proper key, (b) pecking continued on that key until 8–13 consecutive responses were emitted thereon, after which (c) a single peck was directed to the other key. Percentage of reinforced runs was determined by dividing the number of reinforced runs by the total number of runs begun and multiplying by 100. Control data (C) represent mean performance of individual pigeons across all sessions immediately prior to drug administration; vertical lines indicate the range over these sessions. Lines drawn through the drug data represent mean group performance.

case for clonazepam. At the doses tested by Picker *et al.*, this drug produced dose-dependent decreases in percentage of reinforced runs and rate of responding under both versions of the *FCN* schedule. However, the magnitude of these decreases was generally greater in subjects tested without the added discriminative stimulus. Although ethosuximide produced dose-dependent decreases in rate of responding, it had little effect on percentage of reinforced runs under either *FCN* variation. These findings are in accordance with previous reports indicating that clonazepam, but not ethosuximide, substantially interferes with the performance, as well as the learning, of complex conditional discriminations. The ability to interfere with such discriminations appears to represent a major component of the behavioral mechanism of action of the former compound.

Techniques that engender stimulus-controlled responding frequently are used to examine drug effects on *sensory acuity*, or perception. For example, certain aminoglycoside antimicrobials have been shown to produce ototoxicity and consequent loss of behavioral control by stimuli requiring auditory pitch discrimination (Stebbins & Coombs, 1975), whereas high doses of depressants such as ethanol impair general sensory acuity and stimulus control. The two classes of drugs produce very different behavioral outcomes, due in part to their dissimilar mechanisms of action as regards stimulus control.

While drug-induced alterations in stimulus-controlled responding may reflect changes in sensory acuity, it is not always so. As Appel and Dykstra (1977) note:

> While the effects which humans report following LSD or morphine might indeed reflect drug-induced changes in acuity, threshold, or other index of ability to detect the presence or absence of visual or painful stimuli, we cannot objectively study such changes except by measuring some correlated change in behavior which is assumed to indicate the subject's "capacity to discriminate." But such behavior may also be altered by these same drugs; thus, it becomes difficult, if not impossible, to separate the effect of the drug on discriminatory processes (sensitivity) from its effect on the subject's behavior or response criterion (bias) in the presence of the discrimination situation. (p. 141)

Signal detection theory (Green & Swets, 1966) was devised to separate the effects of nonpharmacological variables on sensitivity as opposed to response bias and has been employed occasionally to study drug–behavior interactions (see Appel & Dykstra, 1977). However, the assumptions and methods of signal detection theory are rather complex—in fact, too complex to be covered here—and signal detection analyses of drug effects require the collection of much data under a range of conditions. For these reasons, signal detection theory has yet to play a major role in most behavioral pharmacologists' thinking about drug effects.

Many such individuals do recognize, however, that drug effects on stimulus-controlled responding are determined by multiple factors and frequently reflect the complex interplay of pharmacological (e.g., drug type, drug dose, and the schedule of drug administration) and behavioral variables (e.g., response rate in the absence of drug, the physical characteristics of the stimuli controlling responding, the training procedures employed, the degree of stimulus control evident in the absence of drug, and whether the stimulus-controlled response is well learned or is just being acquired). Nonetheless, as Laties (1975) and Thompson (1978) indicate, behavior that is strongly controlled by a discriminative stimulus is as a general rule less affected by drugs than similar behavior that is stimulus-controlled to a lesser degree. Like nondrug response rate, degree of stimulus control in the absence of drug is apt to modulate a drug's behavioral activity, although it rarely is the sole determinant thereof.

Rate-Dependent Drug Effects

Dews (1955) was the first investigator to report that a drug's behavioral effects were strongly influenced by the ongoing rate of behavior in the absence of drug, that is, were rate-dependent. In that study, pigeons' rates of keypecking maintained under an FR 50 schedule of food delivery were increased by doses of pentobarbital that reduced responding maintained under an FI 90-minute schedule. Nondrug response rates under the *FR* schedule were much higher than those maintained under the *FI* schedule. Subsequent studies reported rate-dependent effects for amphetamines, benzodiazepine anxiolytics, opioids, phenothiazine neuroleptics, and tricyclic antidepressants (Cook & Kelleher, 1962; Kelleher, Fry, Deagan, & Cook, 1961; Marr, 1970; Richelle, Xhenseval, Fontaine, & Thone, 1962; Smith, 1964; Thompson, Trombley, Luke, & Lott, 1970; Waller & Morse, 1963). Not all drugs with rate-dependent effects mimic pentobarbital's ability to increase high-rate responding at doses that reduce low-rate responding.[2] The rate-dependent effects of *d*-amphetamine, for example, are opposite to those of pentobarbital. At low-to-moderate doses, *d*-amphetamine increases low-rate operant responding but reduces high-rate operant responding (Dews & Wenger, 1977).

Many studies have reported rate-dependent effects for *d*-amphetamine, and for other amphetamines as well (Dews & Wenger, 1977). As Sanger and Blackman (1976) point out, one technique for studying rate-dependent drug effects involves giving drugs to subjects exposed to schedules that engender very different response rates, for example, short *FR* and long *FI* schedules of food delivery. Another common technique involves a detailed analysis of drug effects on responding maintained under *FI* schedules. Animals responding under such schedules typically emit few responses early in the interval but respond much more rapidly as the interval progresses. Hence, if each fixed interval is divided temporally into a number of sequential segments (e.g., 10), a range of baseline rates will be evident.

In most studies concerned with rate-dependent drug effects,

---

[2]According to Kelleher and Morse (1969), low-rate operants are separated in time by more than one second; shorter interresponse times are indicative of high-rate responding. However, this standard is not ubiquitously applied. One criticism of rate dependency as an explanatory construct is that high and low rates are sometimes defined after the fact, e.g., rates increased by a moderate dose of amphetamine are "low," whereas those reduced by the same dose are "high." This criticism loses force if rate dependency is properly envisioned as purely descriptive.

data are plotted as shown in Figure 14. Here, drug-induced proportional changes in response rates (i.e., drug rates expressed as a percentage of control rates) are plotted on logarithmic coordinates as a function of control rates, and data are interpreted as showing rate dependency if the data fall along a straight line with a slope other than zero.

When data concerning the effects of *d*-amphetamine on schedule-controlled responding are graphed as just described, the regression line that best fits the data frequently has a slope of about −1 (Gonzales & Byrd, 1977a, b). In such cases, response rate in the presence of drug is constant regardless of control rate, and control and drug rates are independent of one another. In view of this, Gonzales and Byrd (1977a) have proposed *rate con-*

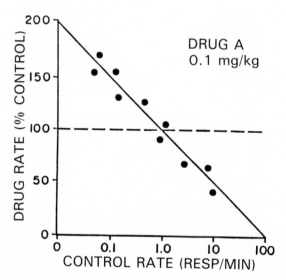

Figure 14. Data showing what commonly are considered as rate-dependent effects for a hypothetical drug. Each data point represents the effects of administering the drug on a single occasion under a condition associated with a particular response rate in the absence of drug. Note that the magnitude and direction of the change in response rate induced by the drug are dependent on the rate of behavior in the absence of drug.

stancy as an alternative to the rate-dependency "hypothesis." Byrd (1981) describes rate constancy as follows:

> According to rate constancy, a drug reduces the variability in the rate at which the behavior occurs, and responding approaches a more constant rate. The higher the drug dose, within limits, the more constant and uniform the rate. (p. 85)

Advocates of the rate constancy analysis recommend that data be plotted with absolute drug rate along the *y*-axis and absolute control rate (both plotted in logarithmic coordinates) along the *x*-axis (Byrd, 1981). This suggestion has as yet been followed but rarely.

To date, research concerning rate-dependent drug effects has almost exclusively involved nonhuman subjects. While there is no good reason to believe that rate-dependent drug effects cannot be observed with humans in their usual environment, those who hope to extend the rate-dependency analysis of drug effects to human behavior should recognize that rate dependency is an explanatory construct only in that it describes a relation between two variables: the relative change in response rate following drug administration and the nondrug response rate. As McKearney and Barrett (1978) contend:

> It is important to note that neither in its initial statement nor in its later elaboration by Dews or his colleagues was this [the rate-dependency analysis] any more than a description of the effects of certain drugs, and as a factor that might predict drug effects in certain situations. It did not, and indeed does not, directly "explain" the effects of drugs. It is still a descriptive statement, not a "theory" or "hypothesis," and its generality and biological significance, rather than truth or falsity, are what should be elaborated experimentally. (p. 26)

Moreover, as Dews and Wenger (1977) note:

> The theory of rate-dependency may be considered under four propositions:
>   1. The weakest proposition is that with all other possible variables unchanged, a change in rate of responding may change the behavioral effect of a drug.
>   2. A stronger proposition is that not only *may* differences in rate of responding lead to differences in the behavioral effect of a drug, but that in general differences in rates *will* determine differences in the effects of a drug, and that there will be a systematic relationship between the rate of responding and the effect of a drug.

3. The third proposition adds a quantitative constraint to the second: the control rate of responding relates to the effect of a drug so that the log of the effect is a linear function of the log of the control rate.

4. The strongest proposition is that the rate of responding completely determines the effect of a given dose of a drug, other variables influencing the drug effect only indirectly by affecting rates of responding. (p. 169, reprinted by permission of Academic Press)

It appears that the first proposition holds for most drugs and that the fourth holds for none. The effects of a drug on schedule-controlled behavior depend upon a variety of factors, including: (1) whether the response in question is punished, (2) whether the response in question is strongly under the control of discriminative stimuli, and (3) which schedule and which reinforcer maintain the response (see McKearney, 1981; Sanger & Blackman, 1976). Despite this, it is abundantly clear that the rate of behavior in the absence of drug can powerfully influence the relative change in response rate produced by the drug. Such an action can be observed under seemingly homogeneous conditions, as occurred in a study by Urbain *et al.* (1978).

This study investigated the effects of relatively low doses of *d*-amphetamine on rats' lever pressing maintained under an *FI* schedule of food delivery. For one group of subjects, exposure to the *FI* was preceded by training under an *FR* schedule; for a second group, an *IRT* > *t* schedule was in effect before the *FI*. *d*-Amphetamine's effects on *FI* responding varied as a result of operant history: The drug typically increased response rates in animals initially exposed to the *IRT* > *t* schedule but reduced rates in animals first trained under the *FR*. These findings appear to reflect rate-dependent effects of *d*-amphetamine, since in the absence of drug animals with *FR* histories responded much more rapidly under the *FI* schedule than did those with *IRT* > *t* histories.

Although the conceptual status and heuristic value of rate-dependent analyses of drug effects have been subject to some debate in recent years (e.g., Thompson, Dews, & McKim, 1981), realization that control response rate is a potent determinant of drug-induced changes in behavior was prerequisite to studying other important determinants of the behavioral effects of drugs. Furthermore, although knowledge of control rates alone frequently is insufficient to predict the effects of drugs with precision, the ubiquity with which rate-dependent effects are observed is striking. McKearney (1981) puts it well when he writes, with respect to the behavioral effects of drugs:

> Rate is important and must *always* be considered, even though it may not be influential in *all ways*. Dews expressed the same thing when he said that "an influence can be all pervading without being all embracing" (Dews, 1963, p. 148). Rates have pervasive influences that will operate whenever they are free to do so. As a concept or principle, "rate-dependency" is neither right nor wrong, but response rate is more or less influential and more or less useful in understanding the effects of drug. It clearly does not "explain," nor can it be expected to predict everything. (p. 98)

Consequence-Dependent Drug Effects

Behavioral pharmacologists have long recognized that response rate can influence qualitative as well as quantitative aspects of drug action. It appeared, in fact, that the rate and temporal patterning of responding was a much more powerful and general determinant of drug effect than the consequences that were maintaining behavior. This was demonstrated in early studies of nonhumans (e.g., Cook & Catania, 1964: Kelleher & Morse, 1964) in which roughly comparable rates of responding were maintained under schedules of food delivery, escape from electric shock, or termination of a stimulus associated with forthcoming shock. In the Cook and Catania study, only *FI* schedules were examined, whereas Kelleher and Morse used both *FI* and *FR* schedules. In both studies, the effects of several drugs (chlordiazepoxide, chlorpromazine, *d*-amphetamine, and imipramine) did not depend on the consequences that maintained behavior. However, in the Kelleher and Morse investigation, the effects of both chlorpromazine and *d*-amphetamine differed under the *FR* and *FI* schedules. The former evoked considerably higher response rates than did the latter, thus these findings are consistent with the notion that the effects of certain drugs are rate-dependent, irrespective of the consequences maintaining behavior.

More recent investigations "provide overwhelming evidence that the type of event controlling behavior can be an important aspect of the environment contributing to the behavioral effects of a number of drugs" (Barrett, 1981, p. 175). This is evident in the results of a study by Barrett (1976), who found that pentobarbital, ethanol, and chlordiazepoxide increased monkeys' responding maintained by food delivery but decreased similar rates of responding engendered by shock presentation. Cocaine, in contrast, similarly affected responding maintained by the two events.

Drugs that act as deprivation-altering events, that is, as establishing operations (EOs), are likely to affect selectively responding maintained by particular reinforcers. Insulin injections may well increase food-seeking behaviors and eating but probably will not similarly strengthen mate-seeking and sexual activity.

A special kind of consequence-dependent drug effect involves the ability of certain drugs selectively to increase punished responding. Benzodiazepines (e.g., chlordiazepoxide, or Librium), for instance, at moderate doses typically increase low rate responding, but the magnitude of this effect is much greater if the responding is punished than if it is not (Sanger & Blackman, 1981). Many drugs said to have "disinhibitory" properties attenuate the effects of punishment, and this may be a major aspect of their behavioral mechanism of action.

As an aside, *disinhibition* historically has referred to an increase in a physiological process as the result of decreased activity in a system that, when active, inhibits the process. Heart rate, for instance, can be increased by decreasing activity in the vagus nerve by administration of large doses of atropine, since vagal imputs slow (inhibit) heart rate (Goth, 1974). Disinhibition when applied to the behavioral effects of drugs usually has no obvious physiological referant but refers on the one hand to a set of imprecisely defined responses to the drug and on the other to a hypothetical mechanism allegedly responsible for these responses. This is an obvious, and unfortunate, error of reification.

Conditioned reinforcement appears to play an important role in the maintenance of many human behaviors and, although this possibility has rarely been examined, certain drugs may differentially affect behavior maintained by primary and conditioned reinforcers. Moreover, the presence of conditioned reinforcers can modulate observed drug effects. McGuire, (1975) has shown, for example, that methadone reduced responding to a lesser degree under schedules of reinforcement that deliver strong conditioned reinforcers (i.e., food-paired brief stimuli) than under similar schedules without strong conditioned reinforcers.

Conditioned reinforcement is involved in much rule-governed behavior. Although rule-governed and contingency-shaped responding may be topographically indistinguishable, it is not clear whether drugs similarly affect the two types of behavior. Comparison of drug effects on rule-governed and contingency-shaped behavior is an interesting line of research yet to be pursued, perhaps because it cannot be done readily in the nonhuman laboratory.

Extinction is a condition in which previously reinforced operant responses are no longer rewarded. Responding during extinction may be selectively affected by drugs, as in a study by Thompson (1962), who demonstrated that doses of chlorpromazine that decreased rats' rates of lever-pressing under an FR 1 schedule of food delivery increased responding during extinction. Extinction-specific drug effects have rarely been studied but appear to be a significant example of consequence-dependent drug effects.

Concluding Comments

It should by now be apparent to the reader that many factors, not all intuitively obvious, interact to determine a drug's behavioral effects. As emphasized in this chapter, these factors include response rate in the absence of drug, the consequences that maintain (or suppress) behavior, and the degree to which responding is stimulus-controlled. The topography of the behavior in question may also influence a drug's effects, as when a compound that induces tremor disrupts performance of an operant response that requires fine-motor skill but has no such effect when only gross responses are demanded. A drug's stimulus properties also dictate its behavioral effects, as do pharmacological variables such as dosage and schedule of administration.

Since drug effects depend upon a wide range of factors, both currently operative and historical, it stands to reason that a given drug can produce dramatically different behavioral actions in different people, or in the same individual at different times and places. Consider two mentally retarded adolescents who engage in self-injurious biting, for which each is treated with the same dose of a neuroleptic drug. Self-injury allows one adolescent to terminate aversive encounters with staff but enables the second to prevent such encounters. Here, biting would be maintained as an escape response for the first client and as an avoidance response for the second. It would not be surprising if the drug's effects on self-biting differed in these individuals, for neuroleptics often interfere with avoidance responding at doses that have no effect on escape responding. If this held true in the present example, Client 1's self-biting would be unaffected by doses of a neuroleptic that suppressed the response in Client 2. This is perfectly lawful and comprehensible if the role of behavioral and environmental variables in determining drug effects is acknowledged, but a mystery if they are ignored. A drug's behavioral effects are rarely simple, but they are always lawful. Making this point clear and isolating the factors that contribute to a drug's behavioral actions are two major contributions to the understanding of drug effects in humans that have arisen from the efforts of behavioral pharmacologists.

CHAPTER

6

Clinical Drug Assessment

In 1900, about 150,000 "mentally ill" Americans occupied hospital beds. This population had grown to 500,000 individuals by 1955, the year before chlorpromazine was introduced into psychiatric practice. With that introduction, the number of hospitalized mentally ill Americans began a steady decline, falling to below 200,000 in 1975 (Berger, 1978). As Lickey and Gordon (1983) point out, "The decline in the number of hospitalized patients has not resulted from a decrease in the rate of new hospital admissions. Rather, the new drugs have made it possible to leave the hospital after a much briefer stay" (p. 4).

Hospitalization data are provocative but provide only a crude and indirect measure of the effects of pharmacotherapeutic agents. Precise determination of how drugs affect clinically significant behaviors is possible only through controlled research. The Food, Drug, and Cosmetic Act, passed in 1938 and amended in 1962, has since the latter date required that drugs marketed in the United States be both safe and effective for the conditions listed on the label or packaging brochure. Specific requirements for approval are set forth in Title 21 of the Code of Federal Regulation:

> The Code . . . demands that the safety and effectiveness of a new drug be established by "substantial evidence," derived from "ade-

quate and well-controlled investigations, including clinical investigations (conducted) by experts qualified by scientific training and experience." (Leber, 1983, p. 5)

In view of these requirements, one might suppose that the behavioral effects of pharmacotherapeutic agents have been adequately
studied and can be confidently specified.

Surely there has been no shortage of attempts to evaluate
most pharmacological agents: Drugs developed after 1962 must
be evaluated for safety in nonhumans, then tested for safety and
effectiveness in Phase 1, 2, and 3 clinical trials with humans.
Phase 1 clinical trials involve giving very small doses of the drug to
healthy volunteers, in whom side effects and pharmacokinetics of
the drug are evaluated. Phase 2 involves determining the safety
and effectiveness of the drug in a few individuals afflicted with the
condition the drug is designed to treat. Phase 3 trials involve
further evaluation in a larger number of individuals (usually 500–
3,000). If, after these tests are completed, the drug appears to
have an acceptable risk-to-benefit ratio, the Food and Drug Administration allows it to be conditionally marketed. Figure 15
provides a summary of the phases of drug development in the
United States.

Developing a new drug takes years and may cost $50 million
to $70 million (Ray, 1983), but required clinical and preclinical
trials do not necessarily detect serious side effects of a particular
agent, reveal all of the conditions in which it is useful, or disclose
the factors which modify its efficacy (Karch & Lasagna, 1975;
Melmon & Morelli, 1978; Melmon et al., 1980). Therefore
postmarketing studies play an important role in the evaluation of
all drugs. Moreover, they play a crucial role in evaluating the safety and efficacy of drugs developed prior to the passage and amendment of the Food, Drug, and Cosmetic Act, which includes agents
used to manage behavior (see Chapter 1).

Unfortunately, although there have been many evaluations of
the majority of behavior-change medications currently on the
market, obvious methodological flaws characterize many reported
studies. For example, Klein and Davis (1969) found only 11 of
over 12,000 published evaluations of chlorpromazine to be meth-

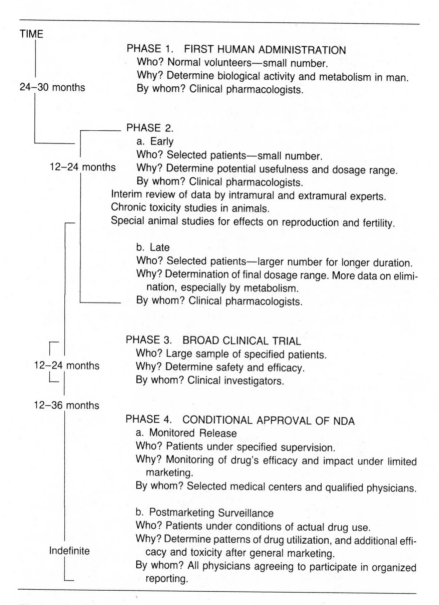

TIME

PHASE 1.   FIRST HUMAN ADMINISTRATION
Who? Normal volunteers—small number.
Why? Determine biological activity and metabolism in man.

24–30 months   By whom? Clinical pharmacologists.

PHASE 2.
a. Early
Who? Selected patients—small number.

12–24 months   Why? Determine potential usefulness and dosage range.
By whom? Clinical pharmacologists.
Interim review of data by intramural and extramural experts.
Chronic toxicity studies in animals.
Special animal studies for effects on reproduction and fertility.

b. Late
Who? Selected patients—larger number for longer duration.
Why? Determination of final dosage range. More data on elimi-
nation, especially by metabolism.
By whom? Clinical pharmacologists.

PHASE 3.   BROAD CLINICAL TRIAL
Who? Large sample of specified patients.

12–24 months   Why? Determine safety and efficacy.
By whom? Clinical investigators.

12–36 months

PHASE 4.   CONDITIONAL APPROVAL OF NDA
a. Monitored Release
Who? Patients under specified supervision.
Why? Monitoring of drug's efficacy and impact under limited
marketing.
By whom? Selected medical centers and qualified physicians.

b. Postmarketing Surveillance
Who? Patients under conditions of actual drug use.
Why? Determine patterns of drug utilization, and additional effi-

Indefinite   cacy and toxicity after general marketing.
By whom? All physicians agreeing to participate in organized
reporting.

Figure 15. The phases of drug development in the United States. Taken from
Melmon *et al.* (1980) and reproduced by permission of Macmillan Publishing
Company.

odologically sound. Marholin and Phillips (1976) subsequently found even these 11 to involve serious methodological flaws, especially with respect to the definition and evaluation of therapeutic change. Similarly, Sulzbacher (1973) found that over 70% of published pharmacological studies with children were inadequately controlled in that they lacked either double-blind conditions or placebo controls. Other authors have also found methodological errors to be ubiquitous in studies of drug effects in mentally retarded as well as mentally ill participants (e.g., Aman & Singh, 1980; Breuning & Poling, 1982; Lipton, DiMascio, & Killam, 1978; Poling, Picker, & Wallace, 1984; Sprague & Werry, 1971).

Beyond rendering findings difficult or impossible to interpret, methodological errors seem to increase the likelihood that a drug will reportedly produce beneficial effects in a given study (Sulzbacher, 1973). Given this, it appears that poor research is worse than no research at all: Uncontrolled investigations may indicate a particular drug to be effective (or ineffective), and subsequent clinical judgments may rest upon this report, even though the findings are actually erroneous. The purpose of the present chapter is to discuss important methodological issues in evaluating the effects of drugs prescribed to improve behavior.

Psychiatric Diagnosis

Behavior-change medications are prescribed to deal with problems: An individual receives pharmacotherapy because something she or he is (or is not) doing is deemed changeworthy, either by the affected person or by other members of society. In most cases, prior to receiving medication a patient will by virtue of his or her behavioral characteristics be assigned to a global diagnostic category. Assignment is frequently based on criteria described in the *Diagnostic and Statistical Manual of Mental Disorders* published by the American Psychiatric Association (1980), and generally referred to as *DSM-III*. The diagnosis of schizophrenia provides a good illustration of how this manual is employed and of the problems associated with psychiatric diagnosis. (To facilitate exposition, only the general category of schizophrenia will be considered, although *DSM-III* deals with a number of subcategories.)

DSM-III (1980, pp. 181–224) lists six diagnostic criteria for schizophrenia; each must be present for an individual to be so classified. These criteria are:

1. One of the following must occur during the illness:
   a. Bizarre delusions.
   b. Somatic, grandiose, religious, nihilistic, or other delusions without persecutory or jealous content.
   c. Delusions with persecutory or jealous content, accompanied by hallucinations.
   d. Auditory hallucinations (two types are described).
   e. Incoherence, loosening of associations, markedly illogical speech if associated with inappropriate affect, delusions or hallucinations, or grossly disorganized behavior.
2. Deteriorations from previous level of functioning in such areas as work, social relations, and self-care.
3. Duration of at least six months. Prodromal and residual phases are also described.
4. Any full depressive or manic syndrome developed after any psychiatric symptom even if brief in duration.
5. Onset of illness before age 45.
6. Illness not due to an organic mental disorder or mental retardation.

Although these criteria are further described in *DSM-III*, even with book in hand they are vague and amorphous. As Lickey and Gordon (1983) emphasize:

> A reliable system of diagnosis will achieve at least two goals. First, it will clearly define each illness by specifying its symptoms. Second, it will specify the methods for determining whether a patient has a particular symptom. (p. 39)

DSM-III represents a significant advance over earlier editions in that it is the first version in which specific diagnostic criteria are specified. However, the manner in which these criteria are to be applied—that is, what exactly a person must do to earn a particular diagnostic label—is unclear. At present, it is charitable to describe the nosological aspect of psychiatry as imprecise. Expert testimony in the bizarre court case of John Hinkley, President Reagan's would-be assassin, exemplifies this imprecision: Psychiatrists for the defense testified (and convinced the jury) that the accused suffered from schizophrenia and was driven to attempted murder by the delusion that killing the president would earn him the love of an actress named Jodie Foster. As might be expected, psychiatrists for the prosecution argued otherwise. In their opinion, John Hinkley was perfectly rational, capable of premeditated murder but free of delusional love.

Less newsworthy but perhaps more compelling demonstrations of the vagaries of psychiatric diagnosis have been provided in a number of empirical studies, (Kanfer & Saslow, 1969; Lickey & Gordon, 1983). These studies indicate that in some circumstances (a) clinicians who assign patients to diagnostic categories often disagree over appropriate placement (American psychiatrists seem to favor schizophrenia, their British counterparts personality disorder; see Lickey and Gordon, 1983, p. 39) and (b) there are significant differences in the actions of persons given the same diagnosis as well as very similar behaviors in individuals given different diagnoses.

In view of the foregoing, it is not surprising that individuals who share a common psychiatric diagnosis frequently evidence different responses to a particular drug. Although it is the case that psychiatric diagnosis is related to the likelihood that a given drug class will produce the desired result, a fact reflected in the way in which behavior-change medications are classified (e.g., as antidepressants), it is not presently possible to predict accurately which patients assigned to a diagnostic category will respond favorably to a particular medication. All that can be done is to assert that, across similarly diagnosed individuals, one kind of drug (e.g., a neuroleptic) is more likely to prove useful than is another (e.g., a stimulant).

Such probability statements are an invaluable guide for the clinical practitioner and firmly indicate that, despite obvious shortcomings, current methods of psychiatric diagnosis are adequate to allow for meaningful communication among researchers and clinicians and to aid in clinical practice. It is grossly unfair to dismiss psychiatric diagnosis as meaningless, but it nonetheless must be recognized that the classifications of *DSM-III* are nothing more than shorthand descriptions of a set of behaviors. In the words of Craighead, Kazdin, and Mahoney (1981):

> Psychological or psychiatric diagnosis seems to provide little information about behavior beyond that which was known when the diagnosis was made. Specifically, little information is given about the etiology, treatment of choice, and prognosis. (p. 102)

In the final analysis, drugs are not prescribed to deal with an underlying disease state of schizophrenia, depression, anxiety, or character disorder, but rather to deal with troublesome behaviors. Though schizophrenics may be characterized by unusually high levels of dopaminergic activity in certain areas of the brain, the schizophrenic is labeled as such on the basis of unusual behavior, not unusual neurochemistry. Overt behavior is therefore the appropriate starting point for the evaluation of pharmacotherapeutic agents. Initial psychiatric diagnosis provides a crude and summary indication of the kinds of problem behaviors an individual is exhibiting and may suggest the class of drug which is most likely to prove useful in dealing with these behaviors. However, as discussed in the next section, something more than traditional psychiatric diagnosis is required to determine whether an individual is deriving benefit from a behavior-change medication.

Target Behaviors and Their Assessment

The sole objective of clinical drug assessment is to determine whether the independent variable, drug administration, significantly improved some targeted aspect(s) of the client's behavior, the dependent variable. Despite the potential complexities of clinical drug evaluation, the essential features of a sound evaluation can be simply stated:

1. The behavior to be changed must be adequately defined and measured.
2. The treatment must be consistently administered according to the selected protocol.
3. The sequencing of conditions (experimental design) and method of data analysis must allow observed changes in the dependent variable to be attributed with confidence to the treatment.

If these three conditions are met, the evaluation is in principle sound.

Since pharmacotherapies are employed with the avowed intent of changing a patient's behavior, they are successful only to the extent that behavior changes in the desired direction and to the desired extent. Whether this has occurred can be ascertained only if the procedure (i.e., the assessment instrument) used to quantify behavior is *valid, reliable,* and *sensitive.* In a general sense, an assessment instrument is valid to the extent that it measures what it purports to measure. Validity cannot be directly assessed but is rather inferred on the basis of whether the measure (a) is logically defensible, (b) is similar in concept and outcome to other accepted measures of the same behavior, and (c) is accepted by experts in the area of concern.

A measure of behavior is reliable to the extent that it yields consistent, repeatable data. Salvia and Ysseldyke (1981) emphasize the worthlessness of an unreliable instrument by comparing it to a stretchable rubber ruler. Such a ruler would not produce consistent measurements, even if a single board was repeatedly measured under seemingly consistent conditions; the length obtained would depend mostly on how hard the ruler was stretched, not on the physical dimensions of the board. To extend the ruler analogy further, an invalid measure would be exemplified by the use of a rigid ruler to quantify weight. If used consistently, such a ruler would yield repeatable data (i.e., be reliable) and would be perfectly adequate for assessing length, but this dimension would have no necessary relation to weight, and it would be most unfortunate if weight and length measures were confused.

A sensitive measure is simply one which is affected by the independent variable. The sensitivity of a measure is ultimately determined by empirical test, although it is clear that a measure can be sensitive only when it is free either to increase or to decrease as a function of drug administration. For example, if a hyperactive child not receiving drug averaged 98% correct on math tests, this performance could not significantly improve if the child were medicated. Thus, it would be an inappropriate measure for assessing the effects of a medication intended to improve academic performance.

Target behaviors have been assessed in several ways in evaluations of pharmacotherapeutic agents. *Global clinical impression* is perhaps the most common method. It also is generally unsatisfactory, for it is rarely apparent what aspects of a patient's repertoire a clinician is assessing, or whether his or her assessment is valid and reliable. In view of these factors, it has been argued (e.g., Wysocki & Fuqua, 1982) that global clinical impressions can no longer be justified as an index of drug effects.

Standardized tests also appear to be of limited value in assessing drug effects, since they provide only an indirect measure of the actual behaviors medication is prescribed to improve and are often of limited sensitivity. However, an incredibly wide range of personality and achievement inventories are available and some of them are occasionally useful in drug evaluations. When such tests are used, one must ensure that they are valid and reliable when employed with the population of concern. Many intelligence tests, for example, are of unknown validity and reliability when administered to mentally retarded individuals (Poling, Parker, & Breuning, 1984).

Checklists and rating scales are rather widely used in assessing drug effects. For example, hyperkinesis is frequently evaluated through the use of the Conners Teachers Rating Scale (Conners, 1969), and severity of depression is commonly indexed by the Hamilton Rating Scale (Hamilton, 1967). The one essential requirement when checklists are used is correspondence between raters' evaluations of an individual and important aspects of that person's behavior. Such correspondence should not be assumed but rather proven by comparing the results of direct observations of behavior with checklist ratings of the same response. When it can be convincingly demonstrated that checklists or rating scales provide accurate measures of important behaviors, they represent a simple, uniform, and low-cost means of assessment.

Physiological assessment involves directly monitoring bodily function. This can often be done with automated equipment which, although costly and sometimes prone to break, increases the overall objectivity and accuracy of measurement. (*Accuracy* is a dimension of measurement that includes components of both validity and reliability: "A measure is accurate to the extent that it reflects the 'true value' of that which is being measured" [Wysocki & Fuqua, 1982, p. 141]). Physiological measures are important for indexing deleterious side effects of drugs and have also been used to measure anxiety and other clinical states. It is revealing that when physiological, motoric, and self-report data are collected simultaneously to index a particular clinical problem (e.g., a phobia), treatment often fails to produce equivalent effects across the three dimensions (Hersen & Barlow, 1976). As Paul (1967) contends, "While multiple measures of outcome are necessary, the dependent variable in any outcome evaluation must be . . . change in the disturbing behavior which brought the client to treatment" (p. 112).

Self-reports are troublesome indices of change, since they rarely involve public events and are quite sensitive to nondrug factors. However, patient reports of discomfort may be responsible for initiating or terminating pharmacotherapy, especially when anxiolytics or antidepressants are considered, and therefore they play an important role in drug evaluation. What a person says about his or her present condition is significant behavior and merits attention. Nonetheless, from a methodological perspective, self-reports provide relatively weak data which should be supported by more objective measures. Mahoney (1977) and Bellack and Schwartz (1976) overview the problems associated with self-reports and offer some suggestions to minimize their influence.

Analogue methods involve assessing behavior outside the environment in which an individual's behavior is of clinical importance. Analogue methods simulate the situation of concern in a way which allows behavior to be easily controlled and monitored. The essential problem with analogue methods is generalizability of results: Are the effects observed in the analogue situation a veridical reflection of happenings in the actual situation of concern? When they are, analogue methods can be quite useful in assessing drug effects. For example, laboratory indices of short-term memory have been profitably employed to analyze the effects of several pharmacotherapeutic agents (e.g., Davis, Poling, Wysocki, & Breuning, 1982; Sprague & Sleator, 1977; Wysocki, Fuqua, Davis, & Breuning, 1981). Several general overviews of analogue methods have been provided (e.g., Epstein, 1986; McFall, 1977; Nay, 1977).

Direct observation of behavior (or its outcome) is an especially useful method for evaluating drug effects. In direct observation, another person actually watches the client and records his or her behavior. To facilitate recording and quantification, *time sampling* and *intermittent time sampling*[1] procedures are commonly used. In time sampling, an observational period is divided into discrete intervals and the observer records whether or not the behavior appeared in each interval, whereas in intermittent time sampling observation occurs in only a few intervals, typically selected at random. With either observational system, *partial interval* or *whole interval* recording may be used. In partial interval recording, an observer scores (i.e., indicates that the target behavior occurred in) any interval in which the response definition was met, regardless of the duration of occurrence of the behavior.

---

[1]Several different terms have been used to describe each of the various methods of data collection employed in behavioral pharmacology (see Repp *et al.*, 1976), and inconsistencies are frequently apparent in the way a particular descriptor is used by different writers. Therefore one must pay close attention to how behavior actually was quantified in an investigation, regardless of the name assigned to the method of data collection.

In whole interval recording, an interval is scored only if the response definition was met throughout the interval.

Figure 16 depicts how a hypothetical response would be scored during baseline (no drug) and treatment (drug administered) conditions under partial interval time sampling, whole interval time sampling, partial interval intermittent time sampling, and whole interval intermittent time sampling procedures. Also presented in this figure are the values that would be obtained if the response were quantified according to frequency or duration of occurrence. Data presented in the figure indicate that, depending on mode of assessment, drug administration appeared to increase, decrease, or have no effect on the target behavior. The take-home message is that the treatment evaluator cannot afford to be cavalier with regard to specific aspects of direct observation, they do make a difference.

The cardinal rule in selecting an observation system is to be sure that the system adopted maximally reflects the aspects of behavior that are changeworthy. Beyond this, systems that arrange frequent observation are to be preferred to those that fail to do so, for the more frequently behavior is sampled (i.e., observation is arranged), the greater the likelihood that obtained data will actually reflect the level of occurrence of the behavior. Finally, since all drugs can deleteriously affect behavior, an acceptable observational system must make provision for the detection of countertherapeutic effects.

Marholin and Phillips (1976) have rightly criticized the traditional practice of considering drug treatments as successful on the basis of a reduction in undesirable behavior alone. This, they argue, is inadequate unless it is evident that the control of undesirable behavior is not accompanied by a dimunition in adaptive responding (e.g., an impairment in learning). Others (e.g., Wysocki & Fuqua, 1982) have echoed this sentiment, and the need for assessing how drugs affect desirable as well as undesirable behavior appears beyond debate.

Unfortunately, since the range of potential behavioral and physiological side effects is wide and the range of behaviors that an investigator can monitor limited, it is practically impossible

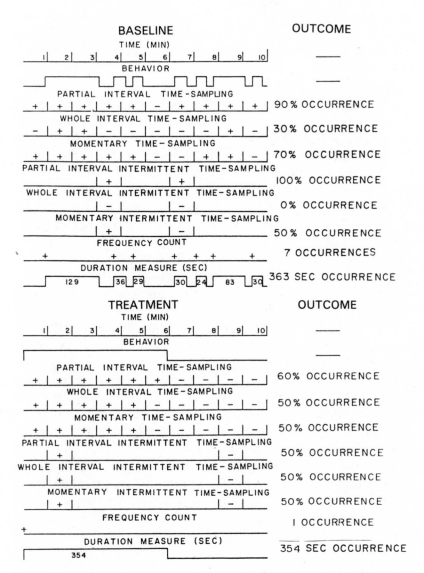

Figure 16. Results that would be obtained if a hypothetical behavior were quantified using various strategies of direct observation.

ever to be sure that a drug is not producing some undesirable side effect. Perhaps the best that a clinical investigator can do is to become familiar with the known phsysiological and behavioral actions of the drug being evaluated and to search systematically for undesirable manifestations of these actions. Neuroleptics, for instance, are known to be associated with weight gain, corneal edema, Parkinsonian reactions, akathisia, and tardive dyskinesia (Baldessarini, 1980). Anyone evaluating such drugs, whether in the context of research or everyday clinical practice, should look for these side effects throughout the period of drug administration. A conscientious investigator would also take steps to ascertain whether the drug was interfering with the acquisition or performance of appropriate behavior. Such side effects can best be detected through the direct observation of a range of target behaviors, but self-reports and nonsystematic clinical observations are often useful in their initial detection.

One easily overlooked potential side effect of pharmacotherapies involves their ability to influence the outcome of nonpharmacological interventions. Assessing the interaction of medications and other treatments is in principle simple enough—the effects of each intervention on the behavior(s) of interest are determined and compared to the effects of the two together—but may pose practical problems. This is evident when one considers that each of the treatments should be evaluated at a number of parametric values (e.g., several drug doses should be assessed) and their interactions at all combinations of parameters studied. Doing so would entail considerable time and effort and probably could not be accomplished in many clinical settings. In such cases, it might appear possible to diminish effort by considering only the most effective value of each treatment. Yet this cannot be accomplished without parametric evaluation, for how else can the most effective treatment values be determined?

Assessment of side effects, like desirable outcomes of treatment, requires careful definition of the condition of concern. A good response definition is objective, clear, and complete (Kazdin, 1982). A definition is *objective* to the extent that it specifies observable events, *clear* to the extent that it unambiguously describes the physical form of these events, and *complete* insofar as it delineates the boundaries for inclusion and noninclusion.

Even if the behaviors of interest are well defined and the conditions of observation carefully chosen, data garnered through direct observation may lead to erroneous conclusions. As Poling, Cleary, and Monaghan (1980) indicate:

> As transducers, humans are invariably suspect. Folklore suggests that lay observations are an imperfect reflection of actual happenings, and a large and growing body of data indicates that allegedly scientific observations sometimes provide an inaccurate index of the variables being considered (Bailey, 1977; Johnson & Bolstad, 1973; Johnston & Pennypacker, 1980). Among the factors demonstrated to influence reported observations are the observer's motivation and expectations (e.g., Rosenthal, 1966), the specifics of the observational situation (e.g., Johnson & Bolstad, 1973), the observational and data recording techniques that are used (e.g., Repp, Roberts, Slack, Repp, & Beckler, 1976), and the characteristics of the behavior being monitored (e.g., Johnston & Pennypacker, 1980).(p. 243)

To control partially for the fallibility of human observers, it is often recommended that "blind" observers, unaware of experimental conditions, be employed. If this is not done, evaluation of clients' behavior, and even the clients' behavior itself, may be affected by the observer's expectations concerning the effects of treatment. Unfortunately, some drug treatments allow observers to detect their presence or absence easily, and in such cases a truely blind experiment cannot be arranged. However, this certainly does not justify informing observers as to both conditions and expected outcomes.

Beyond utilizing blind observers, the treatment evaluator probably ought to ensure that occasionally two (or more) observers independently and simultaneously monitor performance so that a measure of *interobserver agreement* can be calculated (for methods of calculation see Kazdin, 1982, Hawkins & Dotson, 1975, or Page & Iwata, 1986). Despite arguments to the contrary, a high degree of interobserver agreement does not prove that either observer is accurately rating a client's behavior, nor that the observational procedure is valid or reliable as these terms are traditionally used (for a discussion of why this is so see Hawkins & Dotson, 1975). Nonetheless, as Kazdin (1982) indicates, calculation of interobserver agreement is worthwhile for at least three reasons. First, a high degree of interobserver agreement suggests that the target behavior is adequately defined. Second, using multiple observers and repeatedly checking interobserver agreement over time provides a partial check on the consistency with which response definitions are applied. Third, when multiple observers are used in the course of a drug evaluation, it is necessary that the rating of behavior be consistent across observers. If not, behavior will appear variable across time as a function of the different observers who are scoring it. Such imposed variability may obscure any effects of treatment. Requiring high levels of interobserver agreement decreases the likelihood that the idiosyncracies of individual observers will confound treatment effects.

In some instances, automated equipment makes it relatively simple to record a particular behavior and can be substituted for direct observation. The time a hyperactive child spends seated during an educational session may, for instance, be readily determined by affixing a contact-operated microswitch to the chair's seat and having this switch activate a running time meter when operated. Automated recording has been used in a few drug evaluations (e.g., Hollis & St. Omer, 1972; Sprague & Toppe, 1966) and has much to recommend it. The difficulty, of course, is that some responses are not readily quantified by machines.

Further discussion of techniques for quantifying behavior is beyond the scope of this chapter; a number of texts (Ciminero, Calhoun, & Adams, 1977; Cone & Hawkins, 1977; Haynes, 1978; Hersen & Barlow, 1976) are solely devoted to the topic and should be consulted by the interested reader. However, it must be emphasized that the manner in which behavior is quantified strongly influences the probable outcome of a drug evaluation and that a major weakness of many clinical drug evaluations involves a failure to provide an adequate measure of outcome. Hypothetical data were used earlier in this chapter to demonstrate the role of observational technique in treatment outcome. That this variable actually affects the outcome of published investigations is indicated by data presented by Sulzbacher (1973), who found that the probability of beneficial drug effects being reported in pediatric psychopharmacology was highly related to the type of response measure employed. In his study, the probability of beneficial effect's being reported was .88 when global clinical impressions were used, .57 with rating scales, .41 with direct measurement of behavior, and .17 when psychological tests were used to quantify outcome. Given such apparent confounding of response measure and reported outcome, clear interpretations of drug efficacy are simply impossible.

Any clinical drug assessment which fails to ensure that the dependent measure is a valid, reliable, and sensitive measure of the behavior(s) which the drug is prescribed to alter is of questionable worth. Although any of several assessment techniques may meet these criteria, it appears that direct observation of behavior, employing strategies developed and popularized by applied behavior analysts, may be especially useful in assessing drug effects. These strategies have been employed in a number of recent studies (e.g., Ayllon, Layman, & Kandel, 1975; Marholin, Touchette, & Stewart, 1979; Pelham, Schnedler, Bologna, & Contreras, 1980; Shafto & Sulzbacher, 1977: Wulbert & Dries, 1977) which evidence their worth.

Experimental Designs and Strategies

There is no mystery to drug evaluation: One determines whether any independent variable (including medication) affects behaviors of interest by comparing levels of behavior (the dependent variable) when the independent variable is and is not operative, or is operative at different levels. Factors other than the independent variable are held constant across conditions, thus if levels of the dependent variable differ when treatment is and is not present (or is present at different levels), it is logical to assume that behavior changes as a function of treatment, which is therefore deemed active.

Two general tactics can be adopted in drug evaluation. In one, treatment levels are varied and comparisons made between individuals. In the other, treatment levels are varied and comparison made within individuals. Experiments that employ the former strategy involve *between-subjects designs;* those that employ the latter strategy involve *within-subject designs.* The primary purpose of the present section is to describe specific experimental designs that may be appropriate for evaluating pharmacotherapies. Within-subject designs will be the primary focus, for they have much to recommend them and generally are favored by behavioral pharmacologists.

Before considering specific experimental designs, it must be emphasized that there is no one best way to conduct a drug evaluation, no panacean design that succeeds where others fail. The manner in which a researcher evaluates medications will depend on several factors. One, and not the least important, is a scientist's training and theoretical persuasion. A traditional clinician well versed in statistical analysis is unlikely to favor the same designs as an applied behavior analyst for whom statistics are anathema. A second is the research question that the study is attempting to answer. An investigator concerned with whether methylphenidate interacts with a response cost procedure in managing off-task behavior is obliged to use a different design than the researcher who is asking whether thioridazine reduces head-banging in a mentally retarded adolescent. As discussed subsequently, all research designs are limited with regard to the kinds of information they can provide; matching research design to research question, therefore, is of no small consequence. A third factor that influences experimental design is the availability of resources—personnel, time, money, equipment, and subjects. Pragmatism is of necessity the guiding philosophy of the treatment evaluator.

Experiments can be considered along a number of dimensions; three of particular significance are depicted in Figure 17.

This figure, which is quite similar to one previously developed by Huitema (1976), emphasizes that experiments can differ with respect to whether (1) demonstration of a treatment effect depends primarily upon a comparison of (a) the behavior of the same subject(s) under different conditions or (b) the behavior of different subjects under different conditions; (2) a subject's behavior under each experimental condition is observed (a) a single time or (b) repeatedly; and (3) data are analyzed through (a) inferential statistics or (b) visual inspection.

Discussions of experimental designs frequently do not clearly differentiate these three dimensions. Instead, within-subject and between-subjects designs are generically contrasted. Between-subjects designs are presented as involving single observations of each subject's performance and statistical data analysis, whereas repeated observations and visual (graphic) data analysis are represented as features of within-subject designs. If one reads the psychological literature, there is some justification for this conception. For example, most studies published in *JABA* involve a

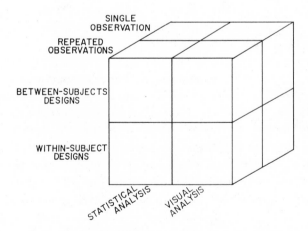

Figure 17. Classification of experimental strategies along three significant dimensions.

within-subject experimental design, repeated observations of behavior across conditions, and visual analysis of data. Such studies are represented by the lower right front cell in Figure 17 and
are often compared to the kinds of studies represented by the
upper left rear cell in that figure. This comparison helps to differentiate two general, and very different, approaches to research
and is of heuristic value. However, each of the cells in Figure 17
represents an experiment that could be conducted. Nothing prevents one from statistically analyzing data from within-subject
designs, utilizing repeated measures in between-subjects designs, or combining within-subject and between-subjects comparisons in the same study. The manner in which subjects are
exposed to the various conditions of interest and the manner in
which data are analyzed should be determined by the kind of
information the researcher desires. No one approach to research
is infallible, or suitable for all applications. To be fully satisfacto-
ry, an experiment must be designed so as to (1) fit the research
question, (2) provide information that is useful to the intended
research consumer, (3) be compatible with the characteristics of
the drug being evaluated, (4) be compatible with the available
subject population, (5) effectively utilize available temporal and
financial resources, and (6) be ethically acceptable.

Experimental designs that involve the intensive study of individuals, each of whose behavior in one condition (e.g., when drug
is given) is compared to his or her behavior in another, different
condition (e.g., when drug is not given) are termed within-subject
designs. They are also sometimes designated as "single subject"
or "single case" designs, but it is in fact rare for one and only one
person to be the subject of an investigation. Though studies of
one person can certainly generate meaningful results, those that
do appear are often derided as "nothing more than case studies,"
regardless of methodological sophistication. Therefore the ap-
pellation "within-subject design" will be used herein.

Whether a drug improves, worsens, or has no effect on a person's behavior can be determined only by comparing her or his
performance when drug is and is not given, that is, through the

use of a within-subject design. At its simplest, the comparison involves initially recording behavior during a no-drug, or baseline, condition, then administering drug and continuing to monitor behavior during this phase. In the shorthand conventionally used to describe experimental designs, the letter *A* is employed to denote a baseline phase, the letter *B* to designate an initial treatment. Other letters, beginning with *C*, are used to refer to subsequent treatments. In this notation, the configuration described above is an *A–B* design.

The primary advantage of an *A–B* design is the ease with which it can be arranged. In medicine, as in psychology, it is common practice to first assess and quantify a client's problem, then to implement a treatment designed to alleviate it. Assessment continues while treatment is in effect, and a comparison of measures taken before and during treatment declares the worth of the intervention. This is much like what a person with a headache does when she or he takes a single 5-grain aspirin tablet and attempts to determine whether it alleviates pain. The strategy is compelling enough to convince most of us whether aspirin is of value in dealing with our headaches, although conservative sufferers might wish to test the drug a number of times before reaching a firm conclusion. Of course, if one wanted to describe aspirin's effects to a friend, some method would have to be devised for quantifying the magnitude of the perceived pain at various times before and after it was taken. Even if this were done and the headache's magnitude progressively declined from the time the tablet was swallowed, a skeptic could argue that this did not prove anything about the drug's action: Pain might simply have begun to diminish at the time the drug was taken, regardless of whether or not aspirin was ingested. Thus the skeptic has no faith in the analgesic action of aspirin, though the headachy individual remains a staunch advocate of the drug.

This example, though unusual textbook fare, makes a number of points about experimental design. First, a drug evaluation that convinces one person may not convince another. Clinical drug evaluation can be very conservative, adhering to the

many dictates of scientific analysis, or more liberal, even haphaz-
ard. What constitutes an adequate drug evaluation depends upon
the consequences of an erroneous outcome and the audience who
is going to use the data collected. Second, as noted earlier, a drug
cannot be adequately evaluated unless the behaviors of interest
are appropriately measured. Third, when an observed relation
between drug treatment and a particular outcome can be repeated, faith that the relation is real grows. Fourth, some experimental designs are such that observed changes in the dependent variable cannot be attributed with confidence to treatment. The *A–B*
design falls in this category.

This is the design's primary weakness: Due to its logical
structure, the *A–B* design can provide only weak and equivocal
confirmation of a drug's behavioral effects. When this design is
used, one can never be sure that a change in behavior that occurs
coincidentally with intervention is not the result of other, unknown factors (*extraneous variables*) that become operative coincidentally with drug administration. Consider a situation in
which frequent physical assaults by a mentally retarded student
are the problem a medication, perhaps thioridazine, is prescribed
to alleviate. Physical assaults are appropriately defined and quantified through direct observation. During the seven days of baseline, in which an inactive placebo is administered, an average of
23 assaults occur per day, with a range across days of 12–37. A
daily average of 6 assaults occur over the ten days when drug is
given; the daily range during this period is 0–9. Given these data,
it can safely be asserted that the problem behavior occurred less
frequently when the student was medicated. However, it is by no
means obvious that thioridazine was responsible for the observed, and quite real, improvement.

Assume that at the start of the assessment period the student
was perfectly healthy. Beginning with the eighth day, however,
the child became ill with a viral infection. This illness generally
reduced activity, including physical assault, and was responsible
for the lessened frequency of the target behavior when drug was
administered.

Certainly this specific scenario is unlikely, for the extraneous variable of illness should be readily apparent, but many other factors, not all easily detected, can produce effects like those desired of treatment (see Campbell & Stanley, 1966). The A–B design does not adequately control for any of these extraneous variables and for that reason is of limited value in research.

The same is true of the case study design, a common but unappealing form of within-subject analysis. As the name applies, this design involves descriptions, often in the form of nonempirical narratives, of potentially relevant details of a subject's condition and treatment. Characteristically confounded by multiple treatment variables, poor definitions of treatment components, and weak measures of improvement (e.g., global clinical impression), this technique generates records of questionable value. Authoritative sources (e.g., Boring, 1954) have deemed designs similar to the case study method devoid of scientific worth, but it is true that case studies can generate hypotheses worthy of rigorous test (Hersen & Barlow, 1976).

The case study is what Campbell and Stanley (1966) term a pre-experimental design, and it is not adequate for demonstrating that a particular treatment actually is responsible for an observed change in behavior. The same is true of A–B and B (treatment only) designs. Although the A–B design is logically superior to the B and case study designs, each suffers from what Campbell and Stanley term "threats to their internal validity." Such uncontrolled threats include changes in the target behavior due to maturation of the subject, history effects, and unknown variables that impose upon the subject coincidentally with treatment.

Although these potential extraneous variables limit the credibility of B and A–B designs, conditions do exist in which stronger designs cannot readily be employed. This is frequently the case in clinical practice, when a physician may wish to document the value of a prescribed medication but has neither the desire nor the wherewithal to conduct a sound experimental evaluation. In this situation, quasi-experimental designs like the B and A–B can be utilized in the hope that some suggestion of a treatment effect may be gleaned from carefully collected data (for suggestions as to how the likelihood of this happening can be enhanced, see Hersen and Barlow, 1976). These designs are certainly preferable to nonempirical guesses about the effects of medications, even though they do not allow observed changes in target behaviors to be attributed with confidence to the treatment.

Withdrawal Designs

Adding a final baseline (A) phase to the A–B design strengthens the design immensely. The A–B–A design is a withdrawal[2] design, and its logic, like that of all such designs, is straightforward and compelling: If the dependent measure changes appreciably from the baseline level when treatment is implemented and returns to at or near the initial baseline level when treatment is terminated, there is good reason to believe that the observed changes in the target behavior reflect the actions of the treatment of interest. It is, of course, possible that some extraneous variable begins to impose upon the subject when treatment is introduced, remains operative throughout the course of treatment, and ceases when treatment is terminated. Unless the extraneous variable is actually associated with treatment, the odds that this might happen are small and grow smaller with each additional implementation and termination of treatment. Repeatedly exposing a subject to treatment and evaluating performance during treatment relative to pre-treatment and posttreatment baseline levels can be conceptualized as replicating an experiment.

Sidman (1960) used the term *direct replication* to refer to the "replication of a given experiment by the same investigator" (p. 73) and noted that replicating an experiment with the same subject increases confidence in the reliability of findings but does not preclude the possibility that the individual is more or less sensitive to treatment than other persons. Direct replication of an

---

[2]Such designs are also commonly referred to as reversal designs. However, as Hersen and Barlow (1976) discuss, this designation seems to imply that conditions are actually reversed during the course of an investigation, as under the crossover design.

experiment with additional subjects also increases confidence in the reliability of findings and, in addition, begins to address the issue of generalizability of results, a topic to which we will return shortly. It is important to realize that in direct replications, either within or across subjects, conditions must be kept relatively constant. That is, treatment parameters and outcome measures must be consistent, and, in direct intersubject replications, subjects should be as homogeneous as possible with respect to the behavior of interest and characteristics likely to affect its modifiability. If this is done, "interpretation of mixed results, where some clients benefit from the procedure and some do not, can be attributed to as few differences as possible, thereby providing a clearer direction for further experimentation" (Herson & Barlow, 1976, p. 318). While there is no standard for the number of direct intersubject replications required for findings to be generally accepted, Hersen and Barlow (1976) judiciously suggest that one successful experiment (i.e., drug evaluation in a single subject) and three successful replications across other participants provide sufficient support for the efficacy of treatment to merit tests by other researchers, in other settings, and with other kinds of clients.

When used appropriately, withdrawal designs suffice for comparing the effects of different treatments (e.g., drug versus behavior modification) and for determining the interaction of two or more treatments, as well as simply evaluating a single drug. A good example of the use of a withdrawal design in assessing medication effects is a study by Marholin *et al.* (1979), who used a *B–A–B* design to examine how chlorpromazine affected four mentally retarded adults. (A fifth person also was studied under a similar but more complex withdrawal design; for simplicity, this subject will not be considered here.) Several behaviors were carefully measured in workshop and ward settings, among them compliance to verbal requests, accuracy and rate of performance of workshop tasks, time on task, eye contact, talking to self, talking to others, standing, walking, being within three feet of others, being in bed, approaching others, and touching others. During the first 19 days of recording, chlorpromazine was given. This was followed in order by a 23-day drug-free (placebo) phase and a 25-day period in which drug treatment was reinstated.

Some of the data collected by Marholin *et al.* are shown in Figure 18. The effects of withdrawing chlorpromazine differed appreciably across subjects (a point that might well have been overlooked by investigators employing a between-subjects design), but some desirable behaviors did emerge when chlorpromazine was withdrawn. Certainly the drug was not producing consistently beneficial effects: "Changes in the behavior of these severely retarded adults which we attributed to chlorpromazine

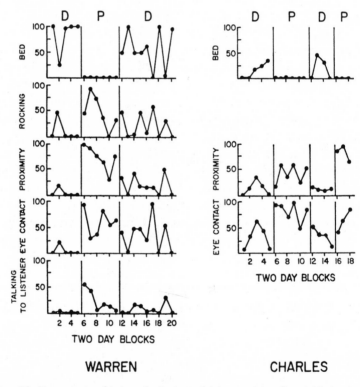

WARREN   CHARLES

Figure 18. Percentage of intervals during which a variety of social behaviors occurred during drug (*D*) and placebo (*P*) conditions. Taken from Marholin *et al.* (1979) and reproduced by permission of the Society for the Experimental Analysis of Behavior.

were diverse and generally of no clear relevance to the patients' well being, access to the environment, or physical or psychological comfort" (Marholin *et al.*, 1979, p. 169). In passing, it might be noted that these findings are in line with those of a number of other investigations which have shown that, with few exceptions, neuroleptic drugs are ineffective in improving the deportment of mentally retarded individuals (see Aman & Singh, 1983; Breuning & Poling, 1982), although these same compounds are of recognized value in treating the mentally ill (Berger, 1978; Lickey & Gordon, 1983).

Two basic rules apply to the use of all withdrawal designs. First, conditions should not be changed until behavior is relatively stable over time (i.e., variability is acceptably low and there is no significant upward or downward trend in the data). Second, only one variable should be altered at a time. In addition, withdrawal designs cannot be used to evaluate the effects of drugs that irreversibly alter the behavior(s) of interest, or in situations where a return to baseline conditions (and resultant behavioral deterioration) cannot be ethically justified. Finally, some critics (e.g., Kiesler, 1971) have argued that all within-subject designs assess only how a particular subject or set of subjects responds to a treatment and do not allow for predictions concerning the treatment's probable effects in other individuals.

The truth of this assertion for the results of a particular study can only be answered empirically: The results of any investigation, regardless of design, are generalizable (or *externally valid*) only insofar as they can subsequently be reproduced.

Generalizability of Results and Within-Subject Designs

Systematic replication (Sidman, 1960) is the term used to describe attempts to assess the range of conditions under which a treatment is valuable.

> We can define systematic replication in applied research as an attempt to replicate findings from a direct replication series, varying settings, behavior change agents, behavior disorders, or any combination thereof. It would appear that any successful systematic rep-

lication series in which one or more of the above-mentioned factors is varied also provides further information on generality of findings across clients since new clients are usually included in such efforts. (Hersen & Barlow, 1976, p. 339)

Researchers who employ within-subject experimental designs attempt to specify which individuals do and do not improve as a function of treatment and, in addition, to ascertain the variables which are responsible for the differential outcome. If it becomes apparent in an investigation that individuals who are homogeneous on some dimension consistently benefit from a medication, whereas others do not, this information provides a basis for determining who is likely to benefit from that medication in subsequent investigations and in clinical practice. The basis for inferring generalizability of results from within-subject experiments is specificity of outcome in subjects with definable characteristics, not overall outcome in a sample of subjects assumed to represent some heterogeneous population, as is typical when between-subjects designs are used. Put differently, generalizations based on within-subject analyses apply only to individuals who are very similar to those actually studied, but typically they are highly valid for those individuals.

It is important to realize that between-subjects and within-subject designs provide fundamentally different kinds of information about treatment effects and their generalizability. It appears that within-subject designs, with their emphasis on changes in individuals and specific predictors of expected outcomes, hold great promise for providing clinically useful information about pharmacotherapies. As yet, however, this promise has not been fulfilled. This reflects the obvious fact that few such studies have appeared, but it may also be an indication that complete within-subject drug analyses involve two stages, and most of the studies published to this point have focused on the first stage. That is convincingly demonstrating whether or not a drug produces the desired behavior change in a client or set of clients. The second phase involves determining the factors responsible for the variable success of treatment that inevitably occurs as diverse subjects are tested.

As noted in previous chapters, behavioral pharmacologists refer to the aspects of a person's behavior that are altered by a drug as the drug's behavioral locus of action (Thompson, 1981), and ascertaining a medication's behavioral locus of action is the first stage of drug evaluation. The importance of clearly documenting what behaviors a drug alters in each individual who receives it cannot be overemphasized; the foremost question in evaluating a medication is, Does the observed behavioral locus of drug action match the desired locus? However, a complete understanding of drug effects, and the rational decisions concerning when a particular compound should be prescribed afforded by such understanding, requires knowledge of mechanisms as well as loci of action.

In a general way, mechanisms of action refer to the processes whereby a drug produces its behavioral effects. In traditional pharmacology, these processes commonly involve events that occur at the biochemical level, for example, changes in neurochemical activity (see Chapter 2). Although this level of analysis has proved profitable, during the past fifteen years considerable emphasis has been placed on determining the behavioral mechanisms of action of many drugs.

> Specifying the behavioral mechanism(s) responsible for an observed effect involves a) identifying the environmental variables which typically regulate the behavior in question, and b) characterizing the manner in which the influence of these variables is altered by the drug. In some instances, the drug assumes the status of a behavioral variable, per se, rather than modulating an existing environmental variable. (Thompson, 1981, p. 3)

General strategies for exploring behavioral mechanisms of action were considered in Chapter 4. By way of review, there are clear examples of drugs affecting learning and performance differently (Thompson & Moerschbaecher, 1979); of drugs selectively affecting behavior under weak stimulus control (Laties, 1975); of drugs differentially affecting behaviors maintained by unlike positive reinforcers (Barrett, 1981); of drugs selectively influencing responding under the control of punishment (McMillan, 1975) or avoidance (Cook & Catania, 1964); and of drugs serving as positive reinforcers, negative reinforcers, discriminative stimuli, and unconditional stimuli (Thompson & Pickens, 1971). To date, such effects are rarely searched for in clinical drug evaluations, perhaps because the environmental variables controlling the problem behaviors drugs are prescribed to manage are rarely if ever known.

This is not likely to change in the near future, but it certainly is possible to arrange conditions artificially so that the variables controlling behavior can be specified and manipulated. For example, video games (which many individuals would play with little inducement) could easily be programmed so that behavior at a given point in time is under the control of punishment contingencies, or of stimuli removed in time from the responses they control. Evaluations of drug effects under such conditions should provide theoretically important information about behavioral mechanisms of drug action. Moreover, they might well uncover significant behavioral effects likely to be missed in more naturalistic assessments. Finally, it is possible that subjects' responses to drugs in controlled laboratory assays will correlate highly with therapeutic outcome, rendering laboratory assays valuable as screening procedures. Since attempts to systematically assess the clinical behavioral pharmacology (locus and mechanism of action) of medications prescribed to deal with problem behaviors can easily be incorporated into evaluations of clinical response (all that would be required is the inclusion of more response measures; design would be unchanged) and may yield significant data, they deserve special consideration by all researchers designing within-subject drug evaluations, regardless of the specific design employed.

Multiple-Baseline Designs

The multiple-baseline design involves a sequence of A–B manipulations staggered in time. In this design, a number of dependent measures, typically three or four (Kazdin & Kopel, 1975), are taken. These dependent measures can represent different behaviors of a single individual, the same or different behaviors of two or more individuals, or the same behavior of a single individual in different circumstances. Each dependent measure must require change in the same direction, and all dependent measures should be independent (i.e., changing one ought not affect the others).

The multiple-baseline design typically begins with all dependent measures being taken during baseline (treatment absent) conditions. When performance stabilizes (i.e., shows no trend and little variability over time), treatment is implemented for one dependent variable. When a drug is used as treatment, it usually cannot be applied to a single behavior in the same sense that a behavioral procedure (e.g., reinforcement) can be applied to that behavior. Hence the "across behaviors" version of this design is rarely useful in drug evaluation. The multiple-baseline "across situations" is also of limited value in assessing most pharmacological interventions, for the effects of clinically significant drugs usually cannot be confined to a single situation. However, this version of the design certainly could be gainfully employed to evaluate short-acting drugs, such as cocaine.

The real strength of the multiple-baseline design in assessing medication rests with the "across subjects" version. This variant involves the temporally staggered introduction (or withdrawal) of drug with several different subjects. In most cases, the dependent variable is first measured under placebo conditions in all subjects. Drug is then administered to one subject at a time until all are eventually receiving medication. Usually a drug is not administered to an additional subject until the previously treated individual's behavior has stabilized. Thus the onset of treatment is temporally staggered across subjects. The strength and generality of the treatment effect is demonstrated by showing that changes in the dependent measure occur when and only when each subject receives medication (or when doses otherwise change).

At the present time, multiple-baseline designs rarely are used in clinical drug studies, but a few exceptions have appeared. For instance, Davis *et al.* (1981) used such a design to evaluate the effects of withdrawing the antiepilepsy drug phenytoin on the workshop and matching-to-sample performance of mentally retarded subjects. As indicated in Figure 19, in all instances work-

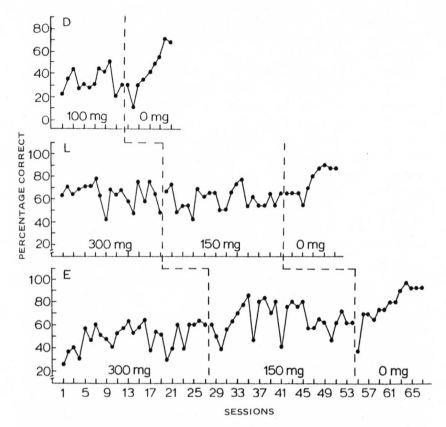

Figure 19. Percentage cf correct responses per session at each dose of phenytoin for the three subjects on the matching-to-sample task. From Davis *et al.* (1981) and reproduced by permission of the authors.

shop performance improved only after the drug was totally withdrawn. Similar results were obtained with respect to matching-to-sample performance, as shown in Figure 20. The correspondence between laboratory and clinical data is interesting, but of greater practical import is the finding that none of the participants experienced seizures when phenytoin was withdrawn. This suggests that these particular individuals were deriving no benefit from the drug, which actually interfered with their performance of certain desired responses. However, it is grossly inappropriate to generalize this finding to epileptic individuals, who by virtue of the seizure control afforded by the drug might derive great benefit from phenytoin.

With the multiple-baseline design, a drug's efficacy is evident when each dependent measure changes when and only when treatment is implemented for that behavior. If two or more behaviors are apparently affected when treatment is implemented for one of them, the design's logic dictates that this effect cannot unambiguously be attributed to treatment. This is because such data might simply reflect a nonindependence of the behaviors, but it also could involve the action of some extraneous variable coincidentally activated at the onset of treatment. These two possibilities can be evaluated by terminating treatment and ascertaining whether both behaviors return to pretreatment levels. If

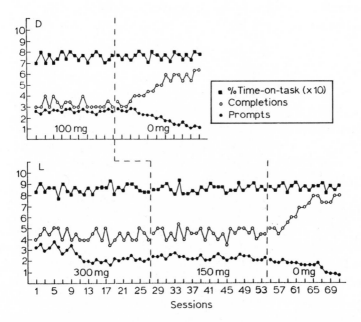

Figure 20. Percentage of time on task (× 10), number of brake assemblies completed, and mean prompts score per session at each dose of phenytoin for two subjects performing a workshop task. From Davis *et al.* (1981) and reproduced by permission of the authors.

so, it is reasonable to conclude that treatment is effective and the two behaviors nonindependent. If not, the action of an extraneous variable cannot be ruled out, and the intervention's efficacy remains moot.

The multiple-baseline design is not limited by the two shortcomings of withdrawal designs: It can be used to evaluate drugs that produce irreversible effects (so long as the dependent measures are independent), and it does not require countertherapeutic behavior change to show the value of treatment. However, since the multiple-baseline is essentially an A–B design with replications staggered in time, it is less compelling that withdrawal designs, although many behavioral psychologists (e.g., Baer, Wolf, & Risley, 1968) contend that the multiple-baseline design is capable of demonstrating a functional relation between independent and dependent variables. Kazdin and Kopel (1975) provide detailed coverage of this design and offer a number of useful recommendations for its use.

Crossover Design

The crossover design is generally considered to be adequate for clinical drug evaluations (e.g., Sprague & Werry, 1971). This design combines within-subject and between-subjects features, although it is commonly discussed in the context of group designs (e.g., Whalen & Henker, 1986). When a crossover design is employed, one randomly selected group of subjects initially receives medication while a second group receives placebo. The behaviors of interest are measured, usually repeatedly across time, under these conditions. After this, conditions are reversed so that members of the initial placebo group now receive drug while members of the initial drug group receive placebo. The behaviors of interest continue to be measured during this second phase, wherein conditions are "crossed over," or reversed across groups, relative to the first phase.

If medication was in fact effective for an individual, a within-subject data analysis would reveal higher levels of desired behavior during the phase when drug was given, regardless of whether that was the first or second condition to which the person was exposed. Moreover, if medication were generally effective across individuals, a between-subjects data analysis would reveal that the average performance of the group that received drug was superior to that of the group that received placebo. Thus, one set of subjects (the initial drug group) would exhibit superior performance during the first phase of the study, whereas the other group would perform better during the second phase (when they received drug). Although the between-subjects analysis afforded by the crossover design allows for reasonable conclusions concerning the overall effects of treatment, the design allows for only a weak analysis of treatment effects in individuals, since each person is actually exposed to an *A–B* or *B–A* configuration.

Since all subjects eventually receive treatment under the crossover design, its employment obviates the problem of an untreated control group, which is a necessary part of many between-subjects configurations. However, if a drug actually is producing beneficial behavior change, the design is ethically defensible only if both groups are given medication at the end of experimentation, a convention not demanded by the design's logic but by no means incompatible with it.

Increasing the levels of the independent variable employed in the crossover design can enhance its efficiency. For example, several different drugs plus placebo could be compared using a number of groups. The order of presentation of the drugs would necessarily be counterbalanced, and all possible combinations of orders would be arranged. Between-subjects data analyses, in which all data collected under one condition (e.g., when Drug A was given) are compared to all data collected under other conditions (e.g., when Drug B and Drug C are given), would in a statistical sense control for order effects, although such effects can never be prevented. As does the simple crossover design, this more elaborate configuration requires that the effects of the test drug (or drugs) be reversible. If not, effects of an initial drug treatment will "carry over," thereby obscuring any effects of the second manipulation.

Sprague and Sleator (1977) used a crossover design in an

elegant study of the effects of methylphenidate in hyperkinetic children. They compared the effects of three doses of methylphenidate, 0.0 (placebo), 0.3, and 1.0 mg/kg, on several dependent measures including accuracy and latency of response in a picture recognition task, activity, heart rate, and teachers' ratings of social behavior. Each of these dependent variables was carefully defined and the rating scale (Conners Teachers Rating Scale) had previously been validated. Each dose of methylphenidate was given to each of three groups of children for a three-week period. The sequence of doses was randomized across groups, and the subjects and the observers were unaware of the particular dose being given at any given time (i.e., double-blind, placebo controlled conditions were in effect).

Some of the data collected by Sprague and Sleator appear in Chapter 2 (Figure 3). In summary, they found that performance in the picture recognition task was best when 0.3 mg/kg methylphenidate was given but that social behavior was rated as most acceptable at the highest (1.0 mg/kg) dose. Although these findings have important implications for the clinical management of hyperkinesis, the study is noteworthy apart from the data obtained because of its rigorous methodology.

Multielement Baseline Design

The multielement baseline design, also known as the alternating treatments design (Barlow & Hayes, 1979), involves the repeated measurement of behavior under alternating values of the independent variable (Ulman & Sulzer-Azaroff, 1975). The levels of the independent variable may alternate either within a measurement session or from one measurement session to the next, and the sequencing of levels may be regular or unpredictable. A unique exteroceptive stimulus typically is paired with each level of the independent variable, thus the design resembles a multiple schedule. Assessment of the treatment's effects involves comparing performance under the various treatment (and stimulus) conditions.

The multielement baseline design is actually a withdrawal

(A–B–A–B . . .) design that alternates rapidly between conditions. In addition to the strengths of all withdrawal designs, discussed previously, the multielement baseline design has a number of appealing features (see Barlow & Hayes, 1979; Ulman & Sulzer-Azaroff, 1975).

One alleged advantage of the multielement baseline design is in the analysis of highly variable behavior. In clinical settings, a dependent variable often fluctuates widely across time; behavior may also consistently improve or worsen without treatment. In such cases, a phase change is not appropriate when multiple-baseline or typical withdrawal designs are employed. With the multielement baseline design, conditions change irrespective of the subject's behavior, and a comparison can legitimately be made between conditions (e.g., drug and placebo) even though the dependent measure improves or worsens under both conditions. So long as behavior is consistently and appreciably better (or worse) when drug is given than when it is not, variability across time does not preclude making a gross statement about the medication's value. However, when behavior does not inevitably differ greatly across conditions, the appropriate interpretation is unclear. The multielement baseline design deals effectively with variability only when independent variables produce such large effects as to overshadow other sources of variability, and the actions of such variables are usually evident regardless of experimental design. The multielement baseline design differs from other within-subject designs primarily in allowing phase changes when behavior is fluctuating; it does not allow a treatment effect to be gleaned from chaotic data.

A second advantage of the multielement baseline design is the speed with which meaningful data can be generated when it is employed. Unlike multiple-baseline and conventional withdrawal designs, the multielement baseline design allows for early initiation of treatment, rapid changes in the level of the independent variable, and a quick evaluation of the success of treatment. Meaningful data (i.e., those that allow for a comparison of behavior under all of the conditions of interest) are generated very early in a study with this design, and all is not lost if the experiment terminates prematurely. In addition, the multielement baseline design allows many levels of the independent variable (e.g., drug doses) to be tested, or diverse treatments compared, within a reasonable amount of time.

Because this design does provide for the rapid alternation of conditions, it has two major shortcomings with respect to drug evaluations. The first is that brief exposure to a drug, as would be arranged under a multielement baseline design, may be insufficient for its true actions to be observed. Tricyclic antidepressants, for instance, often alleviate depression only with chronic exposure of two weeks or more (Berger, 1978). These and all other medications given chronically cannot be adequately evaluated with this design.

A second shortcoming of the multielement baseline design is that treatments with long-lasting effects, which include the majority of drugs used to manage behavior, cannot be adequately assessed with this design, since their actions will persist into, and confound, subsequent conditions. These two limitations severely restrict the usefulness of the multielement baseline design for evaluating medications, and it is rarely used in this capacity. Nevertheless, the design is exceptionally useful for certain applications (e.g., comparing the effects of short-acting drugs to those of a behavioral procedure).

Several other within-subject designs have been developed and are occasionally useful in evaluating behavior-change medications, although their range of application is not so wide as that of withdrawal, crossover, and multiple-baseline configurations. Other authors (e.g., Hersen & Barlow, 1976; Johnston & Pennypacker, 1980; Kazdin, 1980, 1982) provide more comprehensive coverage of within-subject designs than the present overview.

General Methodological Considerations

Strong experimental designs and appropriate quantification of dependent measures are necessary but not sufficient for a methodologically sound clinical drug evaluation. Among the other factors that contribute to the methodological rigor of a study are

(a) the use of double-blind conditions, (b) the employment of placebo controls, (c) adequate quantification of the independent variable, (d) appropriate data analysis, and (e) collection of follow-up data. Why these features are important in clinical drug evaluation is discussed briefly below and at greater length elsewhere (e.g., Gadow & Poling, 1986).

Placebo Control. To prevent nonspecific factors such as subject or staff expectations and observer bias from confounding the drug effect, an inactive substance similar to the drug being evaluated in size, shape, color, and taste should be administered during nondrug sessions. Inclusion of a no-drug condition as well as a placebo phase allows for an evaluation of possible placebo effects that appear in both placebo and drug conditions. The importance of using a placebo control has been demonstrated in many kinds of patients (see Gadow, White, & Ferguson, 1986a, 1986b).

Double Blind. Further to prevent bias and expectancy from confounding treatment, neither the subject nor the observers should be able to discriminate experimental conditions (i.e., each should be "blind"). In some instances, however, discriminable effects of the drug itself may break the double blind. Subjects probably can, for instance, readily ascertain whether they have received amphetamine or an inert placebo. However, as noted earlier, this does not justify informing subjects or observers as to expected drug effects.

Adequate Quantification of the Independent Variable. For the results of a study to be interpretable, all medications being evaluated must be described in unambiguous terms. This includes not only a specification of dose in terms of units drug per unit body weight per unit time (e.g., mg/kg/day), but includes as well the schedule of administration, the form of the drug (e.g., as a capsule or syrup), and whether the dose refers to the drug's salt or base form. Obtained drug blood levels are well correlated with therapeutic response with some drugs (e.g., anticonvulsants, lithium) and should be specified in addition to the dose administered when such compounds are evaluated.

The actions of many drugs are influenced by concurrent administration of other compounds. Thus, whenever possible, all drugs not used as independent variables should be withheld during the course of an investigation. When this is not feasible, all drugs taken by each subject should be clearly specified.

The best drug evaluations will include dose–response determinations within subjects, since the actions of all medications vary critically with dose and individual differences in sensitivity to a given dose are appreciable. Unless there is good reason for doing otherwise, the range of doses evaluated should fall within the usual therapeutic range. Administration schedule (i.e., time and route of administration) in an experiment should parallel therapeutic practice; acute evaluations of a drug prescribed chronically in clinical practice are likely to yield results of limited utility.

When chronic regimens are studied, care must be taken to ensure that the medication is given for a sufficient period to allow for adequate assessment. This includes the detection of any tolerance or physical dependence that might occur, as well as short- and long-term side effects. It must be recognized that the deleterious side effects of certain compounds emerge only with protracted exposure, years in the case of the tardive dyskinesias (involuntary, uncontrollable movements) frequently associated with neuroleptics. Such long-term side effects will be overlooked in the great majority of studies unless their existence was established by nonsystematic observation or through prior report. Finally, baseline (no-drug) periods must be long enough to allow the effects of any prior drug administrations to dissipate completely.

It is obvious that medications are unlikely to prove beneficial unless received by the patient at the dose and time intended. Data suggest that patients asked to self-administer medications often fail to follow instructions for doing so. Patient noncompliance may involve full or partial omission of scheduled doses, administration of inappropriate doses, or premature termination of drug therapy (Swinyard, 1980). A number of factors are known to influence the likelihood of noncompliance, among them the kind of medication involved, the treatment environment, the problem being treated, and the degree to which the importance of compliance is stressed by the physician (Swinyard, 1980). It is not possible to predict accurately who will be noncompliant, but it appears that a sizable proportion of psychiatric patients will fail to self-administer medications according to their treatment plan. This is shown in the results of a study conducted by Hare and Wilcox (1967), who examined noncompliance in a psychiatric hospital. They found that 19% of inpatients, 37% of day patients, and 48% of outpatients were noncompliant.

Although the problem of noncompliance may appear to be obviated when staff monitor inpatients to ensure that medications are taken at the proper times and doses, this is not always so. More than a few mentally ill and mentally retarded individuals become quite adept at appearing to swallow pills that are actually held under the tongue for later disgorgement; others regurgitate just swallowed medications. In addition, instructing staff as to proper administration of drugs does not prevent their making errors or instituting well intentioned but ill-informed changes in treatment. Thus it seems that an important component of evaluating any pharmacological intervention is to do everything possible to maximize the likelihood of patient compliance. If this is not done, the integrity of the independent variable is doubtful and it is unclear whether obtained results can be attributed to the intended treatment (cf. Peterson, Homer, & Wonderlich, 1982). Swinyard (1980) and Moore and Klonoff (1986) consider strategies for assessing and increasing patient compliance.

Appropriate Data Analysis. Data obtained in a clinical drug evaluation are typically analyzed by the use of inferential statistics or by visual inspection. The former method is usually associated with experiments that employ between-subjects designs, the latter with those employing within-subject designs, although as noted earlier this reflects precedent as much as logic.

Regardless of whether data are analyzed statistically or by visual inspection, the initial question to be answered is, Did behavior differ across conditions? The researcher attempting to answer this question can err in two ways, by (1) reaching the conclusion that behavior did differ across conditions (i.e., that medication had an effect), when in fact it did not or (2) reaching the conclusion that behavior did not differ across conditions (i.e., that medication had no effect), when in fact it did. Errors of the former sort are conventionally termed Type 1 errors, those of the latter kind Type 2 errors. As Kazdin (1982) explains:

> Researchers typically give higher priority to avoiding a Type 1 error, concluding that a variable has an effect when the findings may have occurred by chance. In statistical analyses the probability of committing a Type 1 error can be specified (by the level of confidence of the statistical test). With visual inspection, the probability of a Type 1 error is not known. Hence, to avoid chance effects, the investigator looks for highly consistent effects that can be readily seen. By minimizing the probability of a Type 1 error, the probability of a Type 2 error is increased. Investigators relying on visual inspection are more likely to commit more Type 2 errors than are those relying on statistical analyses. Thus, reliance on visual inspection will overlook or discount many reliable but weak effects. (p. 242)

A treatment is *statistically significant* (or, synonymously, *experimentally significant*) to the extent that a researcher is confident that it altered performance. It is clinically significant to the extent that the alteration in performance actually improved the lot of treated individuals.

Clinical significance can be demonstrated in three ways:

1. By comparing levels of behavior during treatment with criterion levels set before treatment. These criterion levels (treatment objectives) constitute solution of the behavioral problem which medication is hoped to relieve.
2. By comparing the performance of the individual(s) undergoing treatment with that of similar individuals who do not manifest the behavioral problem for which treatment was applied. This demands a between-subjects comparison and poses the problem of selecting an appropriate comparison group.
3. By having those who defined the problem evaluate the success of its treatment.

These strategies and their attendant strengths and weaknesses are fully described by Wolf (1978) and Van Houten (1979).

As noted above, when treatments produce nonspecific effects, as drugs inevitably do, evaluation of clinical significance requires consideration of deleterious side effects as well as desired alterations in behavior; in essence, this is a risk–benefit analysis. Whether any undesirable side effects of a pharmacotherapeutic agent are offset by treatment gains can be adequately determined only by comparison with the relative costs and benefits of alternative treatments. In view of the potentially restrictive (harmful) nature of pharmacotherapies, Sprague and Baxley (1978) have recommended that drug treatments always be compared to some other treatment, preferably the best alternative available. This recommendation is not only prudent but mandated by law when drugs are employed to manage the behavior of members of certain populations, such as the institutionalized mentally retarded (see Sprague, 1982).

When inferential statistics are used to analyze data, it is essential that the appropriate test be employed and that the assumptions underlying that test not be violated. Although obvious, this convention has often been violated in clinical drug evaluations (see Sprague & Werry, 1971).

Regardless of how data are analyzed, the response of each individual to medication should not be overlooked. When data are statistically evaluated, results for several individuals are frequently averaged and then compared for differences. Such mathematical manipulations can mask variability between subjects exposed to the same treatment. Perhaps a medication is extremely helpful to some individuals, rather harmful to others, and of no benefit or detriment to some. A statistical comparison may reveal that, overall, the behavior of these individuals did not differ during drug and placebo conditions or, alternatively, the average performance of these individuals when medicated did not differ from that of an untreated control group. This outcome would obscure the clinically important fact that some individuals did improve as a function of the medication. Since individual differences in responsiveness to behavior-change medications are widely acknowledged as real and significant, the use of within-subject research designs and the within-subject data analyses which they make possible appear to provide the best means of evaluating pharmacotherapeutic agents.

Collection of Follow-up Data. When an individual's initial response to a medication is favorable, it is essential to assess the persistence across time of the desired changes in behavior. Doing this requires collection of follow-up data, that is, data collected after short-term treatment evaluation has been completed. Since it is well established that treatment gains associated with behavior-change medications may persist after drug withdrawal, follow-up data should be collected under placebo as well as active medication conditions. Drug-free periods, sometimes termed *drug holidays,* should be of sufficient duration to allow for active drug to be eliminated from the body and for reversible changes in behavior induced by drug withdrawal to disappear. For example, the tardive dyskinesias associated with neuroleptics often appear only after years of treatment, and their appearance frequently is precipitated by termination of the drug regimen or a reduction in dosage. In such cases, the appearance of tardive dyskinesias may appear to indicate that the afflicted individual requires continued medication. However, this is not necessarily so, for a protracted drug-free period will result in a disappearance of the dyskinesias of many individuals.

Concluding Comments

In summarizing the results of their 1971 review of drug studies involving mentally retarded individuals, Sprague and Werry (1971) wrote:

> It is quite clear from this review that very few empirically verified generalizations can be made about psychotropic drugs with the mentally retarded; yet it is just as clear that this series of methodologically weak, experimentally poor, and statistically inept studies have not provided a fair, sensitive measure of the behavioral effects of the drugs, effects which are routinely assumed to be present considering the wide-spread use of these prescribed drugs. (p. 168)

Many studies appearing after 1971 in which drug effects were evaluated in mentally retarded individuals are subject to similar criticism, a point made in several recent reviews (e.g., Aman &

Singh, 1983: Breuning & Poling, 1982). Methodologically weak drug evaluations with mentally ill individuals are also common. However, enough sound investigations have appeared to demonstrate beyond reasonable doubt that drugs are useful in managing a range of behavioral problems. It is not, however, currently possible to predict accurately the response of any individual to a particular pharmacotherapeutic agent. Therefore it behooves the clinician to determine carefully whether a patient actually receives benefit from a prescribed medication. Techniques commonly used by applied behavior analysts to evaluate nonpharmacological interventions appear to be well suited to this task. They also appear to be appropriate for more formal drug evaluations, as discussed in this chapter.

The development of effective behavior-change medications has literally revolutionized psychiatric practice, and the use of such medications is widespread. So widespread, in fact, that: (1) "In 1980, 20% of the prescriptions written in the United States were for medications intended . . . to sedate, stimulate, or otherwise change mood, thinking, or behavior" (Baldessarini, 1980, p. 391). (2) Between 1953 and 1963, over 50 million patients received chlorpromazine (Ray, 1983). (3) In 1975 alone, Americans spent nearly half a billion dollars on anxiolytic drugs, primarily chlordiazepoxide and diazepam (Cant, 1976). (4) Each school year, 600,000 to 700,000 students receive stimulants for the treatment of hyperactivity (O'Leary, 1980). These figures underscore the popularity of pharmacotherapies. And, despite recent judicial pronouncements limiting carte blanche drug use with institutionalized populations, mentally retarded individuals in particular (see Sprague, 1982), there is no reason to believe that the use of drugs to treat behavioral problems will diminish significantly in the near future.

Unfortunately, far too little is known concerning (1) the variables (e.g., kinds of subjects, specific behavior problems) that determine whether a given compound will produce a therapeutic effect, (2) the behavioral side effects of psychotropic agents, and (3) the comparative value of specific pharmacotherapies relative to nondrug treatments, such as contingency management. This is not to say that drugs have not been studied in detail. Some surely have. For instance, studies of neuroleptics' effects in psychotic patients are legion, although as mentioned earlier many are methodologically flawed. A sufficient number of sound evaluations have nonetheless appeared to convince many scientists that neuroleptics can often be of great value in this population (e.g., Berger, 1978).

Often is a critical qualifier here, for it is certain that not all patients, psychotic or otherwise, benefit from neuroleptics. Within-subject research performed in the applied behavior analysis tradition should prove particularly useful in clarifying who does and does not benefit from this drug. In this regard, it is worth repeating the conclusions of a review of neuroleptic drug effects in mentally retarded individuals. The authors of that review, Ferguson and Breuning (1982), write:

> A fairly impressive number of studies have been conducted in an attempt to examine the efficacy of antipsychotic drug use with the mentally retarded. However, the overwhelming majority of these studies are methodologically inadequate and the results are largely uninterpretable. The results of the methodologically stronger studies suggest that compared to a placebo, a few antipsychotic drugs may be effective in reducing some inappropriate behaviors. The most impressive evidence (while not overwhelming) for efficacy is from studies showing that thioridazine can reduce self-stimulatory behaviors. However, these same studies have shown that merely engaging the mentally retarded in another activity is at least as effective as the drug. (p. 199)

Beyond emphasizing how little is actually known concerning the actions of neuroleptic drugs in a population which often receives them, Ferguson and Breuning's summary indicates the need for, and potential value of, comparative research.

It is noteworthy that four of the studies of drugs as independent variables that have appeared in the past decade in *JABA* compared medication to behavioral treatments. These studies (Ayllon *et al.*, 1975; Pelham *et al.*, 1980; Shafto & Sulzbacher, 1977; Wulbert & Dries, 1977) evaluated methylphenidate relative to contingency management in controlling the behavior of hyperactive children. Although medication alone produced at least some beneficial effects in each study, contingency management also facilitated desired behavior. In addition, in three studies (Ayllon *et al.*, 1975; Shafto & Sulzbacher, 1977; Wulbert & Dries, 1977) medication was at least occasionally associated with adverse behavioral changes, whereas contingency management was not reported to produce such effects. However, Pelham *et al.* (1980) did not observe deleterious side effects with methylphenidate alone, or with combined drug and behavioral treatment, which they found to be more effective than either component alone.

These studies do not resolve the complex issue of how hyperactivity ought to be managed (for a discussion of this issue see O'Leary, 1980), but they do demonstrate conclusively that the research philosophy and methodology characteristic of behavioral psychology, and hence of behavioral pharmacology, can be used to compare pharmacotherapies to alternative treatments, as well as to assess the main and side effects of pharmacological interventions.

CHAPTER

7

Drug Abuse

Some patterns of drug self-administration harm the user or other individuals without producing offsetting therapeutic or other benefit. The harm may involve direct physical damage, as when chronic high-dose alcohol intake eventually leads to cirrhosis, or indirect physical damage, as when an intoxicated driver maims innocents in an automobile accident. The unwise use of drugs is a major cause of suffering and death; in 1977 alone, the lives of 500,000 Americans ended prematurely due to the misuse of cigarettes, alcohol, and other drugs (Pollin, 1979).

Even when they do not lead to physical damage, changes in behavior associated with drug self-administration can compromise an individual's ability to function in a manner that is acceptable to that person or to society at large and be in that sense harmful. Heroin use in America is troublesome in part because the drug is so expensive that users must engage in illegal behaviors, such as theft, to obtain sufficient funds to purchase it. These behaviors are vexatious to society at large and constitute a significant part of the heroin problem.

Several terms, among them drug abuse, substance abuse, drug addiction, and drug dependence, have been used to refer to troublesome patterns of drug self-administration. Unfortunately, each of these terms has multiple definitions, all typically so vague and mentalistic as to be of questionable value (Davidson, 1982). Consider the following definition of *drug abuse*, which is similar to most:

> Drug abuse refers to the use, usually by self-administration, of any drug in a manner that deviates from the approved medical or social patterns within a given culture. The term conveys the notion of social disapproval, and it is not necessarily descriptive of any particular pattern of drug use or its potential adverse consequences. (Jaffe, 1980, p. 535)

The obvious problem with this definition is determining what constitutes an approved pattern of drug use. As Jaffe (1980) points out, "For any particular drug there is a great variation in what is considered abuse, not only from culture to culture but also from time to time and from one situation to another within the same culture" (p. 535). Despite this fact, some progress has been made toward the provision of standards for determining whether a particular pattern of drug intake constitutes abuse. For example, *DSM-III* provides diagnostic criteria for a number of substance use disorders, which for most drugs are divided into substance abuse and substance dependence.

According to *DSM-III*, three criteria distinguish nonpathological substance use from *substance abuse;* these criteria appear in Table 6. *DSM-III* also provides diagnostic criteria for *substance dependence*, which

> generally is a more severe form of substance use disorder than substance abuse and requires physiological dependence, evidenced by either tolerance or withdrawal. Almost invariably there is also a pattern of pathological use that causes impairment in social or occupational functioning, although in rare cases the manifestations of the disorder are limited to physiological dependence. (American Psychiatric Association, 1980, p. 165).

As generally used, *physical dependence* and *drug addiction* are approximate synonyms for substance dependence as defined by *DSM-III*, whereas *psychological dependence* usually refers to repeated drug self-administration not accompanied by physical dependence. The reader should nonetheless realize that these terms may have other connotations or denotations when used by writ-

Table 6
DSM-III Criteria That Distinguish Substance Use from Abuse[a]

A pattern of pathological use. Depending upon the substance, this may be manifested by: intoxication throughout the day, inability to cut down or stop use, repeated efforts to control use through periods of temporary abstinence or restriction of use to certain times of the day, continuation of substance use despite a serious physical disorder that the individual knows is exacerbated by use of the substance, need for daily use of the substance for adequate functioning, and episodes of a complication of the substance intoxication (e.g., alcoholic blackouts, opioid overdose).

Impairment in social or occupational functioning caused by the pattern of pathological use. Social relations can be disturbed by the individual's failure to meet important obligations to friends and family, by display of erratic and impulsive behavior, and by inappropriate expression of aggressive feelings. The individual may have legal difficulties because of complications of the intoxicated state (e.g., car accidents) or because of criminal behavior to obtain money to purchase the substance. (However, legal difficulties due to possession, purchase, or sale of illegal substances are highly dependent on local customs and laws, and change over time. For this reason, such legal difficulty on a single occasion should not be considered in the evaluation of impairment in social functioning for diagnostic purposes.)

Occupational functioning can deteriorate if the individual misses work or school, or is unable to function effectively because of being intoxicated. When impairment is severe, the individual's life can become totally dominated by use of the substance, with marked deterioration in physical and psychological functioning. Incapacitation is more frequently associated with chronic Opioid and Alcohol Dependence than with dependence on other substances.

Frequently individuals who develop Substance Abuse Disorders also have preexisting Personality Disorders and Affective Disorders with concomitant impairment in social and occupational functioning. It is therefore necessary to determine that the social or occupational impairment associated with the diagnosis of Substance Abuse or Dependence is actually due to the use of the substance. The best clue is a change in functioning that accompanies the onset of a pathological pattern of substance use, or the development of physiological dependence.

Duration. Abuse as used in this manual requires that the disturbance last at least *one month.* Signs of the disturbance need not be present continuously throughout the month, but should be sufficiently frequent for a *pattern* of pathological use causing interference with social or occupational functioning to be apparent. For example, several episodes of binge drinking causing family arguments during a one-month period would be sufficient even though between binges the individual's functioning was apparently not impaired.

[a]Taken from *DSM-III* (1980, p. 164) and reproduced by permission of the American Psychiatric Association.

ers of differing theoretical persuasions. Moreover, the name assigned to a drug-related problem almost never clarifies the nature of the problem, its causes, or its appropriate treatment. When one attempts to deal with human drug self-administration and its related problems, the *nominal fallacy*, assuming a phenomenon once named is explained, and reification are tempting but tragic errors of logic.

From a behavioral perspective, a drug is abused when its use creates a problem for the individual who self-administers the drug or for those who have a legitimate interest in that person's activities. A problem in this sense is a current state of affairs that is described as needing change in a particular direction. Such change, if affected, is reinforcing and constitutes solution of the problem. Those with a legitimate interest in a person exhibiting drug-related problems include all who are, or might be, harmed by the irresponsible drug use and hence have a legal and generally recognized right to work toward its abolition. Parents, for instance, have a legitimate interest in their children's drug-related problems, as do spouses in their mate's. Society at large has an accepted interest in many drug-related problems; laws exist and are enforced to ensure that this interest is realized. Although decisions concerning whether a particular pattern of drug intake is abusive, and therefore merits treatment, ultimately involve value judgments, not purely objective, data-based decisions, there is within a given culture some consensus as to whether particular patterns of intake are harmful. Moreover, if this is not otherwise apparent, social validation techniques (described in Chapter 6) can be used to determine whether a particular pattern of intake is abusive, as well as to evaluate the goals and success of treatment.

As suggested by the *DSM-III* definition of substance abuse, drug-related problems can take several forms, which vary greatly in their specifics. A high school sophomore busted three times for possession of marijuana has a drug-related problem, but it is of a very different kind from that of a cirrhotic wino, or a junior executive whose profligate cocaine use has lead to familial and financial ruin. There is, however, one element common to these and all other examples of drug abuse: Inappropriate drug-seeking and drug-taking behaviors create a problem that can be solved only if these behaviors are changed. Drug abuse inevitably involves, and is in fact defined by, inappropriate drug-seeking and drug-taking. Behavioral pharmacologists recognize that drug abuse problems reflect exposure to particular environments, not ethical weaknesses or medical diseases, and that they should be conceptualized and treated no differently from undesirable behaviors controlled by other response-produced events. The purpose of the present chapter is to consider the variables that affect drug self-administration and how these variables might operate to produce abusive patterns of intake.

Drugs as Positive Reinforcers

It was pointed out in Chapter 4 that drugs which maintain self-administration, and this includes all abused compounds, are serving as positive reinforcers. Studies examining the reinforcing properties of drugs in nonhumans have long been an important part of behavioral pharmacology. Over 40 years ago, Shirley Sprague observed that chimpanzees made physically dependent on morphine would learn to select one of two boxes if the experimenter then injected the animal with morphine contained in a syringe hidden under the box, and Headlee, Coppeck, and Nichols demonstrated that intraperitoneal injections of morphine served as a reinforcer for physically dependent rats (Thompson & Pickens, 1969; Weeks, 1975).

For unknown reasons, neither of these reports generated appreciable interest or led to further investigations. However, 20 years after Sprague's work, development of a technology for studying intravenous drug self-administration in monkeys evoked considerable scientific interest. Two factors probably contributed to this interest. One was a growing awareness on the part of scientists and laypersons alike that drug abuse was a major, and expensive, problem. The second was the increasing popularity of behavioral psychology as a means of analyzing the events that influence organisms' activities. Given a strong concern with drug abuse plus faith in behavioral psychology, the study of drug self-administration by nonhumans appears quite reasonable. Nevertheless, early reports of drugs serving as positive reinforcers for nonhumans were not always applauded. Travis Thompson, who worked with Charles Schuster at the University of Maryland in conducting some of the first studies in this area,[1] recalls that their initial data showing that drug-naive monkeys regularly self-administered morphine were viewed with considerable skepticism (Thompson, personal communication). But with time, the contention that morphine and other drugs would reliably maintain the drug-seeking and drug-taking behaviors of nonhumans was upheld. The apparatus and procedures devised by these researchers also stood the test of time. They continue to be used today with only slight modifications.

The technique used to study intravenous drug self-administration involves surgically implanting a chronically indwelling catheter into a large vein, such as the jugular, of a rat or monkey. Flexible tubing attached to the catheter passes out of the vein and runs beneath the animal's skin to a point atop the shoulders, where it exits in a location not readily accessible to the subject. The tubing is protected by a harness and is connected to a motor-driven syringe which allows a solution of choice to be infused directly into the vein. In demonstrating a drug's ability to serve as a positive reinforcer, occurrence of a response, such as depressing a lever, activates the syringe motor, which results in the injection of a known dose of the drug. If lever pressing occurs more frequently in this situation than when the drug does not follow presses, the drug is functioning as a positive reinforcer.[2] Although in early studies animals were restrained in primate chairs or other devices,

---

[1]Similar studies with monkeys were conducted independently at about the same time by Yanagita (e.g., 1970), and with rats by Weeks (e.g., 1962).

[2]In some cases, a drug's direct response-altering actions can mask its reinforcing effects, as when a relatively high dose of a CNS depressant is delivered under an *FR* 1 schedule. Here, the drug would rapidly accumulate in the body, limiting the subject's ability to respond and thereby obscuring the drug's reinforcing action. Such confounding can be avoided by making the drug available under an intermittent schedule whereby many responses are required for drug delivery.

technical advances now make gross restraint unnecessary and allow incannulated animals to move about experimental chambers with relative freedom.

Procedures have been devised that allow compounds to be delivered to nonhumans through the respiratory system as well as intragastrically, intraperitoneally, intraventricularly, or intramuscularly. These procedures allow drugs to be self-administered by nonhumans through the route preferred by humans. For example, in one series of studies, monkeys were trained to smoke hashish from a pipelike device that projected from the side of the experimental chamber (Pickens, Thompson, & Muchow, 1973). No surgery was involved and the subjects were not encumbered by harnesses or other apparatus. However, the intravenous preparation remains favored for the study of parenteral drug intake.

Humans take many drugs by mouth, and oral preparations are commonly used with nonhumans, especially for examining alcohol (ethanol) self-administration. The oral route is simple and humane but meets with two difficulties: The onset of drug effects following oral drug intake is comparatively slow, and many drugs have an unpleasant taste. These factors make it somewhat difficult to establish ethanol and other drugs as reinforcers for nonhumans when administered by the oral route. Although the problem of delayed effects cannot be overcome readily, researchers have sometimes attempted to solve the problem of bad-tasting drugs by administering them in flavored masking solutions (Meisch, 1977). Unfortunately, using this technique poses another problem: when a compound is administered in a vehicle, it is necessary to determine whether it is the drug or simply the vehicle that serves as a reinforcer. Put another way, are monkeys drinking orange juice because of, or in spite of, its alcohol content? This question can be answered empirically, and most attempts to establish drugs as positive reinforcers by presenting them in palatable solutions have been unsuccessful (Meisch, 1977).

The use of certain procedures that involve exposing food deprived subjects to dry food at a time when a solution of ethanol and tap water is available has been successful in establishing ethanol as a reinforcer. These procedures, one of which involves delivering small bits of food under an intermittent schedule, evoke sufficient ethanol consumption to produce intoxication. (The copious fluid intake engendered in food-deprived animals by intermittent delivery of small bits of food is termed *schedule-induced polydipsia*, and is an interesting phenomenon in its own right.) When food is withdrawn, subjects continue to ingest ethanol and to emit responses leading to its presentation, as shown in Figure 21. Thus it may appear that inducing animals to consume enough ethanol to experience its pharmacological actions is a necessary and sufficient condition for establishing the compound as a positive reinforcer. But this analysis is overly simple, for monkeys that drink ethanol to avoid electric shocks consume enough to become intoxicated, yet the drug does not serve as a positive reinforcer for animals so trained (Meisch, 1977).

Even in circumstances when food-deprived animals given access to water preferentially consume ethanol it may not be the pharmacological properties of the substance that control behavior. Ethanol is a source of calories and it is possible that hungry animals consume it for this reason (Freed & Lester, 1970). It has, however, been demonstrated that rats given unlimited access to both food and water will respond to receive an ethanol solution which is readily consumed (Beardsley, Lemaire, & Meisch, 1978). Thus the pharmacological effects of the substance, apart from its food value, are in some instances sufficient to maintain non-humans' drug-seeking and drug-taking. As an aside, food deprivation does significantly increase the reinforcing value of ethanol and of a wide range of other drugs as well, including those without caloric value or known anoretic actions (Carroll & Meisch, 1984). The mechanism responsible for this phenomenon is unclear, but its existence provides clear evidence that a drug's effects can be modulated by unexpected, and easily overlooked, variables.

Over 100 compounds have been tested to determine whether they serve as positive reinforcers for nonhumans (see reviews by Griffiths, Bigelow, & Henningfield, 1980; Griffiths, Brady, & Bradford, 1979). Table 7 lists several drugs that are reliably self-administered by nonhumans. In general, there is good correspon-

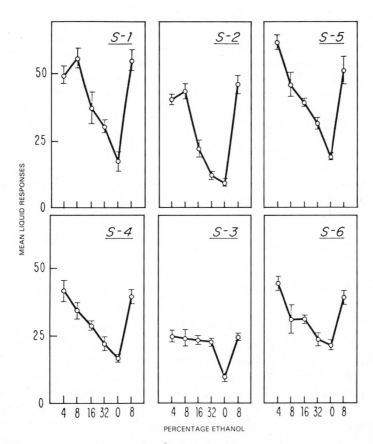

Figure 21. Mean number of liquid-reinforced responses (lever presses) emitted by six individual rats (±1 standard error) during one-hour sessions in which food was not concurrently available. During each condition, liquid was available under an *FR* 1 schedule during seven consecutive sessions. Ethanol concentration was varied across conditions in the order listed, and prior to the sessions shown all subjects were exposed to an intermittent (i.e., *FI* 26-sec) food delivery schedule with ethanol concurrently available. From Poling and Thompson (1977), reproduced by permission of the Society for the Experimental Analysis of Behavior.

Table 7
Representative Drugs
That Are Self-Administered by
(i.e., Serve as Positive Reinforcers for)
Nonhumans[a]

Opioids	Stimulants
Codeine	Amphetamine
Heroin	Cocaine
Meperidine	Ephedrine
Methadone	Methylphenidate
Propoxyphene	Phentermine
CNS depressants	Others
Amobarbital	Phencyclidine
Methohexital	Diphenhydramine
Methaqualone	Nitrous oxide
Pentobarbital	Ketamine
Thiomylal	Procaine

[a]From Griffiths *et al.* (1980).

dence between those drugs which serve as positive reinforcers in nonhumans and those which are self-administered, and abused, by humans. A noteworthy exception to this pattern are hallucinogenic compounds such as LSD, mescaline, and psilocybin. No data indicate that nonhumans will behave in ways leading to the delivery of these drugs; rather, behavior that prevents their delivery is strengthened (Hoffmeister, 1975; Hoffmeister & Wuttke, 1973). Of course, these relations may not be obtained in all circumstances: LSD certainly could serve as a positive reinforcer for nonhumans given special, and as yet unspecifiable, training. It has been suggested (e. g., Poling & Appel, 1982), however, that social factors, primarily the way in which a group reacts to drug taking by its members, are uniquely important in controlling humans' intake of hallucinogens. Such social factors are not manipulated in nonhuman studies.

Nonetheless, it must be reemphasized that a variety of opiates, CNS depressants, stimulants, and other drugs will maintain the drug taking of nonhumans in environments devoid of obvious predisposing factors. That is, rats and monkeys need not be stressed, food-deprived, provided with nondrug reinforcement, or treated in any unusual manner to establish drug self-administration. All that is needed with many compounds (drugs obviously differ in their reinforcing capacity and some serve as positive reinforcers only with special training) is experience in a situation in which a response leads to drug delivery. In these circumstances, the behavior leading to drug delivery occurs often and high levels of intake appear. For example, monkeys allowed to press a bar producing intravenous injections of morphine self-administer enough of the drug to produce physical dependence (Thompson & Schuster, 1964). Moreover, monkeys will acutely administer enough morphine or d-amphetamine to produce death (Johanson, Balster, & Bonese, 1976): most experimenters therefore arrange protective contingencies that limit the amount of drug that a subject can receive. Further, behavior leading to drug delivery will persist even when such deliveries occur infrequently across time or are dependent on many repeated occurrences of the behavior (Thompson & Pickens, 1969).

Studies of drug self-administration by nonhumans have provided abundant evidence that many drugs can exercise powerful control over behavior even in creatures as ostensibly simple as the rat. In addition, physical dependence is not a prerequisite for the development and maintenance of drug intake even in the case of drugs that are capable of producing this effect. Finally, drug-maintained operant behavior is sensitive to variables that affect behavior maintained by other kinds of events. Important variables known to affect drug self-administration are the history of the organism, the kind of drug employed, drug dose, and schedule of drug delivery (see Goldberg, 1976; Griffiths et al., 1980; Johanson, 1978; Schuster & Thompson, 1969).

Studies of drug self-administration by nonhumans are important for two reasons. First, by extrapolation they provide information concerning the factors that control human drug use and abuse. These factors include pharmacological and behavioral variables and may work either to increase or decrease drug intake. Variables with the latter effect can of course be examined with respect to their potential utility for treating drug-related problems (see Poling & Appel, 1979). Second, drug self-administration procedures provide a preclinical means of assessing the abuse potential of new compounds. In principle, a drug's abuse potential in humans is directly related to its strength as a positive reinforcer for nonhumans, although the actual prediction of abuse potential rarely is so simple as this relation suggests (see Thompson & Unna, 1977).

The relevance of data collected with nonhumans to understanding human drug self-administration depends upon the extent to which (1) drugs that serve as positive reinforcers for nonhumans serve a similar function for humans, (2) humans and nonhumans are similarly sensitive to the effects of the self-administered drugs, and (3) similar variables control humans' and nonhumans' drug intake. After reviewing the drug self-administration literature, Johanson (1978) and Griffiths et al. (1980) contend that these assumptions are generally well supported. Although it is beyond the scope of this chapter to review the many studies that deal with drug self-administration by nonhumans, the results of such studies, as well as those of controlled laboratory research with humans and less systematic clinical observations, provide strong clues to the factors that contribute to human drug abuse and to the techniques that should prove effective in combatting it. As shown in the following section, drug abuse is a learned operant response and as such is a function of past and present environmental circumstances. From this perspective, a logical way to deal with drug abuse is to alter those factors responsible for its development and maintenance. Techniques for treating drug abuse are described in the final section of this chapter.

Drug Abuse as an Operant Response

Most theories of drug abuse are mentalistic; their framers construe inappropriate drug taking as a reflection of aberrant psychodynamic function, or of a personality disorder (e.g., Chein, Gerard, Lee, & Rosenfeld, 1964; Hill, Haertzen, & Glazer, 1960).

Such conceptions lack merit. One major weakness is a lack of agreement as to what kinds of personality traits, or intrapsychic maladies, cause drug abuse. Some studies have, for example, found differences in the personality profiles of heroin abusers and other "deviant" groups (e.g., Kurtines, Hogan, & Weiss, 1975: Sutker, 1971), but others have not (e.g., Gendreau & Gendreau, 1973; Platt, 1975). Moreover, by focusing attention on events assumed to take place at some other level of analysis, mentalistic models turn attention away from the inappropriate drug-taking and drug-seeking behaviors that are the crux of all drug abuse. Finally, cause and effect are easily confused in such models, and they provide no rational basis for developing treatments.

An alternative model posits that drug self-administration is an operant response, hence learned, and can be studied and explained in the same manner as any other learned response. This viewpoint, advocated by several authors (e.g., Griffiths *et al.*, 1980; Schuster & Thompson, 1969; Wikler & Pescor, 1967), is widely favored by behavioral pharmacologists. At its heart is the conviction that self-administered drugs are positive reinforcers; they strengthen responses that lead to their delivery. The same classes of variables that affect operant responses maintained by other reinforcers control drug-maintained behavior. In some cases, these variables act to produce a pattern of self-administration that in one way or another constitutes a drug abuse problem.

Obviously, no one abuses a drug without having been exposed to it.[3] If a drug is available, the initial decision to self-administer and the original pattern of use depend upon at least three factors: (1) the kind of rules concerning appropriate drug intake and expected drug effects with which the individual has been provided (2) the extent to which historical events favor following these rules, and (3) the degree to which current circum-

---

[3]Although failure to take a prescribed medication as directed is both commonplace and troublesome (Chapter 5) and might therefore be considered as *drug abuse*, only drug-related problems that result from excessive drug administration will be considered in this chapter.

stances (i.e., contingencies of reinforcement and punishment) support or weaken drug taking. Every person when first presented with the option to try a drug will have been given, or will self-generate, rules concerning its proper use and likely effects. Consider a college freshman to whom a friend proffers cocaine with the accompanying commendation, "It's great stuff—a real upper, no hangover." This is not quite like Mom and Dad's rule: "Cocaine use is bad—it's expensive, immoral, and a road to ruin." Which rule is followed, that is, whether or not cocaine is self-administered, depends upon the sophomore's experience with respect to drugs and parents' versus friends' pronouncements concerning them, as well as the circumstances in which the drug is offered. If all party goers are snorting cocaine and encouraging the novice to do so, the likelihood that the response will occur is increased. No process more complicated than shaping is needed to account for this.

Only nondrug reinforcement can control initial drug taking, and such reinforcement plays a role that persists well beyond initial exposure. As explained in Chapter 4, many drugs that are not positively reinforcing upon early exposure come to be so if self-administration continues. Reinforcement directly provided by peers often plays a role in this process; an example is youths' applauding (reinforcing) their friends' early attempts at cigarette smoking, which eventually becomes reinforcing in its own right. So-called self-reinforcement may also play a role in early drug administration, as when a young person praises her or his own smoking, which is consistent with a rule stating, "cigarette smoking is good—it makes me look cool and grown-up." Note that there is nothing capricious in how a person responds when first offered a drug; this behavior is a function of historical and concurrent variables that, although complex, act in lawful fashion.

Variables with orderly actions continue to control drug self-administration once a compound is serving as a positive reinforcer in and of itself. As operant behavior, drug seeking and drug taking come under the control of discriminative stimuli. These stimuli, which nearly always include individuals who have provided drug in the past, historically are correlated with successful drug seeking, and their presence increases the likelihood that such behavior will occur given the momentary effectiveness of the drug as a reinforcer. One potent determinant of the momentary reinforcing effectiveness of a given drug is degree of drug deprivation. The effects of deprivation are most apparent in physically dependent individuals. For them, drug blood levels fall as time passes without exposure to drug, withdrawal symptoms ensue, and the value of the drug as a positive reinforcer grows. However, changes in drug blood level (i.e., relative deprivation) also can influence patterns of self-administration in the absence of physical dependence. Studies with rats and humans given limited access to cocaine show, for example, that typical subjects rapidly self-administer enough drug to reach a moderately high drug blood level, then space administrations so that this level is maintained (Griffiths *et al.*, 1980; Pickens & Thompson, 1971). When constantly available, stimulants usually are self-administered in a cyclic pattern in which periods of high drug intake lasting several days alternate with periods of low intake during which much time is spent eating and sleeping (see Griffiths *et al.*, 1980). Other drugs are associated with different characteristic patterns of self-administration. Opioids, for example, when constantly available typically are administered in increasing quantities over a period of several weeks, after which a fairly stable level of intake is maintained (see Griffiths *et al.*, 1980). This pattern is evident in Figure 22, which shows morphine intake by a human and heroin intake by a rhesus monkey as a function of days of exposure.

Like other operant responses, drug self-administration is affected by the magnitude of reinforcement (i.e., drug dose) and the schedule of delivery. In controlled situations, the relation between rate of drug self-administration and drug dose describes an inverted U-shaped function, although in general higher doses are more reinforing than (i.e., are preferred to) lower doses (see Griffiths *et al.*, 1980). Humans outside the laboratory regularly exercise considerable control over the doses they self-administer, thus this variable plays a rather small role in determining whether or not drug abuse develops. Schedule of delivery also is frequently within a user's control; with many drugs, a rich schedule with no delay to reinforcement can be readily arranged. With scarce or expensive

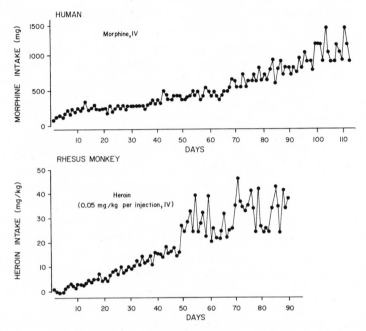

Figure 22. Similar patterns of opioid intake in a human and a rhesus monkey under conditions of continuous drug availability. Each graph shows the amount of drug taken over successive days. The human data are replotted from an experiment in which a volunteer with a history of drug abuse was permitted to self-regulate his intravenous morphine intake (Wikler, 1952). The monkey data are from an unpublished study in which lever-press responses by rhesus monkeys produced intravenous injections of heroin. From Griffiths *et al.* (1980), reproduced by permission of JAI Press and the authors.

drugs, however, much behavior may be required prior to drug delivery. Consider that an average New York City heroin user can easily self-administer $100 worth of the drug per day. Much of such an individual's time is devoted to a long chain of drug-seeking behaviors: theft, fencing of stolen items, contacting a dealer, and preparing a fix may all precede actual drug injection. Although the effects of actual heroin use, including the possibility of accidental overdose death, can be troublesome, a significant part of the general heroin abuse problem reflects the fact that the responses required to obtain the drug—that is, the reinforcement schedules under which it is earned—are undesirable.

Nonpharmacological consequences of drug seeking and drug taking strongly affect these behaviors. In some instances, drug use provides access to reinforcers that otherwise would not be available. As noted earlier, peers may deliver social reinforcers dependent upon drug intake, even if it is abusive. The seducer's saw, "Flowers are good, but liquor's quicker," emphasizes that in certain circles drug use is thought to be associated with increased likelihood of a particular kind of nonpharmacological reinforcer, sexual activity. Although this need not be the case, it sometimes is. Moreover, the *rule* "alcohol + potential partner = sex" can foster drinking in a person for whom sexual activity is a strong reinforcer, even if the rule is untrue.

Pharmacological consequences of drug self-administration surely play a major role in the development and maintenance of nonabusive drug use. Remember that studies with nonhumans show beyond reasonable doubt that many drugs are very potent reinforcers. Why, then, are such drugs not abused by all humans who come into contact with them? The general answer is straightforward: Environmental contingencies foster responsible drug use by many individuals. These contingencies, which are arranged by society at large as well as intimates of the drug user,[4] involve short-term consequences of drug-seeking and drug-tak-ing behaviors; nonabusive self-administration (or abstinence) is reinforced, abusive self-administration punished. In addition, rules describing appropriate durg use are provided, and voicing and following these rules is reinforced. Finally, concurrent oper-ant behaviors incompatible with drug abuse are encouraged and reinforced. The contingencies which a group arranges to prevent abusive drug intake by its members are effective only to the extent that they involve consequences more powerful than those work-ing to produce abusive self-administration.

Unfortunately, in many cases, the powerful and immediate

---

[4]Society at large attempts to control drug abuse so as to protect its members from harm. Most of society's efforts at reducing or preventing drug abuse are less effective than desired because they do not directly contact the individual user or do not involve potent and immediate consequences for particular patterns of drug intake.

reinforcing properties of a drug, coupled with a lack of contingencies sufficiently powerful to reduce drug use, lead to an abusive pattern of intake. As drug self-administration increases and progresses toward abuse, drug-related behaviors can weaken contingencies that otherwise would discourage abusive intake. Envision a happily married couple, one of whom has recently secured employment as a construction laborer. Neither has a drug abuse problem, but the newly hired spouse begins to stop regularly after work to have a few drinks with fellow workers. At first, the drinking involves little time and less alcohol, for the reinforcers associated with home and spouse are preferred to those associated with bar and friends. As days pass, however, the homebound mate wearies of waiting, and begins to behave differently upon the companion's return from work. No longer is dinner kept waiting and plans laid for a happy evening. Arguments, beginning with "Where the hell have you been?" become commonplace as the evening hour grows less pleasant—read "less reinforcing"—for both partners. As the home environment becomes less reinforcing, the bar grows relatively more so. Hence more time is spent at the bar and more alcohol is drunk. This in its turn further increases marital discord in an ever worsening spiral that may well end in a drug abuse problem.

The scenario just described is overly simple, but it does emphasize an important point: Drug-related behaviors may reduce an individual's access to other reinforcers and thereby increase the relative time and effort directed to drug seeking and drug taking. Moreover, at least some individuals who experience drug-related problems have never acquired a behavioral repertoire adequate for attaining any of a range of significant positive reinforcers, such as a good job, a reasonable place of residence, rewarding friends, and satisfying lovers. In the absence of strong competing reinforcers, the relative power of drugs to control behavior is magnified immensely. This has significant treatment implications, for, as Ray (1983) notes, "In fact, treatment for many drug abusers is habilitation, not rehabilitation" (p. 28).

A number of conditioning factors other than those thus far described are known to affect drug self-administration. Stimuli that predictably precede drug administration, such as preparing and injecting heroin, can come to function as conditioned reinforcers and exercise significant control over behavior. Conditioned reinforcement appears to be largely responsible for the "needle freak" phenomenon; individuals who earn this sobriquet report that the act of preparing and injecting their drug of choice is most pleasant. In the words of an occasional heroin user, "Sometimes I think that if I just shot water I'd enjoy it as much" (unnamed, quoted in Powell, 1973, p. 591). Perhaps, but only so long as injections were at least occasionally paired with heroin delivery.

> "Needle freaks" are not commonly encountered. However: There is widespread clinical speculation that rituals and other stimuli associated with drug use become potent conditioned reinforcers which maintain involvement in the drug-using lifestyle and contribute significantly to relapse. For instance, the taste of cigarettes or strong alcoholic drinks are generally considered unpleasant by the inexperienced user; however, after a history involving repeated pairing with the associated drug effects, these tastes apparently become quite powerful conditioned reinforcers in experienced users. (Griffiths *et al.*, 1980, p. 53)

Respondent conditioning plays a role in conditioned reinforcement and also in what Wikler (e.g., 1961, 1973, 1974) has termed *conditioned abstinence*. In brief, conditioned abstinence occurs when an individual repeatedly undergoes withdrawal in the presence of particular stimuli. By virtue of being reliably correlated with the absence of drug (or the presence of an antagonist compound), which leads in a physically dependent organism to the unconditional responses called withdrawal symptoms, these previously neutral conditional stimuli come through respondent conditioning to evoke conditioned withdrawal responses. These responses include but are not limited to drug seeking and subjective craving for drug.

Goldberg and associates have convincingly demonstrated conditioned abstinence in monkeys. In their first study (Goldberg & Schuster, 1967), morphine-dependent monkeys responding under an intermittent schedule of food delivery were occasionally presented with a brief tone followed by delivery of nalorphine, which precipitated withdrawal. After several pairings, presentation of the tone without nalorphine suppressed food-maintained responding and precipated obvious symptoms of withdrawal (i.e., vomiting, salivation, and bradycardia). A subsequent study (Goldberg & Schuster, 1970) found that, even two to four months after termination of physical dependence on morphine, a stimulus once paired with nalorphine (and consequent withdrawal symptoms) suppressed food-maintained behavior and reduced heart rate, although this effect disappeared with repeated exposure (i.e., respondent extinction occurred). Two final studies (Goldberg, Woods, & Schuster, 1969, 1971) demonstrated that morphine self-administration increased during periods of conditioned abstinence.

In a related vein, Wikler (1974) observed that saline injections produced some signs of withdrawal (i.e., yawning, lacrimination, pupillary dilation, rhinnorrhea, cramps, and nausea) in humans who had experienced opioid withdrawal symptoms induced by nalorphine injections. Similar findings also have been reported by O'Brien and colleagues (e.g., O'Brien, 1975; O'Brien, Testa, O'Brien, Brady, & Wells, 1977). In one of these studies (O'Brien, 1975), subjects reported that their subjective craving for drug was greatest in situations in which drug was actually administered, as opposed to situations removed in time from drug administration. Similar data have been reported regarding reported craving for alcohol (Pickens, Bigelow, & Griffiths, 1973). Taken together and in combination with the results of investigations employing nonhuman subjects, these results provide striking evidence of the role that antecedent stimuli play in controlling drug self-administration.

Further evidence of the role that antecedent stimuli play in controlling drug intake comes from a study of rats conducted by Thompson and Ostlund (1965) that is elegant in its simplicity. All subjects in this investigation initially were made physically dependent on morphine, which was dissolved in their drinking water. Next, all animals underwent withdrawal from the drug. For half the subjects, this occurred in the same environment in which morphine was initially presented, whereas a novel withdrawal environment was employed with the other subjects. Finally, all animals were reexposed to morphine, either in the environment in which initial exposure occurred, or in a novel environment. Results were straightforward: Readdiction occurred most readily when the readdiction environment was the same as the initial addiction environment. Clinical observations with human opioid abusers, described in the following section, are consistent with these experimental findings.

Stimuli that increase drug taking through conditioned abstinence are acting as establishing operations (see Chapter 4). These same stimuli, or others, might also increase drug self-administration by acting as discriminative stimuli. Both actions require that the individual have a particular history with respect to the stimuli in question, but establishing operations increase the reinforcing efficacy of a drug, whereas discriminative stimuli increase drug-seeking and drug-taking behaviors only if the drug is momentarily effective as a reinforcer. Unfortunately, as Griffiths *et al.* (1980) point out, few researchers attempt to disentangle the mechanisms whereby antecedent stimuli control drug taking.

Some authors (e.g., Falk & Tang, 1977) have posited that *schedule induction* might play a role in human drug self-administration. In early demonstrations of schedule induction, food-deprived rats intermittently presented with small portions of dry food drank water in gargantuan quantity (e.g., Falk, 1971). Laboratory studies with rats and monkeys (reviewed by Gilbert, 1978) have demonstrated schedule-induced oral consumption of many drugs, and schedule induction frequently is used to establish orally administered drugs as positive reinforcers. There is, however, as yet no clear evidence that schedule induction plays a significant role in the development or maintenance of human drug abuse.

Treating Drug Abuse

Many approaches to the treatment of drug abuse have been evaluated. None is panacean. From the perspective of behavior analysis, drug abuse results from exposure to a particular kind of environment, one in which contingencies operate to support a troublesome pattern of drug self-administration. Altering these contingencies will therefore be a part of any effective treatment program. Holland (1978) makes this point ably:

> A serious effort to solve the social problems involved in drinking is not made by focusing on the so-called "flawed personality" of the unsightly drunk. It is not to be solved by victim blaming. It requires, as every behaviorist should know, a change in the environmental contingencies that constitute daily business and cultural practices. (p. 88)

It is not, however, necessarily easy to determine how contingencies should be changed to eliminate drug abuse by a given individual, nor to bring about those changes that appear necessary. Abusive patterns of drug intake typically harm the user, but the harm often is much delayed relative to the time of drug intake. In contrast, the positively reinforcing effects of drug administration occur with little delay. Since delayed consequences, even if highly undesirable, have little direct effect on behavior, most behavioral approaches to the treatment of drug abuse attempt to arrange short-term consequences which weaken inappropriate drug use or, conversely, strengthen appropriate drug use.

It is rather easy to weaken or eliminate drug self-administration in controlled laboratory situations. Like other operant responses, drug self-administration is sensitive to punishment. Studies with nonhumans have shown, for example, that oral ethanol self-administration by rats (Poling & Thompson, 1977) can be reduced by response-contingent timeout from a food reinforcement schedule and that monkeys' intravenous cocaine intake can be suppressed by response-contingent electric shocks (e.g., Grove & Schuster, 1974). Similar procedures also are effective in reducing human alcohol abusers' drug intake. Wilson, Leaf, and Nathan (1975) have shown, for instance, that response-contingent electric shock suppresses ethanol intake in a research ward setting, whereas Bigelow, Liebson, and Griffiths (1974) have reported similar results with a timeout procedure.

Extinction, which can involve either pharmacological blockade of a drug's effects or simple failure to deliver the drug, eventually reduces drug self-administration in nonhumans (e.g., Davis & Smith, 1976; Gerber & Stretch, 1975) and humans alike (e.g., Griffiths, Bigelow, & Liebson, 1979; O'Brien, 1975; Schuster, 1975). Pairing the taste of a drug with nausea and vomiting in a *conditioned aversion* procedure also reduces drug intake, and such procedures are sometimes used to treat cigarette smoking and alcohol abuse (see Nathan & Lipscomb, 1970; Smith, 1978). Increasing the response requirement for drug delivery is another technique known to reduce drug intake: In general, if response requirement is increased substantially, amount of drug self-administered is inversely related to the magnitude of the response requirement for individual doses (see Griffiths *et al.*, 1980).

Although punishment, extinction, taste aversion conditioning, and increasing response requirements clearly are effective in reducing drug intake, the clinical utility of these procedures outside controlled environments is limited. None of these procedures produce lasting effects; like all contingency management procedures, they affect behavior so long as they are operative and for a limited time thereafter. Once punishment or extinction ends, the pairing of drug and nausea ceases, or response requirements are lowered, behavior typically returns to at or above pretreatment levels. Moreover, humans can discriminate conditions correlated with particular contingencies and behave accordingly. An individual who is taking disulfiram (Antibuse) as part of an alcohol abuse treatment program soon learns that drinking ethanol immediately leads to aversive consequences (i.e., is punished) in the presence of disulfiram, but not in its absence. Punishment can be avoided by not drinking alcohol after taking disulfiram or, similarly, by not taking disulfiram before drinking. In the latter case, the client circumvents the intended treatment as well as punishment. Clients' avoidance or escape of intended therapeutic contingencies is a major problem in the outpatient treatment of drug abuse (Ditman, 1966; Jaffe, 1980; Mottin, 1973).

One tack that can be taken to increase the likelihood that clients will be exposed to therapeutic contingencies is to make these contingencies positively reinforcing. A study by McCaul, Stitzer, Bigelow, and Liebson (1984) provides a good example of the use of positive reinforcement in treating drug abuse. This investigation involved 20 male opioid abusers who were enrolled in an outpatient opioid detoxification program in which methadone doses were gradually decreased over time. Contingency management treatment, which was arranged for 10 men (the experimental group), involved giving a patient $10 and a take-home methadone dose each time he produced an opiate-free urine specimen, and requiring him to participate in an intensive clinical procedure when opioids were present in urine.

As shown in Figure 23, this treatment slowed the relapse to illicit opiate use relative to control subjects who were paid for providing a urine sample, regardless of drug content. It should be noted that methadone was used in the McCaul *et al.* (1984) study to suppress withdrawal symptoms following termination of illicit opiate use. This procedure should not be confused with chronic methadone maintenance programs. By making an alternative opioid that is available dependent upon appropriate behavior (e.g., appearing at the clinic at scheduled times), chronic methadone maintenance programs are intended to reduce problems associated with procuring and administering heroin and similar opioids, which are both expensive and dangerous (for reviews of methadone maintenance programs see Sells, 1979; Simpson, Savage, & Lloyd, 1979; Wilmarth & Goldstein, 1974). As Jaffe (1980) indicates, "This treatment explicitly emphasizes law-abiding and productive behavior rather than abstinence per se, and its relative efficacy in reaching its goals is well documented" (p. 574). However, methadone maintenance alone does not prevent the abuse of other drugs. Perhaps as many as 70% of patients entering methadone maintenance programs return to illicit drugs, although the crime and death rates among those who stay in such programs remain much lower than for similar individuals who do not (Alpern, Sciolino, & Agrest, 1977). Although methadone maintenance programs are of recognized value, they do require chronic exposure to a powerful drug with known behavioral actions. This is considered by many to be less than ideal.

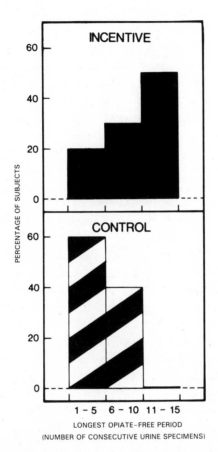

Figure 23. The longest opiate-free period achieved by patients in experimental and control conditions, expressed as the number of consecutive opiate-free urine specimens. Patients provided two specimens per week during the 10-week intervention period, thus patients could achieve a maximum of 20 consecutive opiate-free specimens. Patients in the experimental group received money and methadone contingent on producing an opiate-free specimen, control patients did not. From McCaul *et al.* (1984), reproduced by permission of the Association for the Experimental Analysis of Behavior and the authors.

Several researchers have demonstrated contingency management procedures similar to those used by McCaul *et al.* (1984) effective in reducing abusive drug intake. Contingency contracting, wherein a therapist and client formally agree that specified patterns of drug taking (e.g., abstinence for a given period) will lead to particular consequences, has been demonstrated effective in reducing cigarette smoking (e.g., Winett, 1973), excessive caffeine intake (e.g., Foxx & Rubinoff, 1979), alcohol consumption in chronic alcoholics treated as inpatients (e.g., Griffiths, Bigelow, & Liebson, 1977), and, as shown in Figure 24, barbiturate use by inpatient sedative abusers (e.g., Pickens, 1979).

Numerous other examples of the use of contingency management to treat abusive drug intake are available (see Harris, 1981; Krasnegor, 1979). On balance, it is clear that altering the consequences of drug-related behaviors is an effective method for treating drug abuse in a variety of situations. The primary problem with such procedures is that it is often difficult or impossible to arrange conditions such that a drug abuser is consistently exposed to conditions that prevent drug abuse. Though such conditions can be arranged within a treatment facility, return to the client's normal environment too often results in exposure to the same contingencies that originally resulted in drug abuse, which reappears as a result of their actions.

A commonly cited example of the importance of the posttreatment environment in the reinstatement of drug abuse concerns

---

→

Figure 24. The effects of contingency contracting on drug intake of six subjects with confirmed histories of sedative abuse. Graphs along the left side indicate levels of pentobarbital intake per day prior to treatment. At the start of detoxification, phenobarbital was substituted for pentobarbital (15 mg phenobarbital equivalent to 50 mg pentobarbital) for three days of self-administration. Subjects were then given points (exchangeable for a variety of reinforcers) for successfully reducing drug intake but lost points for failing to do so. Five of six subjects typically met the requirements of the contract and became drug-free. Follow-up data (right panels) indicate that these patients had not returned to drug use two months after detoxification. From Pickens (1979), reproduced by permission of the author.

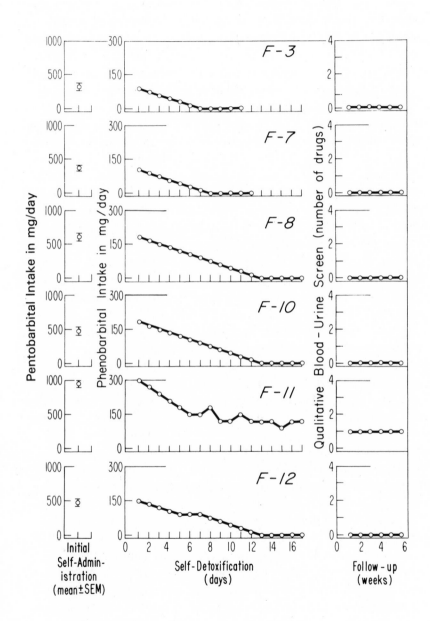

American military personnel who returned from Vietnam with a heroin abuse problem. After treatment, and return to their home country, the vast majority did not return to heroin abuse, presumably because the contingencies that fostered abuse in Vietnam were not present in the home environment (Robins, 1974).

Skinnerians have contended for years that behavioral problems typically cannot be cured by everlasting interventions. Operant behavior changes in orderly response to an altered environment, therefore treatment gains that result from contingency management persist only so long as the environment supports them. Drug taking is operant behavior, and many factors influence how, or if, an individual self-administers drugs. In view of the range of factors that contribute to drug abuse, effective drug abuse treatments are likely to be broad-spectrum, intensive, and of long duration. *Detoxification*, safely weaning a physically dependent person away from drug, is a necessary first step in dealing with drug abuse problems that involve physical dependence and one that is easily accomplished with current technology (Jaffe, 1980).

Once an individual is detoxified, dramatic steps must be taken to alter the consequences of drug taking such that abusive patterns of intake are not supported. How consequences should be changed to deal with a given drug abuse problem depends upon the kind of drug involved, the nature of the abuse problem, the circumstances of the abuser's life and the kinds of contingency management they allow, and the individual's general behavioral repertoire. In general, effective treatment programs are likely to entail teaching appropriate rule-governed behavior concerning drugs, perhaps through the use of what are generically termed *cognitive behavior modification* procedures (see Foreyt & Rathjen, 1978). Training new responses appropriate for gaining nonpharmacological reinforcers also is likely to be necessary. Finally, conditioning factors in the client's daily environment that foster inappropriate drug usage probably will have to be rendered impotent. These include aspects of the environment that increase drug taking by acting as discriminative stimuli and establishing operations, as well as nonpharmacological reinforcers associated with drug self-administration.

Concluding Comments

It is beyond the scope of the present chapter to detail specific drug abuse treatment programs, or to consider their efficacy. In general, treatment programs are less effective than is desired: "A number of recent reports and studies indicate that despite claims for the effectiveness of particular treatment modalities or treatment programs . . . there is very little verified evidence in both the treatment of alcoholism and of drug dependence" (Babow, 1975, p. 73). Nonetheless, some individuals do benefit from specific treatment programs. Those who respond favorably represent the return on a sizable investment. As Ray (1983) indicates, "In 1979 the United States spent $511 million to support the treatment of 235,414 individuals in 3600 treatment units" (p. 27). Offering useful treatment to those experiencing drug abuse problems requires understanding of the variables that contribute to drug abuse and a technology that enables clinicians to manipulate these variables so as to prevent or terminate harmful patterns of self-administration. If nothing else, drug self-administration studies conducted by behavioral pharmacologists have shown that operant and respondent conditioning play a significant role in the development and maintenance of drug abuse and that treatments based on learning principles are both logical and useful. Refining these treatments and arranging for their widespread implementation is a task quite as formidable as it is important.

CHAPTER

8

The Future

Behavioral pharmacology has existed as a discipline for approximately 30 years. Preceding chapters have recounted significant happenings over the course of that brief history. Although accurately predicting future developments in any field is difficult, certain trends are evident in the development of behavioral pharmacology and appear likely to persist into the foreseeable future—say from now until the year 2000.

After considering these trends, Branch (1984) provides a rather unimpressive scenario for the future of behavioral pharmacology:

> To summarize, the future of behavioral pharmacology seems predictable on two fronts but less so on the third. Pharmacologically oriented research using drug-discrimination procedures will continue because the preparation has become a standard part of the pharmacologist's arsenal. Research on drug self-administration will advance because of the obvious social relevance of such work. The picture for the rest of behavioral pharmacology is less clear. (p. 320)

Pharmacologically oriented research using drug discrimination procedures has often attempted to relate the discriminative stimulus properties of drugs to their neuropharmacological actions. Such research is firmly in the tradition of the neurosciences which, with the discovery of endorphins and several types of opiate receptors (e.g., Martin, Eades, Thompson, Huppler, & Gilbert, 1976), have undergone a new wave of popularity. However, even though neuropharmacology provides a theoretical basis for interpreting drug effects, neuropharmacological explanations of behavioral events are reductionistic and nonbehavioral and divert attention from the importance of environmental events as determinants of drug action (cf. Branch, 1984). Moreover, understanding the neuropharmacological mechanisms whereby a drug produces a given behavioral effect is often (though surely not always) of little practical utility. The actions of heroin and morphine indeed may in one sense be explained in terms of their actions at kappa, mu. and sigma receptor sites, but such an explanation is of trifling value to a clinician attempting to treat a heroin abuser.

Despite the fact that more than a few researchers trained in behavioral pharmacology have yielded to the guile of neuropharmacology, it does not appear from this quarter that the best possible future for behavioral pharmacology is as a handmaiden to the neurosciences. Nonetheless, research in this area undoubtably will continue to be popular.

So, too, will drug self-administration research. As discussed in Chapter 7, behavioral analyses are playing a growing role in predicting the abuse potential of newly synthesized medications and in the analysis and treatment of drug abuse. One area of waxing interest involves the role of genetic variables as determinants of drug effects in general and of the positively reinforcing effects of drugs in particular. Current evidence provides, for example, some indication that genotype affects the likelihood that an individual will abuse ethanol, although the mechanism whereby this occurs, its relative potency as a determinant of alcohol abuse, and its implications for the treatment and prevention of alcohol abuse, are unclear (see Goodwin, 1979). Behavioral pharmacologists are beginning to explore genetic contributions to drug abuse (e.g., Pickens, 1985), but it remains to be seen whether their unique skills and analytical perspectives will prove useful in what historically has been a problematic area.

Branch (1984) suggests that, if behavioral pharmacology is to escape becoming a minor arm of pharmacology, researchers should devote greater effort toward assessing behavioral mechanisms of drug action. Assessment of behavioral mechanisms of action typically involves nonhuman subjects but, as described in Chapter 6, can be an integral part of clinical drug evaluations as well. The research methodology characteristic of behavioral pharmacology is very well suited for clinical drug studies, and it appears that a true science of clinical behavioral pharmacology is emerging. If the field is to flourish. It appears that researchers must attend to drug effects on complex behaviors (e., social interactions, rule-governed behavior, learning, self-control), as well as on the simple schedule-controlled responses characteristically examined in nonhuman studies. Moreover, behavioral pharmacologists should respond to the recognized need (e.g., Aman & Singh, 1983; Crook & Ferris, 1986) for methodologically sound evaluations of pharmacological interventions used with special populations, including mentally retarded individuals and geriatric patients. Such evaluations may require considerable refinement of the procedures now commonly employed by behavioral pharmacologists or the development of novel procedures.

Speculation concerning the future of behavioral pharmacology would not be complete without mention of behavioral toxicology. Chemical contamination of all living beings is status quo on planet Earth, but how, or if, particular chemicals harm humans and other species frequently is hard to determine. Nonhuman studies in the tradition of behavioral pharmacology allow for precise assessment of the harmful effects of diverse chemicals. In addition, the exquisitely sensitive procedures employed by behavioral toxicologists can be put to good use in evaluating drug effects in humans unintentionally exposed to putative toxins. As Evans and Weiss (1978) note, "The kind of subjective and objective measures that behavioral scientists are experienced in acquiring could be a vital supplement to the morbidity and mortality data that commonly constitute the epidemiologist's primary criteria" (p. 478).

References

Alpern. D. M., Sciolino, E., & Agrest, S. (1977, February 7). The methadone Jones. *Newsweek*, p. 29.

Aman, M. G., & Singh, N. N. (1980). The usefulness of thioridazine for treating childhood disorders—fact or folklore? *American Journal of Mental Deficiency, 84,* 331–338.

Aman, M. G., & Singh, N. N. (1983). Pharmacological intervention. In J. L. Matson & J. A. Mulick (Eds.), *Handbook of mental retardation* (pp. 317–337). New York: Pergamon Press.

American Psychiatric Association. (1980). *Diagnostic and statistical manual of mental disorders* (3rd edition). Washington, D.C.: American Psychiatric Association.

Annals of the New York Academy of Sciences. (1956). Volume 65 (pp. 247–256).

Appel, J. B., & Dykstra, L. A. (1977). Drugs, discrimination, and signal detection theory. In T. Thompson & P. B. Dews (Eds.), *Advances in behavioral pharmacology* (Vol. 1, pp. 140–166). New York: Academic Press.

Ayllon, T., Layman, D., & Kandal, J. H. (1975). A behavioral-educational alternative to drug control of hyperactive behavior. *Journal of Applied Behavior Analysis, 8,* 137–146.

Babow, I. (1975). The treatment monopoly in alcoholism and drug dependence. *Journal of Drug Issues, 5,* 120–128.

Baer, D. M., Wolf, M. M., & Risley, T. R. (1968). Some current dimensions

217

of applied behavior analysis. *Journal of Applied Behavior Analysis, 1,* 91–97.

Baldessarini, R. J. (1977). *Chemotherapy in psychiatry.* Cambridge: Harvard University Press.

Baldessarini, R. J. (1980). Drugs and the treatment of psychiatric disorders. In A. G. Gilman, L. S. Goodman, & A. Gilman (Eds.), *The pharmacological basis of therapeutics* (pp. 391–447). New York: Macmillan.

Barber, T. X. (1976). *Pitfalls in human research.* New York: Pergamon Press.

Barlow, G. H., & Hayes, S. C. (1979). Alternating treatments design: One strategy for comparing the effects of two treatments in a single subject. *Journal of Applied Behavior Analysis, 12,* 199–210.

Baron, A., Kaufman, A., & Stauber, K. A. (1969). Effects of instructions and performance feedback on human operant behavior maintained by fixed-interval reinforcement. *Journal of the Experimental Analysis of Behavior, 12,* 701–712.

Barrett, J. E. (1976). Effects of alcohol, chlordiazepoxide, cocaine, and pentobarbital on responding maintained under fixed-interval schedules of food or shock presentation. *Journal of Pharmacology and Experimental Therapeutics, 196,* 605–615.

Barrett, J. E. (1981). Differential drug effects as a function of the controlling consequences. In T. Thompson & C. Johanson (Eds.), *Behavioral pharmacology of human drug dependence* (pp. 159–181). Washington, D.C.: U.S. Government Printing Office.

Beardsley, P. M., Lemaire, G. A., & Meisch, R. A. (1978). Ethanol-reinforced behavior of rats with concurrent access to food and water. *Psychopharmacology, 59,* 7–11.

Bellack, A. S., & Schwartz, J. S. (1976). Assessment of self-control programs. In M. Hersen & A. S. Bellack (Eds.), *Behavioral assessment: A practical handbook* (pp. 126–158). New York: Pergamon Press.

Berger, P. A. (1978). Medical treatment of mental illness. *Science, 200,* 974–981.

Berryman, R., Cumming, W. W., & Nevin, J. A. (1963). Acquisition of delayed matching in the pigeon. *Journal of the Experimental Analysis of Behavior, 6,* 101–107.

Bianchine, J. R. (1980). Drugs for Parkinson's disease: Centrally acting muscle relaxants. In A. G. Gilman, L. S. Goodman, & A. Gilman (Eds.), *The pharmacological basis of therapeutics* (pp. 475–493). New York: Macmillan.

Bigelow, G. E., Liebson, I. A., & Griffiths, R. R. (1974). Alcoholic drinking: Suppression by a brief time-out procedure. *Behavior Research and Therapy, 12,* 107–115.

Bijou, S. W., & Baer, D. M. (1961). *Child development. Vol. 1: A systematic and empirical theory.* New York: Appleton-Century-Crofts.

Blackman, D. E., & Sanger, D. J. (1978). *Contemporary research in behavioral pharmacology.* New York: Plenum Press.

Boren, J. J. (1963). Repeated acquisition of new behavioral chains. *American Psychologist, 17,* 421.

Boren, J. J. (1967, April). *The study of performance enhancing drugs with a repeated acquisition technique.* Paper presented at the meeting of the Eastern Psychological Association, Boston.

Boring, E. G. (1954). The nature and history of experimental control. *American Journal of Psychology, 67,* 573–589.

Bradley, C. (1937). The behavior of children receiving benzedrine. *American Journal of Psychiatry, 94,* 577–585.

Branch, M. N. (1984). Rate dependency, behavioral mechanisms, and behavioral pharmacology. *Journal of the Experimental Analysis of Behavior, 42,* 511–522.

Breuning, S. E., & Poling, A. (1982). *Drugs and mental retardation.* Springfield, IL: Charles C. Thomas.

Brody, H. (1980). *Placebos and the philosophy of medicine.* Chicago: University of Chicago Press.

Buskist, W. F., & Miller, H. L., Jr. (1982). The analysis of human operant behavior: A brief census of the literature: 1958–1981. *The Behavior Analyst, 5,* 137–143.

Byrd, L. D. (1981). Quantification in behavioral pharmacology. In T. Thompson, P. B. Dews, & W. A. McKim (Eds.), *Advances in behavioral pharmacology* (Vol. 3, pp. 75–90). New York: Academic Press.

Caldwell, A. E. (1970). *Origins of psychopharmacology: From CPZ to LSD.* Springfield, IL: Charles C. Thomas.

Campbell, D. T., & Stanley, J. C. (1966). *Experimental and quasi-experimental designs for research.* Chicago: Rand McNally.

Cant, G. (1976, February). Valiumania. *The New York Times Magazine,* pp. 34–44.

Carroll, M. E., & Meisch, R. A. (1984). Increased drug-reinforced behavior due to food deprivation. In T. Thompson, P. B. Dews, & J. E. Barrett (Eds.), *Advances in behavioral pharmacology* (Vol. 4, pp. 47–88). New York: Academic Press.

Chein, I., Gerard, D. D., Lee, R. S., & Rosenfeld, E. (1964). *The road to H.* New York: Basic Books.

Chen, E. (1979). *PBB: An American tragedy.* New York: Prentice-Hall.

Ciminero, A. R., Calhoun, K. S., & Adams, H. E. (1977). *Handbook of behavioral assessment.* New York: Wiley.

Claghorn, J. L. (1976). Double blind evaluations in psychopharmacology. In D. Gallant & G. Simpson (Eds.), *Depression: Behavioral, biochemical, diagnostic and treatment concepts* (pp. 250–271). New York: Spectrum.

Cone, J. D., & Hawkins, R. P. (1977). *Behavioral assessment: New directions in clinical psychology.* New York: Brunner/Mazel.

Conners, C. K. (1969). A teacher rating scale for use in drug studies with children. *American Journal of Psychiatry, 126,* 152–156.

Conners, C. K., Taylor, E., Meo, G., Jurtz, M. A., & Fournier, M. (1972). Magnesium pemoline and dextroamphetamine: A controlled study in children with minimum brain dysfunction. *Psychopharmacology, 26,* 321–336.

Cook, L., & Catania, A. C. (1964). Effects of drugs on avoidance and escape behavior. *Federation Proceedings, 23,* 818–835.

Cook, L., & Kelleher, R. T. (1962). Drug effects on the behavior of animals. *Annals of the New York Academy of Sciences, 96,* 315–335.

Craighead, W. E., Kazdin, A. E., & Mahoney, M. J. (1981). *Behavior modification: Principles, issues, and applications.* Boston: Houghton Mifflin.

Crane, G. E. (1957). Iproniazid (Marsilid) phosphate, a therapeutic agent for mental disorders and debilitating disease. *Psychiatric Research Reports, 8,* 142–152.

Crook, T. H., & Ferris, S. (1986). Issues in geriatric psychopharmacology. In K. Gadow & A. Poling (Eds.), *Methodological issues in human psychopharmacology.* Greenwich, CT: JAI Press.

Davidson, R. S. (1982). Addictive behaviors. In D. M. Doleys, R. L. Meredith, & A. R. Ciminero (Eds.), *Behavioral medicine: Assessment and treatment strategies* (pp. 347–369). New York: Plenum Press.

Davis, W. M., & Smith, S. G. (1976). Role of conditioned reinforcers in the initiation, maintenance and extinction of drug-seeking behavior. *Pavlovian Journal of the Biological Sciences, 11,* 222–236.

Davis, V. J., Poling, A., Wysocki, T., & Breuning, S. E. (1981). Effects of phenytoin withdrawal on matching to sample and workshop performance of mentally retarded persons. *Journal of Nervous and Mental Disease, 169,* 718–725.

Desjardins, P. J., Moerschbaecher, J. M., Thompson, D. M., & Thomas, J. R. (1982). Intravenous diazepam in humans: Effects on acquisition and performance of response chains. *Pharmacology, Biochemistry, and Behavior, 17,* 1055–1060.

Desta, B., & Pernarowski, M. (1973). The dissolution characteristics of two clinically different brands of chlorpromazine HCl tablets. *Drug Intelligence and Clinical Pharmacy, 7,* 408–412.

de Villiers, P. (1977). Choice in concurrent schedules and a quantitative formulation of the law of effect. In W. K. Honig & J. E. R. Staddon (Eds.), *Handbook of operant behavior* (pp. 233–287). Englewood Cliffs, NJ: Prentice-Hall.

Dews, P. B. (1955). Studies on behavior: I. Differential sensitivity to pentobarbital of pecking performance in pigeons depending on the schedule of reward. *Journal of Pharmacology and Experimental Therapeutics, 115,* 343–401.

Dews, P. B., & Wenger, G. R. (1977). Rate-dependence of the behaviorial effects of amphetamine. In T. Thompson & P. B. Dews (Eds.), *Advances in behavioral pharmacology* (Vol. 1, pp. 167–229). New York: Academic Press.

Ditman, K. (1966). Review and evaluation of current drug therapies in alcoholism. *Psychosomatic Medicine, 28,* 667–677.

Dornbush, R. L., Freedman, A. M., & Fink, M. (1976). Chronic cannabis use. *Annals of the New York Academy of Sciences, 282:* all.

Downs D. A., & Woods J. H. (1975). Naloxone as a negative reinforcer in rhesus monkeys: Effects of dose, schedule, and narcotic regimen. *Pharmacology Reviews, 27,* 397–406.

Eacker, J. N. (1972). On some elementary philosophical problems of psychology. *American Psychologist, 27,* 553–565.

Epstein, L. H., & Cluss, P. A. (1982). A behavioral medicine perspective on adherence to long-term medical regimens. *Journal of Consulting and Clinical Psychology, 50,* 950–971.

Epstein, R. (1986). Analogue methods. In A. Poling & R. W. Fuqua (Eds.), *Research methodology in applied behavior analysis: Issues and advances* (pp. 127–156). New York: Plenum Press.

Evans, F. J. (1981). The placebo response in pain control. *Psychopharmacology Bulletin, 17,* 72–76.

Evans, H. L., & Weiss, B. (1978). Behavioral toxicology. In D. E. Blackman & D. J. Sanger (Eds.), *Contemporary research in behavioral pharmacology* (pp. 449–488). New York: Plenum Press.

Falk, J. L. (1971). The nature and determinants of adjunctive behavior. *Physiology and Behavior, 6,* 577–588.

Falk, J. L., & Tang, M. (1977). Animal model of alcoholism: Critique and progress. In M. M. Gross (Ed.), *Alcohol intoxication and withdrawal* (Vol. 3, pp. 465–493). New York: Plenum Press.

Ferguson, D. G., & Breuning, S. E. (1982). Antipsychotic and antianxiety drugs. In S. E. Breuning & A. Poling (Eds.), *Drugs and mental retardation* (pp. 168–214). Springfield, IL: Charles C Thomas.

Ferster, C. B., & Skinner, B. F. (1957). *Schedules of reinforcement.* New York: Appleton-Century-Crofts.

Fields, H. L., & Levine, J. D. (1981). Biology of placebo analgesia. *American Journal of Medicine, 70,* 745.

Fisher, S. (1970). Nonspecific factors as determinants of behavioral response to drugs. In A. DiMascio & R. I. Shader (Eds.), *Clinical handbook of psychopharmacology* (pp. 16–39). New York: Science House.

Foreyt, J. P., & Rathjen, D. P. (1978). *Cognitive behavior therapy.* New York: Plenum Press.

Foxx, R. M., & Rubinoff, A. (1979). Behavioral treatment of caffeinism: Reducing excessive coffee drinking. *Journal of Applied Behavior Analysis, 12,* 335–344.

Freed, E. X., & Lester, D. (1970). Schedule-induced consumption of ethanol: Calories or chemotherapy? *Physiology and Behavior, 5,* 555–560.

Gadow, K. D., & Poling, A. (1986). *Methodological issues in human psychopharmacology.* Greenwich, CT: JAI Press.

Gadow, K. D., White, L., & Ferguson, D. G. (1986 a). Placebo controls and double-blind conditions: Part I. In K. E. Gadow & A. Poling (Eds.), *Methodological issues in human psychopharmacology.* Greenwich, CT: JAI Press.

Gadow, K. D., White, L., & Ferguson, D. G. (1986 b). Placebo controls and double-blind conditions: Part II. In K. E. Gadow & A. Poling (Eds.), *Methodological issues in human psychopharmacology.* Greenwich, CT: JAI Press.

Gendreau, P., & Gendreau, L. P. (1973). A theoretical note on personality characteristics of heroin addicts. *Journal of Abnormal Psychology, 82,* 139–140.

Gerber, G. J., & Stretch, R. (1975). Drug-induced reinstatement of extinguished self-administration behavior in monkeys. *Pharmacology, Biochemistry, and Behavior, 3,* 1055–1061.

Gilbert, R. M. (1978). Schedule-induced self-administration of drugs. In D. E. Blackman & D. J. Sanger (Eds.), *Contemporary research in behavioral pharmacology* (pp. 289–324). New York: Plenum Press.

Gilman, A. G., Goodman, L. S., & Gilman, A. (1980). *The pharmacological basis of therapeutics.* New York: Macmillan.

Gilman, A. G., Mayer, S. E., & Melmon, K. L. (1980). Pharmacodynamics:

Mechanisms of drug action and the relationship between drug concentration and effect. In A. G. Gilman, L. S. Goodman, & A. Gilman (Eds.), *The pharmacological basis of therapeutics* (pp. 28–39). New York: Macmillan.

Goldberg, S. R. (1976). The behavioral analysis of drug addiction. In S. D. Glick & J. Goldfarb (Eds.), *Behavioral pharmacology* (pp. 283–316). St. Louis: Mosby.

Goldberg, S. R., & Schuster, C. R. (1967). Conditioned suppression by a stimulus associated with nalorphine in morphine-dependent monkeys. *Journal of the Experimental Analysis of Behavior, 10,* 235–242.

Goldberg, S. R., & Schuster, C. R. (1970). Conditioned nalorphine-induced abstinence changes: Persistence in post morphine-dependent monkeys. *Journal of the Experimental Analysis of Behavior, 14,* 33–46.

Goldberg, S. R., Woods, J. H., & Schuster, C. R. (1969). Conditioned increases in self-administration in rhesus monkeys. *Science, 166,* 1306–1307.

Goldberg, S. R., Woods, J. H., & Schuster, C. R. (1971a). Nalorphine-induced changes in morphine self-administration in rhesus monkeys. *Journal of Pharmacology and Experimental Therapeutics, 176,* 464–471.

Goldberg, S. R., Hoffmeister, F., Schlichting, U. U., & Wuttke, W. (1971). Aversive properties of nalorphine and naloxone in morphine-dependent rhesus monkeys. *Journal of Pharmacology and Experimental Therapeutics, 179,* 268–276.

Goldberg, S. R., Hoffmeister, F., & Schlichting, U. U. (1972). Morphine antagonists: Modification of behavioral effects by morphine dependence. In J. M. Singh, L. Miller, & H. Lal (Eds.), *Drug addiction. I. Experimental pharmacology* (pp. 31–48). Mount Kisco, NY: Futura Publishing.

Goldberg, S. R., Spealman, R. D., & Shannon, H. E. (1982). Psychotropic effects of opioids and opioid antagonists. In F. Hoffmeister & G. Stille (Eds.), *Handbook of experimental pharmacology: Psychotropic agents* (Vol. 55, III, pp. 269–304). New York: Springer-Verlag.

Gonzales, F. A., & Byrd, L. D. (1977a). Mathematics underlying the rate-dependency hypothesis. *Science, 195,* 546–550.

Gonzales, F. A., & Byrd, L. D. (1977b). Rate-dependency hypothesis. *Science, 198,* 1977.

Goodwin, D. W. (1979). Genetic determinants of alcoholism. In J. H.

Mendelson & N. K. Mello (Eds.), *The diagnosis and treatment of alcoholism* (pp. 305–358). New York: McGraw-Hill.

Goth, A. (1974). *Medical pharmacology.* St. Louis: Mosby.

Goth, A. (1984). *Medical pharmacology.* St. Louis: Mosby.

Green, D. M., & Swets, J. A. (1966). *Signal detection theory and psychophysics.* New York: Wiley.

Griffiths, R. R.. Bigelow, G. E., & Liebson, I. A. (1977). Comparison of social time-out and activity time-out procedures in suppressing ethanol self-administration in alcoholics. *Behavior Research and Therapy, 15,* 329–336.

Griffiths, R. R., Bigelow, G. E., & Liebson, I. A. (1979). Human sedative self-administration: Double-blind comparison of pentobarbital, diazepam, chlorpromazine and placebo. *Journal of Pharmacology and Experimental Therapeutics, 210,* 301–310.

Griffiths, R. R., Brady, J. V., & Bradford, L. D. (1979). Predicting the abuse liability of drugs with animal drug self-administration procedures: Psychomotor stimulants and hallucinogens. In T. Thompson & P. B. Dews (Eds.), *Advances in behavioral pharmacology* (Vol. 2, pp. 163–208). New York: Academic Press.

Griffiths, R. R., Bigelow, G. E., & Henningfield, J. E. (1980). Similarities in animal and human drug-taking behavior. In N. Mello (Ed.), *Advances in substance abuse* (Vol. 1, pp. 1–90). Greenwich, CT: JAI Press.

Grossett, D., Roy, S., Sharenow, E., & Poling, A. (1982). Subjects used in *JEAB* research: Is the snark a pigeon? *The Behavior Analyst, 5,* 189–190.

Grove, R. N., & Schuster, C. R. (1974). Suppression of cocaine self-administration be extinction and punishment. *Pharmacology, Biochemistry, and Behavior, 2,* 199–208.

Hamilton, M. (1967). Development of a rating scale for primary depressive illness. *British Journal of School and Clinical Psychology, 6,* 278–296.

Hare, E. H., & Wilcox, D. R. C. (1967). Do psychiatric inpatients take their drugs? *British Journal of Psychiatry, 113,* 1435–1439.

Harlow, H. (1969). William James and instinct theory. In R. MacCleod (Ed.). *William James: Unfinished business* (pp. 21–30) Washington, D.C.: American Psychological Association.

Harris, L. S. (1981). *Problems of drug dependence, 1981.* Washington, D.C.: U.S. Government Printing Office.

Harvey, J. A. (1971). *Behavioral analysis of drug action.* Glenview, IL: Scott, Foresman.

Hawkins, R. P., & Dotson, V. A. (1975). Reliability scores that delude: An Alice in Wonderland trip through misleading characteristics of interobserver agreement scores in interval recording. In E. Ramp & G. Semb (Eds.), *Behavioral analysis: Areas of research and application* (pp. 359–376). Englewood Cliffs, NJ: Prentice-Hall.

Haynes, R. B., Taylor, D. W., & Sackett, D. L. (1979). *Compliance in health care.* Baltimore: Johns Hopkins Press.

Haynes, S. N. (1978). *Principles of behavioral assessment.* New York: Gardner.

Hearst, E. (1967). The behavior of Skinnerians. *Contemporary Psychology, 12,* 402–404.

Hearst, E., & Jenkins, H. M. (1974). *Sign-tracking: The stimulus-reinforcer relation and directed action.* Austin, TX: The Psychonomic Society.

Hersen, M., & Barlow, D. H. (1976). *Single case experimental designs: Strategies for studying behavior change.* New York: Pergamon Press.

Hill, H. E., Haertzen, C. A., & Glazer, R. (1960). Personality characteristics of narcotic addicts as indicated by the MMPI. *Journal of General Psychology, 62,* 127–139.

Ho, B. T., Richards, D. W., III, & Chute, D. L. (1978). *Drug discrimination and state dependent learning.* New York: Academic Press.

Hoffmeister, F. (1975). Negatively reinforcing properties of some psychotropic drugs in drug-naive rhesus monkeys. *Journal of Pharmacology and Experimental Therapeutics, 192,* 468–477.

Hoffmeister, F., & Wuttke, W. (1973). Negatively reinforcing properties of morphine antagonists in naive rhesus monkeys. *Psychopharmacology, 33,* 247–258.

Holland, J. G. (1978). Behaviorism: Part of the problem or part of the solution? *Journal of Applied Behavior Analysis, 11,* 163–174.

Holland, J. G., & Skinner, B. F. (1961). *The analysis of behavior.* New York: McGraw-Hill.

Hollis, J. H., & St. Omer, V. V. (1972). Direct measurement of psychopharmacologic response: Effects of chlorpromazine on motor behavior of retarded children. *American Journal on Mental Deficiency, 76,* 397–407.

Holmstedt, B. (1967). Historical survey. In D. H. Efron (Ed.), *Ethopharmacological search for psychoactive drugs* (pp. 3–32). Washington, D.C.: U.S. Government Printing Office.

Holmstedt, B., & Leljestrand, G. (1963). *Readings in pharmacology.* New York: Pergamon Press.

Honig, W. K. (1966). *Handbook of operant behavior*. New York: Appleton-Century-Crofts.

Hordern, A. (1968). Psychopharmacology: Some historical considerations. In C. R. B. Joyce (Ed.), *Psychopharmacology: Dimensions and perspectives* (pp. 95–148). London: Tavistock.

Huitema, B. E. (1976, May). *The misuse of statistics in behavior modification research*. Paper presented at the meeting of the Midwestern Association of Behavior Analysis, Chicago.

Iverson, S. D., & Iverson, L. L. (1975). *Behavioral pharmacology*. New York: Oxford Press.

Jaffe, J. H. (1980). Drug addiction and drug abuse. In A. G. Gilman, L. S. Goodman, & A. Gilman (Eds.), *The pharmacological basis of therapeutics* (pp. 535–584). New York: Macmillan.

Johanson, C. E. (1978). Drugs as reinforcers. In D. E. Blackman & D. J. Sanger (Eds.), *Contemporary research in behavioral pharmacology* (pp. 325–448). New York: Plenum Press.

Johanson, C. E., Balster, R., & Bonese, S. (1976). Self-administration of psychomotor stimulant drugs: The effects of unlimited access. *Pharmacology, Biochemistry, and Behavior, 4,* 45–51.

Johnson, S. M., & Bolstad, O. D. (1973). Methodological issues in naturalistic observation. In L. A. Hammerlynck, L. D. Handy, & E. J. Mash (Eds.), *Behavior changes: Methodology, concepts, and practice* (pp. 7–67). Champaign, IL: Research Press.

Johnston, J. M., & Pennypacker, H. S. (1980). *Strategies and tactics of human behavioral research*. Hillsdale, NJ: Lawrence Erlbaum.

Jospe, M. (1978). *The placebo effect in healing*. Lexington, MA: Lexington Books.

Julien, R. M. (1978). *A primer of drug action*. San Francisco: Freeman.

Julien, R. M. (1981). *A primer of drug action*. San Francisco: Freeman.

Kanfer, F. H., & Saslow, G. (1969). Behavioral diagnosis. In C. M. Franks (Ed.), *Behavior therapy: Appraisal and status* (pp. 417–444). New York: McGraw-Hill.

Karch, F. E., & Lasagna, L. (1975). Adverse drug reactions: A critical review. *Journal of the American Medical Association, 234,* 1236–1241.

Katahn, M., & Koplin, J. H. (1968). Paradigm clash: Comment on "Some recent criticisms of behaviorism and learning theory with special reference to Breger and McGough and to Chomsky." *Psychological Bulletin, 69,* 147–148.

Kazdin, A. E. (1980). *Research designs in clinical psychology*. New York: Harper & Row.

Kazdin, A. E. (1982). *Single-case research designs*. New York: Oxford Press.

Kazdin, A. E., & Kopel, S. A. (1975). On resolving ambiguities of the multiple-baseline design: Problems and recommendations. *Behavior Therapy, 6*, 601–608.

Kelleher, R. T., & Morse, W. H. (1964). Escape behavior and punished behavior. *Federation Proceedings, 23*, 808–817.

Kelleher, R. T., & Morse, W. H. (1969). Determinants of the behavioral effects of drugs. In D. H. Tedeschi & R. E. Tedeschi (Eds.), *Importance of fundamental principles in drug evaluation* (pp. 1–60). New York: Raven Press.

Kelleher, R. T., Fry, W., Deegan, J., & Cook, L. (1961). Effects of meprobamate on operant behavior in rats. *Journal of Pharmacology and Experimental Therapeutics, 133*, 271–280.

Keller, F. S., & Schoenfeld, W. M. (1950). *Principles of psychology*. New York: Appleton-Century-Crofts.

Kiesler, D. J. (1971). Experimental designs in psychotherapy research. In A. E. Bergin & S. L. Garfield (Eds.), *Handbook of psychotherapy and behavior change: An empirical analysis* (pp. 36–74). New York: Wiley.

Klein, D. F., & Davis, J. (1969). *Diagnosis and treatment of psychiatric disorders*. Baltimore: Williams & Wilkins.

Klein, D. F., Gittelman, R., Quitkin, F., & Rifkin, A. (1980). *Diagnosis and drug treatment of psychiatric disorders: Adults and children*. Baltimore: Williams & Wilkins.

Knobel, M. (1959). Diagnosis and treatment of behavior disorders in children. *Diseases of the Nervous System, 20*, 334–340.

Krantz, D. L. (1971). The separate worlds of operant and non-operant psychology. *Journal of Applied Behavior Analysis, 4*, 61–70.

Krasnegor, N. A. (Ed.). (1979). *Behavioral analysis and treatment of substance abuse*. Washington, D.C.: U.S. Government Printing Office.

Kuhn, R. (1958). The treatment of depressive states with C22355 (imipramine hydrochloride). *American Journal of Psychiatry, 115*, 459.

Kurtines, W., Hogan, R., & Weiss, D. (1975). Personality dynamics of heroin use. *Journal of Abnormal Psychology, 84*, 87–89.

Lal, H. (1977). *Discriminative stimulus properties of drugs*. New York: Plenum Press.

Laties, V. G. (1972). The modification of drug effects on behavior by external discriminative stimuli. *Journal of Pharmacology and Experimental Therapeutics, 183*, 1–13.

Laties, V. G. (1975). The role of discriminative stimuli in modulating drug effects. *Federation Proceedings, 34,* 1880–1888.

Laties, V. G. (1979). I. V. Zavadskii and the beginnings of behavioral pharmacology: An historical note and translation. *Journal of the Experimental Analysis of Behavior, 32,* 463–472.

Laties, V. G., Wood, R. W., & Cooper, R. D. (1981). Stimulus control and the effects of drugs. *Psychopharmacology, 75,* 277–282.

Lattal, K. A., & Poling, A. (1981). Descriptions of response–event relations: Babel revisited. *Behavior Analyst, 4,* 143–152.

Leber, P. (1983). Establishing the efficacy of drugs with psychogeriatric indications. In T. Crook, S. Ferris, & R. Bartus (Eds.), *Assessment in geriatric psychopharmacology* (pp. 1–12). New Canaan, CT: Mark Powley Associates.

Leitenberg, H. (1978). *Handbook of behavior modification and behavior therapy.* Englewood Cliffs, NJ: Prentice-Hall.

Lickey, M. E., & Gordon, B. (1983). *Drugs for mental illness.* San Francisco: Freeman.

Lippmann, L. G., & Meyer, M. E. (1967). Fixed interval performance as related to instructions and to subjects' verbalizations of the contingency. *Psychonomic Science, 8,* 135–136.

Lipton, M. A., DiMascio, A., & Killam, K. F. (1978). *Psychopharmacology: A generation of progress.* New York: Raven Press.

Lowe, C. F., Harzem, P., & Bagshaw, M. (1978). Species differences in the temporal control of behavior. II: Human performance. *Journal of the Experimental Analysis of Behavior, 29,* 351–361.

Lutzker, J. R., & Martin, J. A. (1981). *Behavior change.* Monterey, CA: Brooks/Cole.

Macht, D. L., & Mora, C. F. (1921). Effects of opium alkaloids on the behavior of rats in the circular maze. *Journal of Pharmacology and Experimental Therapeutics, 16,* 219–235.

Mahoney, M. J. (1977). Some applied issues in self-monitoring. In J. D. Cone & R. P. Hawkins (Eds.), *Behavioral assessment: New directions in clinical psychology* (pp. 241–254.). New York: Brunner/Mazel.

Marholin, D., & Phillips, D. (1976). Methodological issues in psychopharmacological research. *American Journal of Orthopsychiatry, 46,* 477–495.

Marholin, D., Touchette, P. E., & Stewart, R. M. (1979). Withdrawal of chronic chlorpromazine medication: An experimental analysis. *Journal of Applied Behavior Analysis, 12,* 150–171.

Marr, M. J. (1970). Effects of chlorpromazine in the pigeon under a second order schedule of food presentation. *Journal of the Experimental Analysis of Behavior, 13*, 291–299.

Marston, M. V. (1970). Compliance with medical regimens: A review of the literature. *Nursing Research, 19*, 312–323.

Martin, W. R., Eades, C. G., Thompson, J. A., Huppler, R. E., & Gilbert, P. E. (1976). The effects of morphine- and nalorphine-like drugs in the nondependent and morphine-dependent chronic spinal dog. *Journal of Pharmacology and Experimental Therapeutics, 197*, 517–532.

Masek, B. J. (1982). Compliance and medicine. In D. M. Doleys, R. L. Meredith, & A. R. Ciminero (Eds.), *Behavioral medicine: Assessment and treatment strategies* (pp. 527–536). New York: Plenum Press.

Matthews, B. A., Shimoff, E., Catania, A. C., & Sagvolden, T. (1977). Uninstructed human responding: Sensitivity to ratio and interval contingencies. *Journal of the Experimental Analysis of Behavior, 27*, 453–467.

Mayer, S. E., Melmon, K. L., & Gilman, A. G. (1980). Introduction: The dynamics of drug absorption, distribution, and elimination. In A. G. Gilman, L. S. Goodman, & A. Gilman (Eds.), *The pharmacological basis of therapeutics* (pp. 1–27). New York: Macmillan.

McCaul, M. E., Stitzer, M. L., Bigelow, G. E., & Liebson, I. A. (1984). Contingency management interventions: Effects on treatment outcome during methadone detoxification. *Journal of Applied Behavior Analysis, 17*, 35–43.

McFall, R. M. (1977). Analogue methods in behavioral assessment: Issues and prospects. In J. D. Cone & R. P. Hawkins (Eds.), *Behavioral assessment: New directions in clinical psychology* (pp. 152–177). New York: Brunner/Mazel.

McGuire, P., (1975). *The effects of acute methadone on fixed-interval schedules of reinforcement in pigeons.* Unpublished doctoral dissertation, University of Minnesota, Minneapolis.

McKearney, J. W. (1981). Rate-dependency: Scope and limitations in the explanation and analysis of the behavioral effects of drugs. In T. Thompson, P. B. Dews, & W. A. McKim (Eds.), *Advances in behavioral pharmacology* (Vol. 3, pp. 91–110). New York: Academic Press.

McKearney, J. W., & Barrett, J. E. (1978). Schedule-controlled behavior and the effects of drugs. In D. E. Blackman & D. J. Sanger (Eds.),

Contemporary research in behavioral pharmacology (pp. 1–68). New York: Plenum Press.

McMillan, D. E. (1975). Determinants of drug effects on punished responding. *Federation Proceedings, 34,* 1870–1879.

Mechner, F., & Latranyi, M. (1963). Behavioral effects of caffeine, methamphetamine, and methylphenidate in the rat. *Journal of the Experimental Analysis of Behavior, 6,* 331–342.

Meisch, R. A. (1977). Ethanol self-administration: Infrahuman studies. In T. Thompson & P. B. Dews (Eds.), *Advances in behavioral pharmacology* (Vol. 1, pp. 35–84). New York: Academic Press.

Melmon, K. L., & Gilman, A. G. (1980). Drug interactions. In A. G. Gilman, L. S. Goodman, & A. Gilman (Eds.), *The pharmacological basis of therapeutics* (pp. 1738–1752). New York: Macmillan.

Melmon, K. L., & Morelli, H. F. (1978). Drug reactions. In K. L. Melmon & H. F. Morelli (Eds.), *Clinical pharmacology: Basic principles in therapeutics* (pp. 951–981). New York: Macmillan.

Melmon, K. L., Gilman, A. G., & Mayer, S. E. (1980). Principles of therapeutics. In A. G. Gilman, L. S. Goodman, & A. Gilman (Eds.), *The pharmacological basis of therapeutics* (pp. 40–55). New York: Macmillan.

Michael, J. L. (1980). Flight from behavior analysis. *The Behavior Analyst, 3,* 1–24.

Michael, J. L. (1982). Distinguishing between discriminative and motivational functions of stimuli. *Journal of the Experimental Analysis of Behavior, 37,* 149–155.

Moore, D. J., & Klonoff, E. A. (1986). Assessment of compliance. In K. E. Gadow & A. Poling (Eds.), *Methodological issues in human psychopharmacology.* Greenwich, CT: JAI Press.

Mottin, J. C. (1973). Drug-induced attenuation of alcohol consumption: A review and evaluation of claimed, potential or current therapies. *Quarterly Journal of Studies on Alcohol, 34,* 444–472.

Nathan, P. E., & Lipscomb, T. R. (1979). Behavior therapy and behavior modification in the treatment of alcoholism. In J. H. Mendelson & N. K. Mello (Eds.), *The diagnosis and treatment of alcoholism* (pp. 305–358). New York: McGraw-Hill.

Nathanson, J. A., & Greengard, P. (1978, August). "Second messengers" in the brain. *Scientific American,* 108–120.

National Institute on Drug Abuse. (1978). Behavioral tolerance: Research and treatment implications. Washington, D.C.: U.S. Government Printing Office.

Nay, W. R. (1977). Analogue measures. In A. R. Ciminero, K. S. Calhoun, & H. E. Adams (Eds.), *Handbook of behavioral assessment* (pp. 233–278). New York: Wiley.

Newsweek. (1983, March 7). Storm over the environment.

Nicholson, A. N., & Wright, C. M. (1974). Inhibitory and disinhibitory effects of mitrazepam, diazepam, and flurazepam hydrochloride on delayed matching behavior in monkeys. *Neuropharmacology, 12,* 311–317.

Nicholson, A. N., Wright, C. N., & Ferres, H. M. (1973). Impaired performance on delayed matching in monkeys by heptabarbitone, pentabarbitone sodium and quinalbarbitone sodium. *Neuropharmacology, 12,* 311–317.

O'Brien, C. P. (1975). Experimental analysis of conditioning factors in human narcotic addiction. *Pharmacology Reviews, 27,* 533–543.

O'Brien, C. P., Testa, T., O'Brien, T. J., Brady, J. P., & Wells, B. (1977). Conditioned narcotic withdrawal in humans. *Science, 195,* 1000–1002.

O'Leary, K. D. (1980). Pills or skills for hyperactive children? *Journal of Applied Behavior Analysis, 13,* 191–204.

Page, T., & Iwata, B. (1986). Interobserver agreement: History, theory, and current methods. In A. Poling, R. W. Fuqua, & R. Ulrich (Eds.), *Research methodology in applied behavior analysis: Issues and advances* (pp. 99–126). New York: Plenum Press.

Paul, G. L. (1967). Strategy of outcome research in psychotherapy. *Journal of Consulting Psychology, 31,* 104–118.

Pavlov, I. P. (1910). *Work of the digestive glands.* New York: Griffin.

Pelham, W. E., Schnedler, R. W., Bologna, N. C., & Contreras, J. A. (1980). Behavioral and stimulant treatment of hyperactive children: A therapy study with methylphenidate probes in a within-subjects design. *Journal of Applied Behavior Analysis, 13,* 221–236.

Peterson, L., Homer, A. L., & Wonderlich, S. A. (1982). The integrity of the independent variable in behavior analysis. *Journal of Applied Behavior Analysis, 15,* 477–492.

Pickens, R. (1977). Behavioral pharmacology: A brief history. In T. Thompson & P. B. Dews (Eds.), *Advances in behavioral pharmacology* (Vol. 1, pp. 230–261). New York: Academic Press.

Pickens, R. (1979). A behavioral program for treatment of drug dependence. In N. A. Krasnegor (Ed.), *Behavioral analysis and treatment of substance abuse* (pp. 44–54). Washington, D.C.: U.S. Government Printing Office.

Pickens, R. (1985, May). *Reinforcement susceptibility in families: It isn't only Jordache who has genes.* Paper presented at the meeting of the Association for Behavior Analysis, Columbus, OH.

Pickens, R., & Thompson, T. (1971). Characteristics of stimulant drug reinforcement. In T. Thompson & R. Pickens (Eds.), *Stimulus properties of drugs* (pp. 177–192). New York: Academic Press.

Pickens, R., Bigelow, G., & Griffiths, R. R. (1973). An experimental approach to treating chronic alcoholism: A case study and one-year follow-up. *Behavior Research and Therapy, 11,* 321–325.

Pickens, R., Thompson, T., & Muchow, D. C. (1973). Cannabis and phencyclidine self-administration by animals. In L. Goldberg & F. Hoffmeister (Eds.), *Bayer Symposium IV: Psychic Dependence* (pp. 78–87). Berlin: Springer-Verlag.

Picker, M., & Poling, A. (1984). Effects of anticonvulsants on learning: Performance of pigeons under a repeated acquisition procedure when exposed to phenobarbital, clonazepam, valproic acid, ethosuximide, and phenytoin. *Journal of Pharmacology and Experimental Therapeutics, 230,* 307–316.

Picker, M., Leibold, L., Endsley, B., & Poling, A. (1986). Effects of clonazepam and ethosuximide on the responding of pigeons under a fixed-consecutive-number schedule with and without an external discriminative stimulus. *Psychopharmacology, 88,* 325–330.

Picker, M., White, W., & Poling, A. (1985). Effects of phenobarbital, clonazepam, valproic acid, ethosuximide, and phenytoin on the delayed-matching-to-sample performance of pigeons. *Psychopharmacology, 86,* 494–498.

Platt, J. J. (1975). "Addiction proneness" and personality in heroin addicts. *Journal of Abnormal Psychology, 84,* 303–306.

Poklis, A., & Whyatt, P. L. (1980). Current trends in the abuse of pentazocine and tripelennamine: The metropolitan St. Louis experience. *Journal of Forensic Science, 25,* 72–78.

Poling, A. (1984). Comparing humans to other species: We're animals and they're not infrahumans. *The Behavior Analyst, 7,* 211–212.

Poling, A., & Appel, J. B. (1978). d-Amphetamine and fixed-interval performance: Effects of establishing the drug as a discriminative stimulus. *Pharmacology, Biochemistry, and Behavior, 9,* 473–476.

Poling, A., & Appel, J. B. (1979). Procedures for reducing drug intake: Nonhuman studies. In T. Thompson & P. B. Dews (Eds.), *Advances in behavioral pharmacology* (Vol. 2, pp. 209–228). New York: Academic Press.

Poling, A., & Appel, J. B. (1982). Dependence-producing liability of LSD and similar psychotomimetics. In F. Hoffmeister & G. Stille (Eds.), *Psychotropic agents* (pp. 111–118). Berlin: Springer-Verlag.

Poling, A., & Picker, M. (1986). Behavioral effects of anticonvulsant drugs. In T. Thompson, P. B. Dews, & J. Barrett (Eds.), *Advances in behavioral pharmacology* (Vol. 5). Greenwich, CT: JAI Press.

Poling, A., & Ryan, C. (1982). Therapeutic applications of differential-reinforcement-of-other-behavior (DRO) schedules: A review. *Behavior Modification, 6,* 3–20.

Poling, A., & Thompson, T. (1977). Suppression of ethanol-reinforced lever pressing by delaying food availability. *Journal of the Experimental Analysis of Behavior, 28,* 271–283.

Poling, A., Cleary, J., & Monaghan, M. (1980). The use of human observers in psychopharmacological research. *Pharmacology, Biochemistry, and Behavior, 13,* 243–246.

Poling, A., Kesselring, J., Sewell, R. G., Jr., & Cleary, J. (1983). Lethality of pentazocine and tripellenamine combinations in mice housed individually and in groups. *Pharmacology, Biochemistry, and Behavior, 18,* 103–105.

Poling, A., Parker, C., & Breuning, S. E. (1984). Assessment of institutionalized mentally retarded children. In R. Glow (Ed.), *Advances in the behavioral measurement of children* (Vol. 1, pp. 93–136). Greenwich, CT: JAI Press.

Poling, A., Picker, M., & Wallace, S. (1984). Psychopharmacological research with the mentally retarded: A methodological analysis of thirty-nine studies published from 1970 to 1982. In J. C. Griffin, M. T. Stark, D. E. Williams, B. K. Altmeyer, & H. K. Griffin (Eds.), *Advances in the treatment of self-injurious behavior* (pp. 89–122). Austin, TX: Texas Planning Council for Developmental Disabilities.

Pollin, W. (1979). Foreword. In N. A. Krasnegor (Ed.), *Behavioral analysis and treatment of substance abuse* (pp. v–vi). Washington, D.C.: U.S. Government Printing Office.

Poppen, R. (1982). The fixed-interval scallop in human affairs. *The Behavior Analyst, 5,* 127–136.

Powell, D. H. (1973). A pilot study of occasional heroin users. *Archives of General Psychiatry, 28,* 586–594.

Powers, R. B., & Osborne, J. G. (1976). *Fundamentals of behavior.* St. Paul: West.

Physicians' desk reference. (1982). Oradell, NJ: Medical Economics.

Premack, D. (1959). Toward empirical laws. I. Positive reinforcement. *Psychological Review, 66,* 219–233.

Rachlin, H. (1976). *Behavior and learning.* San Francisco: Freeman.

Ray, O. (1983). *Drugs, society, and human behavior.* St. Louis: Mosby.

Repp, A. C., Roberts, D. M., Slack, D. J., Repp, C. F., & Beckler, M. S. (1976). A comparison of frequency, interval, and time-sampling methods of data collection. *Journal of Applied Behavior Analysis, 9,* 501–508.

Richelle, M., Xhenseval, B., Fontaine, O., & Thone, L. (1962). Action of chlordiazepoxide on two types of temporal responding in rats. *International Journal of Neuropharmacology, 1,* 381–391.

Rickels, K. (1968). *Non-specific factors in drug therapy.* Springfield, IL: Charles C Thomas.

Rilling, M. (1977). Stimulus control and inhibitory processes. In W. K. Honig & J. E. R. Staddon (Eds.), *Handbook of operant behavior* (pp. 432–480). Englewood Cliffs, NJ: Prentice-Hall.

Robins, L. N. (1974). *The Vietnam drug user returns.* Washington, D.C.: U.S. Government Printing Office.

Rosenthal, R. (1966). *Experimenter effects in behavioral research.* New York: Appleton-Century-Crofts.

Sackett, E. L., & Snow, J. C. (1979). The magnitude of compliance and noncompliance. In R. B. Haynes, D. W. Taylor, & D. L. Sackett (Eds.), *Compliance in health care* (pp. 11–22). Baltimore: Johns Hopkins Press.

Salvia, J., & Ysseldyke, J. E. (1981). *Assessment in special and remedial education.* Boston: Houghton Mifflin.

Sanger, D. J., & Blackman, D. E. (1976). Rate-dependent effects of drugs: A review of the literature. *Pharmacology, Biochemistry, and Behavior, 4,* 73–83.

Sankar, R. V. (1975). *LSD—A total study.* Westbury, NY: PJD Publications.

Schuster, C. R. (1975). Drugs as reinforcers in monkey and man. *Pharmacology Reviews, 27,* 511–521.

Schuster, C. R., & Balster, R. L. (1977). The discriminative stimulus properties of drugs. In T. Thompson & P. B. Dews (Eds.), *Advances in behavioral pharmacology* (Vol. 3, pp. 86–139). New York: Academic Press.

Schuster, C. R., & Thompson, T. (1969). Self-administration of and behavioral dependence on drugs. *Annual Review of Pharmacology, 9,* 483–502.

Schuster, L. (1962). *Readings in pharmacology.* New York: Little, Brown.

Seiden, L. S., & Dykstra, L. A. (1977). *Psychopharmacology: A bio-*

chemical and behavioral approach. New York: Van Nostrand Reinhold.

Sells, S. B. (1979). Treatment effectiveness. In R. L. DuPont, A. Goldstein, & J. O'Donnell (Eds.), *Handbook on drug abuse* (pp. 105–118). Washington, D.C.: U.S. Government Printing Office.

Shafto, F., & Sulzbacher, S. (1977). Comparing treatment tactics with a hyperactive preschool child: Stimulant medication and programmed teacher intervention. *Journal of Applied Behavior Analysis, 10,* 13–20.

Showalter, C. V. (1980). T's and blues: Abuse of pentazocine and tripelennamine. *Journal of the American Medical Association, 224,* 1224–1225.

Shapiro, A. K., & Morris, L. A. (197G). The placebo effect in medical and psychological therapies. In S. L. Garfield & A. E. Bergin (Eds.), *Hnadbook of psychotherapy and behavioral change: An empirical analysis* (pp. 439–473). New York: Wiley.

Siegel, S. (1979a). Pharmacological learning and drug dependence. In M. M. Grunberg & J. R. Eiser (Eds.), *Research in psychology and medicine* (pp. 126–153). New York: Academic Press.

Siegel, S. (1979b). The role of conditioning in drug tolerance and addiction. In J. D. Keehn (Ed.), *Psychopathology in animals: Research and treatment implications* (pp. 143–168). New York: Academic Press.

Siegel, S., Hinson, R. E., & Krank, M. D. (1978). *Opiate "overdose" death: Modulation of the lethal effect of opiates by drug-associated environmental cues.* Paper presented at the meeting of the Behavioral Pharmacology Society, Glen Cove, NY.

Sidman, M. (1956). Drug–behavior interactions. *Annals of the New York Academy of Sciences, 65,* 282–302.

Sidman, M. (1960). *Tactics of scientific research.* New York: Basic Books.

Simpson, D. D., Savage, L. J., & Lloyd, M. R. (1979). Follow-up evaluation of treatment of drug abuse 1969 to 1972. *Archives of General Psychiatry, 36,* 772–780.

Skinner, B. F. (1938). *The behavior of organisms.* New York: Appleton-Century-Crofts.

Skinner, B. F. (1948). *Walden two.* New York: Macmillan.

Skinner, B. F. (1953). *Science and human behavior.* New York: Macmillan.

Skinner, B. F. (1957). *Verbal behavior.* New York: Appleton-Century-Crofts.

Skinner, B. F. (1959). Animal research in the pharmacotherapy of mental disease. In J. O. Cole, & R. W. Gerard (Eds.), *Pyschopharmacology: Problems in evaluation* (pp. 224–235). Washington, D.C.: National Academy of Sciences.

Skinner, B. F. (1969). *Contingencies of reinforcement.* New York: Meredith.

Skinner, B. F. (1974). *About behaviorism.* New York: Random House.

Smith, C. B. (1964). Effects of d-amphetamine upon operant behavior of pigeons: Enhancement by reserpine. *Journal of Pharmacology and Experimental Therapeutics, 146,* 167–174.

Smith, C. M. (1978). *Alcoholism: Treatment* (Vol. 2). Montreal: Eden Press.

Solomon, R. L. (1980). The opponent-process theory of acquired motivation. *American Psychologist, 35,* 691–712.

Solomon, S. H. (1984). Drug and neurotransmitter receptors in the brain. *Science, 224,* 22–31.

Sprague, R. L. (1982). Litigation, legislation, and regulations. In S. E. Breuning & A. Poling (Eds.), *Drugs and mental retardation* (pp. 377–415). Springfield, IL: Charles C Thomas.

Sprague, R. L., & Baxley, G. B. (1978). Drugs for behavior management with comment on some legal aspects. In J. Wortis (Ed.), *Mental retardation* (Vol. 10, pp. 92–129). New York: Brunner/Mazel.

Sprague, R. L., & Berger, B. D. (1980). Drug effects on learning performance. In R. M. Knights & D. J. Bakker (Eds.), *Treatment of hyperactive and learning disordered children* (pp. 167–183). Baltimore: University Park Press.

Sprague, R. L., & Sleator, E. K. (1977). Methylphenidate in hyperkinetic children: Difference in dose effects on learning and social behavior. *Science, 198,* 1274–1276.

Sprague, R. L., & Toppe, L. (1966). Relationship between activity level and delay of reinforcement in the retarded. *Journal of Experimental Child Psychology, 3,* 390–397.

Sprague, R. L., & Werry, J. L. (1971). Methodology of psychopharmacological studies with the retarded. In N. R. Ellis (Ed.), *International review of research in mental retardation* (Vol. 5, pp. 147–219). New York: Academic Press.

Stebbins, W. C., & Coombs, S. (1975). Behavioral assessment of ototoxicity in nonhuman primates. In B. Weiss & V. G. Laties (Eds.), *Behavioral toxicology* (pp. 401–428). New York: Plenum Press.

Sulzbacher, S. I. (1973). Psychotropic medication with children: An evaluation of procedural bias in results of reported studies. *Pediatrics, 51,* 513–517.

Sutker, P. B. (1971). Personality differences and sociopathy in heroin addicts and nonaddict prisoners. *Journal of Abnormal Psychology, 75,* 237–251.

Swinyard, E. A. (1980). Principles of prescription order writing and patient compliance instructions. In A. G. Gilman, L. S. Goodman, & A. Gilman (Eds.), *The pharmacological basis of therapeutics* (pp. 1660–1674). New York: Macmillan.

Szostak, C., & Tombaugh, T. N. (1981). Use of a fixed consecutive number schedule of reinforcement to investigate the effects of pimozide on behavior controlled by internal and external stimuli. *Pharmacology, Biochemistry, and Behavior, 15,* 609–617.

Tang, A. H., & Morse, W. H. (1975). Termination of a schedule complex associated with intravenous injections of nalorphine in morphine-dependent monkeys. *Pharmacology Reviews, 27,* 407–417.

Thompson, D. M. (1975). Repeated acquisition of response sequences: Stimulus control and drugs. *Journal of the Experimental Analysis of Behavior, 23,* 429–436.

Thompson, D. M. (1978). Stimulus control and drug effects. In D. E. Blackman & D. J. Sanger (Eds.), *Contemporary research in behavioral pharmacology* (pp. 159–208). New York: Plenum Press.

Thompson, D. M., & Moerschbaecher, J. M. (1979). Drug effects on repeated acquisition. In T. Thompson & P. B. Dews (Eds.), *Advances in behavioral pharmacology* (Vol. 2, pp. 229–260). New York: Academic Press.

Thompson, T. (1962). The effect of two phenothiazines and a barbiturate on extinction-induced rate increase of a free operant. *Journal of Comparative and Physiological Psychology, 55,* 714–718.

Thompson, T. (1981). Behavioral mechanisms and loci of drug action: An overview. In T. Thompson & C. Johanson (Eds.), *Behavioral pharmacology of human drug dependence* (pp. 1–10). Washington, D.C.: U.S. Government Printing Office.

Thompson, T. (1982). Foreword. In S. E. Breuning & A. Poling (Eds.), *Drugs and mental retardation* (pp. vii–xiii). Springfield, IL: Charles C Thomas.

Thompson, T., & Dews, P. B. (1977). *Advances in behavioral pharmacology* (Vol. 1). New York: Academic Press.

Thompson, T., & Ostlund, W. (1965). Susceptibility to readdiction as a function of the addiction and withdrawal environments. *Journal of Comparative and Physiological Psychology, 60,* 388–392.

Thompson, T., & Pickens, R. (1969). Drug self-administration and conditioning. In H. Steinberg (Ed.), *Scientific basis of drug dependence* (pp. 177–198). London: Churchill.

Thompson, T., & Pickens, R. (1971). *Stimulus properties of drugs.* New York: Appleton-Century-Crofts.

Thompson, T., & Schuster, C. R. (1964). Morphine self-administration, food-reinforced, and avoidance behaviors in rhesus monkeys. *Psychopharmacologia, 5,* 97–94.

Thompson, T., & Schuster, C. R. (1968). *Behavioral pharmacology.* Englewood Cliffs, NJ: Prentice-Hall.

Thompson, T., & Unna, K. (1977). *Predicting dependence liability of stimulant and depressant drugs.* Baltimore: University Park Press.

Thompson, T., Trombley, J., Luke, D., & Lott, D. (1970). Effects of morphine on behavior maintained by four simple food-reinforcement schedules. *Psychopharmacologia, 17,* 182–192.

Thompson, T., Dews, P. B., & McKim, W. M. (1981). *Advances in behavioral pharmacology* (Vol. 3). New York: Academic Press.

Thorndike, E. L. (1911). *Animal intelligence.* New York: Macmillan.

Turner, E. G., & Altshuler, H. L. (1976). Conditioned suppression of an operant response using *d*-amphetamine as the conditioned stimulus. *Psychopharmacology, 50,* 139–144.

Ullmann, L. P., & Krasner, L. (1965). *Case studies in behavior modification.* New York: Holt, Rinehart, and Winston.

Ulman, J. D., & Sulzer-Azaroff, B. (1975). Multielement baseline design in educational research. In E. Ramp & G. Semb (Eds.), *Behavior analysis: Areas of research and application* (pp. 377–391). Englewood Cliffs, NJ: Prentice-Hall.

Ulrich, R., Stachnik, T., & Mabry, J. (1966). *Control of human behavior* (Vol. 1). Glenview, IL: Scott, Foresman.

Urbain, C., Poling, A., Millam, J., & Thompson, T. (1978). *d*-Amphetamine and fixed-interval performance: Effects of operant history. *Journal of the Experimental Analysis of Behavior, 29,* 285–292.

Van Houten, R. (1979). Social validation: The evolution of standards of competency for target behaviors. *Journal of Applied Behavior Analysis, 12,* 581–591.

Wagman, W. D., & Maxey, G. C. (1969). The effects of scopolamine hydrobromide and methyl scopolamine hydrobromide upon the discrimination of interoceptive and exteroceptive stimuli. *Psychopharmacologia, 15,* 280–288.

Waller, M. B., & Morse, W. H. (1963). Effects of pentobarbital on fixed-ratio reinforcement. *Journal of the Experimental Analysis of Behavior, 6,* 125–130.

Watson, J. B. (1924). *Behaviorism.* New York: People's Institute.

Webster's New Twentieth Century Dictionary. (1979). New York: Simon & Schuster.

Weeks, J. R. (1962). Experimental morphine addiction: Method for autonomic intravenous injections in unrestrained rats. *Science, 138,* 133–134.

Weeks, J. R. (1975). Environmental influences affecting the voluntary intake of drugs: An overview. *Federation Proceedings, 34,* 1755–1758.

Weiner, N. (1980). Drugs that inhibit adrenergic nerves and block adrenergic receptors. In A. G. Gilman, L. S. Goodman, & A. Gilman (Eds.), *The pharmacological basis of therapeutics* (pp. 176–210). New York: Macmillan.

Weiss, B., & Laties, V. G. (1969). Behavioral pharmacology and toxicology. *Annual Review of Pharmacology, 9,* 297–326.

Weiss, B., & Laties, V. G. (1975). *Behavioral toxicology.* New York: Plenum Press.

Whalen, C. K., & Henker, B. (1986). Group designs. In K. D. Gadow & A. Poling (Eds.), *Methodological issues in human psychopharmacology.* Greenwich, CT: JAI Press.

Wikler, A. (1952). A psychodynamic study of a patient during experimental self-regulated re-addiction to morphine. *Psychiatry Quarterly, 26,* 270–293.

Wikler, A. (1961). On the nature of addiction and habituation. *British Journal of Addictions, 57,* 73–79.

Wikler, A. (1973). Dynamics of drug dependence. *Archives of General Psychiatry, 28,* 611–616.

Wikler, A. (1974). Requirements for extinction of relapse-facilitating variables and for rehabilitation in a narcotic-antagonist treatment program. In M. C. Braude, L. S. Harris, E. L. May, J. P. Smith, & J. E. Villarreal (Eds.), *Advances in biochemical psychopharmacology* (Vol. 8, pp. 399–414). New York: Raven Press.

Wikler, A., & Pescor, F. T. (1967). Classical conditioning of a morphine abstinence phenomenon, reinforcement of opioid-drinking behavior and "relapse" in morphine-addicted rats. *Psychopharmacologia, 10,* 255–284.

Wilkins, W. (1973). Expectancy of therapeutic gain: An empirical and conceptual critique. *Journal of Consulting and Clinical Psychology, 40,* 69–77.

Wilmarth, S. S., & Goldstein, A. (1974). *Therapeutic effectiveness of methadone maintenance programs in the U.S.A.* Geneva: World Health Organization.

Wilson, C. T., Leaf, R. C., & Nathan, P. E. (1975). The aversive control of excessive alcohol consumption by chronic alcoholics in a laboratory setting. *Journal of Applied Behavior Analysis, 8,* 13–26.

Winett, R. A. (1973). Parameters of deposit contracts in the modification of smoking. *Psychological Record, 23,* 49–60.

Wolf, M. M. (1978). Social validity: The case for subjective measurement, or how applied behavior analysis is finding its heart. *Journal of Applied Behavior Analysis, 11,* 203–214.

Wulbert, M., & Dries, R. (1977). The relative efficacy of methylphenidate (Ritalin) and behavior-modification techniques in the treatment of a hyperactive child. *Journal of Applied Behavior Analysis, 10,* 21–32.

Wysocki, T., & Fuqua, R. W. (1982). Methodological issues in the evaluation of drug effects. In S. E. Breuning & A. Poling (Eds.), *Drugs and mental retardation* (pp. 138–167). Springfield, IL: Charles C Thomas.

Wysocki, T., Fuqua, R. W., Davis, V. J., & Breuning, S. E. (1981). Effects of thioridazine (Mellaril) on titrating delayed matching to sample performance of mentally retarded adults. *American Journal of Mental Deficiency, 85,* 539–547.

Yanagita, T. (1970). Self-administration studies on various dependence-producing agents in monkeys. *University of Michigan Medical School Journal, 36,* 216–224.

Young, J. H. (1974). *The toadstool millionaires.* Princeton: Princeton University Press.

Zeiler, M. (1977). Schedules of reinforcement: The controlling variables. In W. K. Honig & J. E. R. Staddon (Eds.), *Handbook of operant behavior* (pp. 201–232). New York: Prentice-Hall.

Index

DATE DUE